THE IRRATIONAL ECONOMIST

THE
IRRATIONAL
ECONOMIST

Making Decisions in a Dangerous World

Erwann Michel-Kerjan AND **Paul Slovic**
editors

PUBLICAFFAIRS
New York

Published in the United States by PublicAffairs™,
a member of the Perseus Books Group.

PublicAffairs books are available at special discounts for bulk purchases in the U.S. by corporations, institutions, and other organizations. For more information, please contact the Special Markets Department at the Perseus Books Group, 2300 Chestnut Street, Suite 200, Philadelphia, PA 19103, call (800) 810-4145, ext. 5000, or e-mail special.markets@perseusbooks.com.

Designed by Brent Wilcox
Text set in 11 point Adobe Caslon

Library of Congress Cataloging-in-Publication Data
The irrational economist : making decisions in a dangerous world / Erwann Michel-Kerjan and Paul Slovic, editors.
    p.   cm.
  Includes bibliographical references and index.
  ISBN 978-1-58648-780-5 (alk. paper)
  1. Economic forecasting.   2. Decision making.   I. Michel-Kerjan, Erwann.
II. Slovic, Paul, 1938-
  HB3730.I77 2010
  330.01'9—dc22

                    2009043477

First Edition

10 9 8 7 6 5 4 3 2 1

ec·o·nom·ics (ĕk'ə-nŏm'ĭks) – *noun*

1. a study of mankind in the ordinary business of life (Alfred Marshall, 1890)
2. the social science that analyzes human behavior as a relationship between the *production, distribution,* and *consumption* of *goods* and *services.*

NOTE TO THE READERS

There is a clear tendency to view our own thoughts, words, and actions as *rational* and to see those who disagree as *irrational.*

CONTENTS

Introduction

An Idea Whose Time Has Come

ERWANN MICHEL-KERJAN AND PAUL SLOVIC

> All the forces in the world are not so powerful as an idea
> whose time has come.
> —Victor Hugo

OUR DANGEROUS AND INTERDEPENDENT WORLD

At a time of immensely consequential choices, it has never been more important to make the right decisions. But how can we be sure we are not making fatal mistakes? How can we be sure we can trust the tools, models, and methods we use to make our decisions?

The Irrational Economist aims to shed light on some important developments in decision making that have occurred in economics and other social sciences over the past few decades, including some of the most recent discoveries. Quite surprisingly, much of the knowledge developed in these fields has yet to be translated from research into actionable decisions in the real world. Our goal in this book is simple: to provide this knowledge in a condensed fashion to help people make better decisions in a world that seems to become more and more uncertain—if not more dangerous—as time passes.

This last statement may seem controversial. Conventional wisdom holds that crises and catastrophes are not new and that the world has seen many great dangers before. The twentieth century alone witnessed one of the deadliest five-year periods in human history: Between 1914 and 1918, World War I killed over 15 million people. And as the war ended, the 1918–1919 influenza pandemic (commonly referred to as the Spanish flu) spread to nearly every part of the world. The flu killed over 50 million, more than the toll of the Black Death in the fourteenth century. Wars and natural disasters have indeed devastated many parts of the world throughout history. Since the industrial revolution, new types of technological risks and deadly weapons have also emerged.

But one of the hallmarks of the twenty-first century will likely be more and more unthinkable events, previously unseen contexts, and pressure to react extremely quickly, even when we cannot predict the cascading impact our actions might have.

That is because the world has been evolving at an accelerating speed. Physical frontiers between economies are disappearing, as described by Thomas Friedman in his best-selling book, *The World Is Flat*. Increasingly widespread social and economic activities have turned our planet into an interdependent village. Communication costs are close to zero, goods and people travel faster and more cheaply than ever before, and knowledge is shared with unprecedented ease on the Internet and through emerging social networks. There are many benefits to this process.

Yet the flip side of this extraordinary transformation has been somewhat underappreciated: Actions taken or risks materializing 5,000 miles away can affect any of us very soon thereafter. Viruses fly business class, too! The financial turmoil that started in 2008 is another example; this blew up the theory of decoupling long supported by many theorists who thought a reduction in the United States' or China's economic growth would not severely affect the rest of the world. Well, as we now know, it did—with profound consequences. We are all interconnected.

The litany of global interdependent risks is almost endless. Events that have surfaced prominently on the social, economic, and political fronts in many countries just since the beginning of 2001 are eye-opening: terrorist attacks; financial crises; global warming; scarcity of water and other resources; hurricanes, floods, tsunamis, heat waves, droughts, earthquakes, and wildfires unprecedented in scale and recurrence;[1] failures of our aging critical infrastructures;[2] repeated genocides and local wars; nuclear threats; pandemics and new illnesses.

This list is long but hardly exhaustive: We trust that if you think for a moment about what is going wrong today, what you are afraid of, or you simply watch news TV, you shall soon add to this list. And as challenging as it is today on a planet with nearly 7 billion people, it is likely to be even more so as the population continues to grow; ever greater concentrations of people and assets at risk set the stage for truly devastating events to happen.

At the heart of the work that led to this somewhat unusual book is this question: Is the series of untoward events that have occurred since 2001 an omen of what the twenty-first century has in store for us? If so—as we believe—it is time to think about the future in a fundamentally different way. What does this mean for us, as individuals and families, private companies, government authorities, and organizations? How might we behave in this new, uncertain, and more dangerous environment? Will our actions be rational or irrational? And what does this last question actually mean?

ARE WE RATIONAL ACTORS OR RATIONAL FOOLS?

We sought the answer to these questions from a group of internationally recognized experts who had worked with or were influenced by the economist Howard Kunreuther, who pioneered the field of decision making and catastrophe management (see the Acknowledgments section). Their work in *The Irrational Economist* examines human decision making from a variety of perspectives and documents the rich and subtle complexities of the concept "rationality." These contributors' perspectives are the result of an important evolution in theory and applied research that has occurred during the past half-century and is now accelerating.

Many mainstream economists in the second part of the twentieth century developed sophisticated mathematical treatments that attempted to model human behavior. But most of these were founded on a very simplistic concept of rationality. Indeed, early views on rationality were dominated by the concept of *homo economicus*: The idea here is that we can all be represented by an *economic man* who is assumed to be completely informed, perfectly responsive to economic fluctuations, and rational in the sense of having *stable-over-time*, *orderly* preferences that maximize economic well-being and are independent of the actions and preferences of others.

Slowly, psychologists and other behavioral scientists began testing this presumption of rationality, which, as noted by Herbert Simon, one of the most influential social scientists of the twentieth century, permitted economists to make "strong predictions . . . about behavior without the painful necessity of observing people."[3]

Simon, both an economist and a psychologist, drew upon empirical research on human cognitive limitations to challenge traditional assumptions about the motivation, omniscience, and computational capacities of "economic man." He introduced the notion of "bounded rationality," which asserts that cognitive limitations force people to construct simplified models of how the world works in order to cope with it. To predict behavior "we must understand the way in which this simplified model is constructed, and its construction will certainly be related to man's psychological properties as a perceiving, thinking, and learning animal."[4]

About the same time that Simon was documenting bounded rationality in the 1960s and 1970s, another psychologist, Ward Edwards, began testing economic theories through controlled laboratory experiments to examine how people process information central to "life's gambles." Early research confirmed that people often violate the assumptions of economic rationality and are guided in their choices by noneconomic motivations. For example, one series of studies showed that slight changes in the way choice options are described to people or in the way they are asked to indicate their preferences can result in markedly different responses. In short, we behave very differently depending on how the information is presented to us, on the nature of the decision-making environment, even on what period of life we are in. Moreover, in many important situations we do not really know what we prefer; we must construct our preferences "on the spot."[5]

Not surprisingly, as often happens with new ideas, economists of the 1960s and 1970s were divided on how to interpret them. Many, rather than trying to understand the psychology, embarked on studies designed "to discredit the psychologists' work as applied to economics."[6] Evidence against the rationality of individual behavior tended to be dismissed by those economists on the grounds that in the competitive world outside the laboratory, rational agents would survive at the expense of others. In this way, the study of irrationality could be downplayed as the study of transient phenomena.

At the same time, and despite very important advances in economic theory that were made possible by the traditional view of *economic man*,[7] there was a growing sense of unease among the general public and other social scientists as well as among policy makers that many economists had been unrealistic in their attempts to always rationalize how people, enterprises, and markets function.

Fortunately, the story did not stop there. Stimulated by creative conceptual, methodological, and empirical work by the more senior authors in *The Irrational Economist* and many others, including Amos Tversky, Daniel Kahneman, and Richard Thaler, the trickle of studies challenging traditional economic assumptions of rationality became a torrent. Nobel prizes in economics awarded to Herbert Simon in 1978, to George Akerlof in 2001, and to Daniel Kahneman and Vernon Smith in 2002 for their contributions toward understanding the behavioral dynamics of economic decisions further contributed to what has become a revolution in thinking.

Today, young scholars, and even those not so young, have become convinced that the secret to improving economic decision making lies in the careful empirical study of how we *actually* make decisions. New multidisciplinary fields have now emerged—many represented in this book by those who pioneered them—including behavioral economics, economic psychology, behavioral finance, decision sciences, and neuroeconomics, to integrate theories and results from economics, psychology, sociology, anthropology, biology, and brain sciences. Applied fields such as management, marketing, finance, public policy, and risk management and insurance are using this new knowledge today in significant ways.

We now recognize that the question "Are people rational or irrational?" is ill-formed. As human beings, we have intuitive and analytic thinking skills that work beautifully, most of the time, to help us navigate through life and achieve our goals, individually and collectively. But sometimes our thinking skills fail us.

The very modes of thought that are highly rational most of the time can get us into big trouble when the nature of the environment surrounding us, or the time horizon on which we make decisions, changes. We are also fundamentally influenced by short-term rewards, by what others do, and by what is at stake and how we feel when we make these decisions. Our emotions (known to economists as "affective feelings" or "affects"), including fear, anxiety, love, trust, and confidence, all of which help us assess risk and reward, are processed swiftly in our minds. These feelings form the neural and psychological substrate of what is important to us and guide many decisions, what economists refer to as "utility." In this sense, reliance on feelings enables us to be rational actors in many important situations. For instance, if you were to see a venomous snake on your vacation trip, you would not pause to calculate the mathematical utility of all the possible harmful consequences multiplied by their associated probability (hard to calculate anyway) in order to decide what to do. Upon seeing the snake, you would act rationally: You would move away fast.

More generally, reliance on our gut feelings works when our experience enables us to anticipate accurately the consequences of our decisions—that is, when we have a good knowledge of the situation and (think we) fully understand our reactions today and in the future. But it fails miserably when the consequences turn out to be very different from what we expected—which is likely to happen quite often in an uncertain world. In the instance of surprise, the rational actor often becomes, to borrow the words of 1998 Nobel Laureate Amartya Sen,[8] the rational fool.

This brings us back to two of our original questions: How might we behave in this new, uncertain, and more dangerous environment? Will our actions be rational or irrational? Our answer is: It depends. Part One of this book—"Irrational Times"—addresses a series of behaviors that many might consider irrational. Yet, when we look at them more closely and try to understand the rationale behind them, they often make sense: Our actions are driven by our feelings, incentives, and the nature of the environment in which we make decisions.

The challenge before us now is to better understand when and how rationality fails in this modern world. The chapters in Part Two—"Are We Asking the Right Questions? Economic Models and Rationality"—consider the growing menu of tools we have at our disposal today to meet this challenge. Part Three—"Individual Decisions in a Dangerous and Uncertain World"—looks at the individual decision processes that arise when people are confronted with small and catastrophic risks, and at how experience, uncertainty, and different time horizons can radically threaten rationality. By understanding these processes and thus avoiding the failures of rationality that sometimes result, people can make better decisions for themselves, and also better decisions for others in our society. Part Four—"Managing and Financing Extreme Events"—analyzes how individual behavior can translate into very good or very poor collective decisions by enterprises, markets, and governments. Natural disasters, climate change, terrorism threats, and financial crises are cited as illustrative examples of uncertain and dangerous environments.

WHAT ROLE FOR THE ECONOMIST?
FROM THE IVORY TOWER TO THE CIRCLE OF POWER

In many ways, the transformation of economics as a discipline that now includes more realistic behavioral models is similar to what happened over the course of several centuries in physics, chemistry, biology, and medicine. Established paradigms evolve with new knowledge, the discovery of which is fueled, at least in part, by the collective desire to explain more accurately the world we live in, and by the aspiration to make it better. Economics is still a young discipline. To mature, it needs to transform itself into one that not only can better *represent* human behavior in the real world (the normative approach) but also can *propose* better remedies to societal issues the world faces (the prescriptive approach).

This leads us to ask: What should be the role of those who study or have a special knowledge of economics and other social sciences in ensuring the success of this transformation? Many pioneers of economics not only were advocates of specific theoretical programs but also participated directly in government. One example is Adam Smith, often cited as the father of modern economics. His work on self-interest was largely prompted by a critique of mercantilism and adherence to a moderate free-market policy (even though his earlier work focused on a morality based on sympathy and benevolence).[9] But he was also one of the leading customs commissioners in Scotland appointed in 1778. Another is James Mill, who made significant contributions to classical British economic theory and was also a high-ranking official of the East India Company that governed India. During the 1830s, he was an influential leader in Parliament. A third is David Ricardo, tutored by Mill; after writing his *Principles of Political Economy and Taxation* in 1817 he entered Parliament as well. And influential laissez-faire economist Michel Chevalier negotiated the free-trade agreement between the U.K. and France in 1860—the same year he became a senator in the French Congress.

This long history of prominent economists influencing policy has continued. For instance, the Italian economist Vilfredo Pareto made important contributions to the study of income distribution and the analysis of individuals' choices; but he was also a militant laissez-faire liberal who battled for free trade. And of course John Maynard Keynes, the very influential British economist, served in several key government posts during the twentieth century. Keynes would spearhead a revolution in economic thinking that was essentially pragmatic, rather than theoretical. He wanted his ideas to work in the world.

It is for the same reason that in a rare moment of collective awareness for our profession, Part Five of this book addresses the ultimate question "What Difference Can We Make?" If we are right in saying that the world is becoming more interconnected, that the potential for catastrophes is more widespread than ever before, and that the effects of any single person or group may be, like the proverbial flap of the butterfly's wing, amplified across the world with potentially vast consequences, then an accurate appreciation of the science of decision making and of catastrophe risk management cannot remain within the ivory towers of universities and specialist institutes. Indeed, this knowledge must be shared—with industries, governments, nongovernmental organizations, philanthropic foundations, investors, the media, and, last but by no means least, all individuals who care to make the best-informed choices to safeguard themselves and their families in this fast-moving, ever-thrilling world that may challenge them with deep adversity and extreme events. This is the goal of *The Irrational Economist*.

As a way of ensuring that this knowledge is shared and used more broadly, we hope to see more and more behavioral scientists being asked to provide top decision makers with their views, or even to take on high-level positions in the public and private sectors. In doing so, they will assume this dual role of researchers/teachers and influential players in the power circles of business and public policy, as other great minds in economics have done before. But this time, not quite as purely rationally.

PART ONE

IRRATIONAL TIMES

IN THESE FIVE OPENING CHAPTERS, the authors contemplate a patch-work of situations where decisions can be viewed as *irrational* (i.e., deviating from what economic rationality would seem to dictate). Each chapter, each anecdote, each piece of evidence provides a touch of color representing an aspect of human behavior either in daily life or during extraordinary times. Together, they provide a mosaic of ideas, integral parts of a surprising painting, that will be discussed in detail in the rest of the book.

For example, why don't many hotels have a thirteenth floor? Or planes a thirteenth row? Should our believing in supra-human forces (superstition and religion) be considered irrational? If so, how do economists study the ways in which it affects human behavior? A cast of remarkable characters—weather forecasters and beautiful people—unexpectedly help us better understand how (misaligned) incentives on Wall Street pushed us into financial chaos. This section will also consider how decisions can be made today about career choices for the next thirty years, given the increasing uncertainties that come with our rapidly changing world. Part One ends with an ounce of behavioral observation about our dangerous world. We ask how compassionate we really are when it comes to helping others in profound distress . . . and learn that caring does not increase proportionally with the number of victims, as economic rationality would suggest, but rather goes in the opposite direction. All the anecdotes and evidence highlighted in Part One give us a sense of how we *really* make decisions—a consideration that is all the more important to appreciate and acknowledge as we contemplate the extraordinary times that lie ahead. The new risk architecture that is now unfolding brings complex interdependencies among nations, companies, and individuals all over the world. How others behave should matter more to you today than ever: Directly or indirectly, you are linked to them, as they are to you.

1 Superstition

A Common Irrationality?

THOMAS SCHELLING

The night before the conference honoring Howard Kunreuther's birthday I stayed in a Philadelphia Hotel. Riding up the elevator I noticed there was no thirteenth floor.

Walking up Madison Avenue in New York recently, for about twenty blocks, I counted more than twenty fortune tellers on one side of the street. I remember that the wife of a president of the United States was reported to have consulted some kind of seer who resided in California. I've been told by what I thought a reliable source that air traffic is below normal on a Friday the thirteenth. Several airlines have no thirteenth row. (What could happen to a passenger in the thirteenth row that would not occur in the fourteenth, I can't imagine.)

And this morning's newspaper carried this advice in the horoscope for (my birth month) Aries:

> Old problems surface. Make progress in this regard so you can avoid sharing the all-too-familiar chorus of your discontent. That tune is tired and loved ones will thank you for not playing it.

I recall that the oracle at Delphi had a reputation for prophecies sufficiently ambiguous to avoid her being proved wrong. (Now that I think of it, I've never checked whether the horoscopes in different newspapers provide similar advice, or whether they are sufficiently specific that their similarity can be judged.)

11

Before many states succumbed to the temptation to use lotteries to enhance their revenue, illegal lotteries, known as "numbers rackets," met the demand and were able to charge higher prices for "lucky" numbers—particular numbers that, unlike one's birth date, were not peculiar to an individual but were widely regarded as somehow blessed.

There is a well-known, and much-studied, "gamblers' fallacy"—actually two of them. One is that if a tossed coin comes up heads four times in a row, it has "exhausted" its heads inventory and is likely to come up tails. The other is that it's on a "roll," and is likely to come up heads again. (If the experimenter pulls a new coin out of his pocket, after the four heads, the new coin is viewed as neutral, offering a 50–50 chance.) My statistically sophisticated colleagues dismiss these expectations with the rhetorical question, "Does the coin remember, does the coin care?" I think the believers must answer, "Someone up there does!"

Many years ago, while driving a son to school with the radio on, I would hear the advertisement of the Massachusetts Lottery Commission urging us to consider that if we concentrated hard enough we might just do better than chance with our ticket. I never knew whether the Commission meant we might *predict* the winning numbers or we might *determine* the winning numbers. (Not all of us, I'm sure, because not all of us could concentrate on the same number!) I marveled that the Commonwealth of Massachusetts would promote extrasensory perception to sell tickets. The market analysis must have led the Commission to believe that some of us could be conned. (Or did the Commissioners believe it themselves; did they even buy tickets themselves and concentrate?)

There are experiments in which people given a modest gift, a coffee mug or a sweatshirt, decline to trade it for some equally "valuable" gift that they might instead have been given. Something happens to "attach" the gift to the recipient. Similarly, people who receive lottery tickets at the door to some event have been found unwilling to trade their tickets for "equally" valuable tickets. (See the work of Ellen Langer, psychologist, Harvard University.) One explanation is that if it's "their" day to win, they don't want to confuse the decision by switching tickets!

In the Theory of Games it is held that in "games against nature," such as deciding whether the weather will turn cold, or rain may ensue, nature is neutral, in contrast to games with human subjects who will act strategically. My impression is that for many people nature is not neutral. I've known someone whose auto collision insurance expired while he was traveling, and he wouldn't drive until his renewed insurance was confirmed. I asked him how many collisions he'd had in some decades of driving, and the answer was none. What's the expected value of the risk of auto damage if you drive, I asked, thinking he could give a statistical answer that would contradict his decision not to drive. Instead he smiled and said, "That's just the day that I'd have the accident!" I think the same goes for driving without one's license: "That's the day I'd get stopped by a cop!"

(Maybe it is not a truly superstitious belief that if I drive without a license I'll be stopped by an officer. It may be that if I drive without a license I cannot stop *thinking* I have no license, and cannot stop looking in the mirror for a police car. It's my imagination I cannot control, not my logic.)

We've been taught by psychologists Daniel Kahneman and Amos Tversky that many people are innocent of statistical sampling, that many get "anchored" by a randomly produced number, that many are seduced by "representativeness," and many don't understand "regression to the mean." You walk into a public library in the suburb of a large city and see a man, dressed in tie and jacket, reading Thucydides; you have already learned that he is either a concert violinist or a truck driver. Which do you guess he is? Considering that there are 10,000 concert violinists in the country and 2 million truck drivers, if 1 in 200 truck drivers is as likely as any single concert violinist to read Thucydides in the public library dressed in jacket and tie, you should guess truck driver, but you (and I) usually don't.

RELIGION AND SUPERSTITION

An article in the magazine of the American Association of Retired People on the prevalence of belief in miracles reported that among 1,300 people over 45 years of age 80 percent believed in miracles. Fully 37 percent said they had actually witnessed one. The article defined a miracle as "an incredible event that cannot be scientifically explained." (What about credible events that cannot be scientifically explained? Believers must find miracles credible, else they'd not believe in them.)

The *American Heritage Dictionary* defines *miracle* as "an event that appears unexplainable by the laws of nature and so is held to be supernatural in origin or an act of god." It defines *superstition* as "a belief, practice, or rite *irrationally* maintained by *ignorance* of the laws of nature or by faith in magic or chance." (Emphasis added.) If *magic* is supernatural, these definitions are distinguished mainly by the somewhat superfluous adjective *irrationally*.

Of course, what is in accordance with the laws of nature can be somewhat ephemeral. Isaac Newton believed in the transmutation of elements; alchemy was not yet against the laws of nature. Eventually the laws of nature made the transformation of one element into another not possible. Then, in the twentieth century, it proved possible to convert Uranium 238 into Plutonium 239 by irradiation.

In 1997, a religious organization called Heavensgate believed that a space vehicle was hidden on the far side of the Hale Bopp comet and could be accessed by the devout if they would commit communal suicide. Seventy-five followers killed themselves. Was their belief "against the laws of nature"? Most of us don't believe they made it to the other side of Hale Bopp but many of us do believe in heaven and hell, which "appear unexplainable by the laws of nature." As miracles go, the Heavensgate project is not uniquely unimaginable, but the media treated it as superstition.

During the New Hampshire Republican primary campaign George H. W. Bush shouted at Ronald Reagan, "That's Voodoo economics!" (I couldn't tell whether he capitalized *voodoo*.) I doubt whether anyone would dare to say, in a New Hampshire primary campaign, "That's Mormon economics" or "That's Seventh Day Adventist economics" or "That's Jehovah's Witnesses economics." There might be a Mormon, or an Adventist, or a Witness in the audience but probably not someone from Haiti registered to vote.

Most people I encounter appear willing to dismiss Voodoo as superstition, are amusedly patronizing of Native American theology, but respectful of monotheisms whether or not they subscribe to one.

All three of the world's great monotheisms entail *prayer*, "a reverent petition made to a deity or other object of worship" (*American Heritage Dictionary*). It is no insult to those who pray to observe that a response to a *reverent petition* would be a *miracle* as defined above, "an event that appears unexplainable by the laws of nature and so is held to be supernatural in origin or an act of god."

I doubt whether the authenticity of prayer can be experimentally disproven. Prayer certainly has been shown to have a placebo effect. Whether the prayer itself can be deemed responsible for the success of the petition depends on whether the outcome can be identified with any certainty as not due to natural causes. Any negative results in an experiment designed for the purpose of testing the deity's responsiveness would surely violate the Third Commandment and could be discarded on that account.

If we have now arrived at the junction of myth, superstition, and religion, it's time for me to close.

P.S. A couple of months after Howard's celebration my wife and I were in the security line at Copenhagen airport and realized that I had no wallet. We cancelled our flight, retrieved our luggage, returned to our hotel, cancelled my credit and ATM cards, talked to all the cab drivers, went back to the airport for a late flight to Warsaw. Our luggage didn't arrive. On checking out of our hotel five days later, we needed to verify the date of our arrival. It turned out to have been Friday the thirteenth!

RECOMMENDED READING

Kahneman, Daniel, Paul Slovic, and Amos Tversky, eds. (1982). *Judgment Under Uncertainty: Heuristics and Biases.* Cambridge: Cambridge University Press, 1982.

Kahneman, Daniel, and Amos Tversky, eds. (2000). *Choices, Values, and Frames.* Cambridge: Cambridge University Press, 2000.

Langer, Ellen J. (1982). "The Illusion of Control." In Daniel Kahneman, Paul Slovic, and Amos Tversky, eds. *Judgment Under Uncertainty: Heuristics and Biases.* Cambridge: Cambridge University Press.

Schelling, Thomas (1996). "Coping Rationally with Lapses from Rationality," *Eastern Economic Journal* (Summer): 251–269. Reprinted in Thomas Schelling, *Strategies of Commitment and Other Essays* (Cambridge, MA: Harvard University Press, 2006.)

2 Berserk Weather Forecasters, Beauty Contests, and Delicious Apples on Wall Street

GEORGE A. AKERLOF AND ROBERT J. SHILLER

No one has ever made rational sense of the wild gyrations in financial prices, such as stock prices.[1] These fluctuations are as old as the financial markets themselves. And yet these prices are essential factors in investment decisions, which are fundamental to the economy. Corporate investment is much more volatile than aggregate GDP, and it appears to be an important driver of economic fluctuations. If we recognize these facts, we are left once again with more evidence that animal spirits are central to the ups and downs of the economy.

The real value of the U.S. stock market rose over fivefold between 1920 and 1929. It then came all the way back down between 1929 and 1932. The real value of the stock market doubled between 1954 and 1973. Then the market came all the way back down. It then lost half of its real value between 1973 and 1974. The real value of the stock market rose almost eightfold between 1982 and 2000. Then it lost nearly 60 percent of its value between 2007 and early 2009, before rebounding again.[2]

The question is not just how to forecast these events before they occur. The problem is deeper than that. No one can even explain why these events rationally ought to have happened even *after* they have happened.

One might think, from the self-assurance that economists often display when extolling the efficiency of the markets, that they have reliable explanations of what has driven aggregate stock markets, which they are just keeping to themselves. They *can* of course give examples that justify the stock price changes of some individual firms. But they cannot do this for the aggregate stock market.[3]

16

Over the years economists have *tried* to give a convincing explanation for aggregate stock price movements in terms of economic fundamentals. But no one has ever succeeded. They do not appear to be explicable in terms of changes in interest rates, subsequent dividends or earnings, or anything else.[4]

"The fundamentals of the economy remain strong." That cliché is repeated by authorities as they try to restore public confidence after every major stock market decline. They have the opportunity to say this because just about every major stock market decline appears inexplicable if one looks only at the factors that logically *ought* to influence stock markets. It is practically always the stock market that has changed; indeed, the fundamentals haven't.

How do we know that these changes could not be generated by fundamentals? If prices reflect fundamentals, they do so because those fundamentals are useful in forecasting future stock payoffs. In theory, the stock prices are the predictors of the discounted value of those future income streams, in the form of future dividends or future earnings. But stock prices are much too variable. They are even much more variable than those discounted streams of dividends (or earnings) that they are trying to predict.[5]

BERSERK WEATHER FORECASTERS

To pretend that stock prices reflect people's use of information about those future payoffs is like hiring a weather forecaster who has gone berserk. He lives in a town where temperatures are fairly stable, but he predicts that one day they will be 150° and on another they will be –100°. Even if the forecaster has the mean of those temperatures right, and even if his exaggerated estimates are at least accurate in calling the relatively hot days and the relatively cold days, he should still be fired.

He would make more accurate forecasts on average if he did not predict that there would be any variation in temperature at all. For the same reason, one should reject the notion that stock prices reflect predictions, based on economic fundamentals, about future earnings. Why? Because the prices are much too variable.

Even this fact, blatant as it is, has not convinced efficient-markets advocates that their theory is wrong. They point out that the movements in stock prices *could* still be rational. They say that such movements could be reflecting new information about some possible major event affecting fundamentals that by chance did not happen in the past century, or the century before that either. In this view the stock market is still the best predictor of those future payoffs. Its gyrations are occurring because something might have happened to fundamentals. They maintain that the mere fact that the major event did not happen cannot be taken to mean that the market was irrational. Maybe they are right. One cannot decisively *prove* that the stock market has been irrational. But in all of this debate no one has offered any real evidence to think that the volatility *is* rational.[6]

The price changes appear instead to be correlated with social changes of various kinds. Andrei Shleifer and Sendhil Mullainathan have observed the changes in Merrill Lynch advertisements. Prior to the stock market bubble, in the early 1990s, Merrill Lynch was running advertisements showing a grandfather fishing with his grandson. The ad was captioned: "Maybe you should plan to grow rich slowly." By the time the market had peaked around 2000, when investors were obviously very pleased with recent results, Merrill's ads had changed dramatically. In one of these was a picture of a computer chip shaped like a bull. The caption read: "Be Wired . . . Be Bullish." After the subsequent market correction, Merrill went back to the grandfather and the grandson. They were again patiently fishing. The caption advertised "Income for a lifetime."[7] Of course, the marketing professionals who concoct such ads believe they are closely tracking public thinking as it changes dramatically over time. Why should we regard *their* professional opinion as less worth listening to than the professional opinion of finance professors and efficient-markets advocates?

THE BEAUTY CONTEST AND DELICIOUS APPLE METAPHORS

In his 1936 book Keynes compared the equilibrium in the stock market to that of a popular newspaper competition of his time. Competitors were asked to pick the six prettiest faces from a hundred photographs. The prize was awarded to the competitor whose choices came closest to the average preferences of all of the competitors as a group. Of course, to win such a competition one should not pick the faces one thinks are prettiest. Instead, one should pick the faces that one thinks others are likely to think the prettiest. But even that strategy is not the best, for certainly others are employing it too. It would be better yet to pick the faces that one thinks others are most likely to think that others think are the prettiest. Or maybe one should even go a step or two further in this thinking.[8] Investing in stocks is often like that: Just as with the beauty contest, in the short run one wins not by picking the company most likely to succeed in the long run but, rather, by picking the company most likely to have high market value in the short run.

The Delicious Apple offers another metaphor for much the same theory. Hardly anyone today really likes the taste of the varietal now called Delicious. And yet these apples are ubiquitous. They are often the *only* choice in cafeterias, on lunch counters, and in gift baskets. Delicious Apples used to taste better, back in the nineteenth century when an entirely different apple was marketed under this name. The Delicious varietal had become overwhelmingly the best-selling apple in the United States by the 1980s. When apple connoisseurs began shifting to other varietals, apple growers tried to salvage their profits. They moved the Delicious Apple into another market niche. It became the inexpensive apple that people think other people like, or that people think other people think other people like. Most growers gave up on good taste. They cheapened the apple by switching to strains with higher yield and better shelf life. They cheapened it by clear-picking an entire orchard at once, no longer choosing the apples as they ripened individually. Since Delicious Apples are not selling based on taste, why pay extra for taste? The general public cannot imagine that an apple could be so cheapened. Nor does it imagine the real reason these apples are ubiquitous despite their generally poor taste.[9]

The same kind of phenomenon occurs with speculative investments. Many people do not appreciate how much a company with a given name can change through time, or how many ways there are to debase its value. Stocks that nobody really believes in but that retain value are the Delicious Apples of the investment world.

RECOMMENDED READING

Allen, Franklin, Stephen Morris, and Hyung Song Shin (2002). "Beauty Contests, Bubbles, and Iterated Expectations in Asset Markets." Unpublished paper, Yale University.

Barberis, Nicholas, and Richard Thaler (2003). "A Survey of Behavioral Finance." In George Constantinides, Milton Harris, and René Stulz, eds. *Handbook of the Economics of Finance*. New York: Elsevier Science.

Campbell, John Y., and Robert J. Shiller (1987). "Cointegration and Tests of Present Value Models." *Journal of Political Economy* 97, no. 5: 1062–1088.

Higgins, Adrian (2005). "Why the Red Delicious No Longer Is." *Washington Post*, August 5, p. A1.

Jung, Jeeman, and Robert J. Shiller (2005). "Samuelson's Dictum and the Stock Market." *Economic Inquiry* 43, no. 2: 221–228.

Keynes, John Maynard. (1936/2009). *The General Theory of Employment, Interest and Money.* Kindle: Signalman Publishing.

LeRoy, Stephen, and Richard Porter (1981). "Stock Price Volatility: A Test Based on Implied Variance Bounds." *Econometrica* 49: 97–113.

Marsh, Terry A., and Robert C. Merton (1986). "Dividend Variability and Variance Bound Tests for the Rationality of Stock Prices." *American Economic Review* 76, no. 3: 483–498.

Shiller, Robert J. (1981). "Do Stock Prices Move Too Much to Be Justified by Subsequent Changes in Dividends?" *American Economic Review* 7, no. 3: 421–436.

Shiller, Robert J. (1986). "The Marsh-Merton Model of Managers' Smoothing of Dividends." *American Economic Review* 76, no. 3: 499–503.

Shiller, Robert J. (2000). *Irrational Exuberance*, 1st ed. Princeton: Princeton University Press.

Shleifer, Andrei, and Robert W. Vishny (1997). "The Limits of Arbitrage." *Journal of Finance* 52, no. 1: 33–55.

3 Subways, Coconuts, and Foggy Minefields

An Approach to Studying Future-Choice Decisions

ROBIN M. HOGARTH

"Future-choice" decisions are decisions that have three important sources of complexity.

First, *actions taken today can have unknown consequences at future horizons that are difficult to specify.*
Second, *decisions imply complex inter-temporal tradeoffs.*
And, third, *it is problematic to specify relevant states of the world, let alone to assess their probabilities.*

Consider, for example, making decisions today that will affect the layout of a city. How far into the future should such decisions look? What volumes of traffic are likely to develop on alternative highways? What unknown technological advances could change costs and benefits? Will public preferences remain stable? What are the possibilities of different natural or social disasters? And so on. The list of possibilities and complications is endless. Imagine further a 23-year-old who is planning a career and ways of acquiring capital across her life. How can she evaluate different career paths? How can she know today what expertise will be in demand in ten or twenty years? How can she predict changes in her personal situation as well as her health?

Today, the standard economic model for dealing with these situations is the discounted utility model. This has the advantage of reducing the net benefits of each alternative stream of actions to a single number so that "rational" comparisons can be made. However, achieving these single numbers implies a series of heroic assumptions that exceed most mortals' capabilities.

In thinking about these issues, I first want to salute the considerable advances made in our understanding due to decision theory. In so doing, however, we need to keep clearly in mind just what decision analysis can and cannot take into account.

Second, I will go on to distinguish two types of uncertainty that characterize decisions labeled "subway" and "coconut" uncertainty, respectively.

Third, the presence of coconut uncertainty essentially implies the breakdown of decision-theoretic and forecasting models and demands a new approach for future-choice decisions. Whereas I cannot offer a new approach yet—or an intellectual breakthrough—I can suggest a *heuristic principle* and metaphor that may help us deal with some of the issues. Perhaps by considering their advantages and disadvantages, we might illuminate some of the problems of future-choice decisions and, at the least, set an agenda for future research.

THE FAILURE OF DECISION THEORY

Like many graduate students of my generation, I was totally seduced by statistical decision theory. But statistical decision theory never really became the universal tool that many imagined it would.

Nor do I believe that decision theory has been handicapped by the fact that many of its axioms are violated by people's choices. Indeed, it is precisely "violations" of this sort that illustrate why a good theory is necessary.

My belief is that statistical decision theory fails in many important problems—particularly future-choice problems—because humans are incapable of characterizing the uncertainties of the world in which they operate. Decision theory applies only to well-defined "small worlds" (Savage, 1954).

In addition, although there can be no doubt that the ability to predict many phenomena has been an important element of human development, when it comes to predicting events in the socioeconomic domain the human predictive track record is, frankly, dismal.

TWO TYPES OF UNCERTAINTY

I think that what really hampers the use of formal analytical techniques for future-choice decisions is that uncertainty can take two forms. In a new book

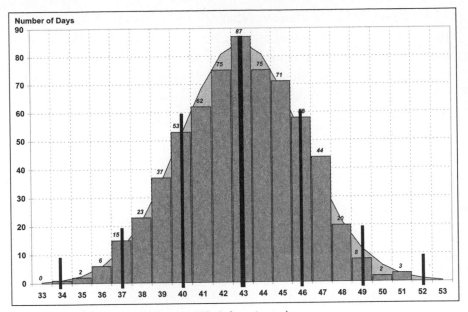

FIGURE 3.1 **Klaus's Travel Time to Work (in minutes)**
Source: Makridakis, Hogarth, and Gaba (2009).

(Makridakis, Hogarth, and Gaba, 2009), my co-authors and I refer to these as "subway uncertainty" and "coconut uncertainty," respectively.

In explaining these concepts, we cite the example of a mythical and obsessive character called Klaus who every day charts his commuting times to and from work (using the subway) so that, over a certain period, he accumulates a statistical representation of his travel times in the form of what is essentially a normal distribution—as shown in Figure 3.1. Indeed, assuming that nothing systematic disturbs the statistical pattern observed, Klaus can use the characteristics of the normal distribution to calculate the probability that his arrival time on any given day will fall within specified limits based on past history. Moreover, he can actually validate his model's predictions every day when he goes to work.

By "subway uncertainty," then, we mean a source of uncertainty whereby the statistical properties are well known and future "surprises" fall within well-specified limits. This kind of uncertainty—or approximations thereof—can be well handled within our decision-theoretic and forecasting models.

By "coconut uncertainty" we mean something quite different. Imagine you are sitting under a palm tree on a South Seas island and a coconut happens to fall on your head, causing considerable distress. Now, there are many disasters that you can imagine in life, but being hit on the head by a coconut when you are on vacation is probably not one of them (until you read this story, at least). In other words, by realizations of coconut uncertainty we mean events that you probably never even imagined could occur—there are so many different ones and you don't know which particular one will happen. Indeed, you might not even have a good handle on the class of events that could be described as coconuts.[1]

Interestingly, although there is a history of coconuts in some domains, people are still surprised by their occurrence. Daily returns on the stock market provide a case in point. Figure 3.2 shows the distribution of daily returns of the Dow Jones Industrial Average (DJIA) for the period from January 1, 1900, to December 31, 2007. As you can see, many observations lie outside the plus-or-minus-three-standard-deviations limits, and this graph does not even contain the observations for the wild market movements that occurred in 2008 and 2009. Parenthetically, if you look at the same data as a time series, there are periods—mainly at "crisis" times (e.g., October 1987 or 2001)—during which there seems to be dependence in the size of fluctuations, rather like the pre- and after-shocks that accompany earthquakes. In principle, in considering the stock market and other financial data one could always model some coconuts; but for some reason, many practitioners fail to do this and inevitably suffer the consequences—as evidenced by the worldwide financial crisis of 2008.

This observation is not limited to the financial markets, however. My point is that for future-choice decisions many variables are inherently unknowable. We cannot characterize the uncertainty because, if we are honest, we cannot even specify the events that might or might not occur. Consider, for example, how few people at the beginning of the 1980s foresaw the widespread use of personal computers and the development of the Internet. If you had been given correct forecasts for these developments at the time, would you have believed them? My contention is that you probably would not have known how to evaluate the forecasts.

What developments will occur over the next twenty-five years? I believe that we are all quite blind with respect to the future—and, moreover, that if we simply extrapolate past trends, huge errors will ensue. The path of social and economic development follows an evolutionary trail and, as is well known,

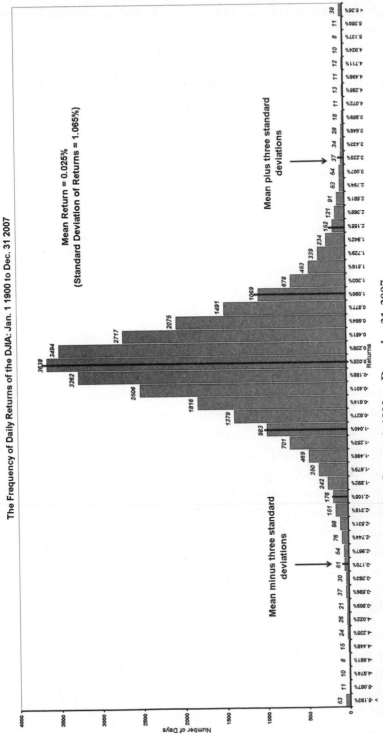

FIGURE 3.2 Dow Jones Industrial Average from January 1, 1900, to December 31, 2007

Source: Makridakis, Hogarth, and Gaba (2009).

although evolution provides a good story for explaining the past, it makes no predictions.

COMMIT ONLY AS FAR AS YOU CAN PREDICT

It would be wonderful to come up with a "good" or "amended" discounted utility model that could be used for long-term future-choice decisions. However, the complexities are such that I think this is not practicable. Instead, I would like to suggest a different strategy: Formulate a number of simple decision rules, or *heuristics*, that people can use to guide their actions when facing future-choice decisions. Whereas we must accept that no rule can be a guarantee, we could at least test such rules through simulation techniques and get some sense of their possibilities and limitations. Thus the rules would depend on more than just common sense.

The essence of the rule I wish to suggest here is to "commit only as far as you can predict." The rationale for this rule was suggested to me by the old joke about a Japanese Airlines pilot who ditched his aircraft in the bay at the San Francisco airport after a flight from Tokyo. "Why did you miss the airport by 200 yards?" a journalist asked. "Well," replied the pilot, "considering I came all the way from Tokyo, 200 yards was not much of an error."

The insight provided by this story is that, normally, when making commitments (here, where to land), a person should match actions with the level of uncertainty that can be managed. Thus, when leaving Tokyo, the pilot was foolish to commit to the precise parameters for landing in San Francisco; all he should have done was to select a path that could be adapted as conditions changed. When close to San Francisco, however, he could commit to a particular landing spot because at this proximity there would be considerably less uncertainty about the specific parameters. In short, the level of commitment should be matched to the level of uncertainty.

What are the implications of this pilot metaphor for future-choice decisions? First, many future-choice decisions have a temporal structure—similar to that of the Tokyo–San Francisco flight path—that can be broken down into several segments. Consider, for example, the many scenarios involved in urban planning or career development. However, in contrast to the Tokyo–San Francisco flight, which has a precise goal (i.e., arrival at a specific spot in San Francisco), the end-states of these future-choice decisions are not necessarily well defined. On the other hand, they undoubtedly are driven by a "direction" or values (e.g., creation of a viable city, achievement of personal and professional success). The important point here is that the time line of all these decisions can be broken down into periods for which it is reasonable to make commitments that can be evaluated.

FROM AIRPLANES TO FOGGY MINEFIELDS

Although it makes this point, the pilot metaphor is too simple for many realistic future-choice decisions. So, instead, I would like to introduce the metaphor of traveling across a minefield in a fog. The general goal—as in life—is to get across the field in good shape, and let's assume that in crossing the field there are various positive rewards that you can collect. But at the same time, your ability to see where you are going is restricted—randomly—by the density of the fog so that, whereas you might be able to see quite far in some cases, this is not always going to be the case. The mines, too, are distributed randomly around the field and vary in terms of how much damage they can inflict. In other words, whereas some are "coconuts," others might be quite containable. Let's say you also have some diagnostic mine-detecting equipment but this is not 100 percent reliable and may be biased for some types of mines.[2]

In the foggy minefield, the goal cannot be precise—it's just to get to the other side in the best possible condition. As for sub-goals, these are going to vary considerably depending on the state of the fog when you make any particular commitment. How, then, should one act?

It should be clear that decision making in the foggy minefield cannot be modeled easily by, say, some form of dynamic programming. The reason is that the characteristics of the environment are not known in advance but are only revealed as you advance. (Sure, you can have some intuitions about how the field is structured, but there will still be events you cannot even imagine.) My contention is that many future-choice decisions are like foggy minefields and, thus, that determining how to handle such environments is an important research agenda.

What research can be done on this topic? I argue that a good starting point would be to take a rule like the one described above—"commit only as far as you can predict"—and see how it performs in simulations that model different variations of the foggy-minefield paradigm. My suspicion—based on the work being done on simple decision rules in conventional environments[3]— is that heuristics that "work well" will be those that match the environment in critical ways.

As an example of such a simulation, imagine the following videogame, which I shall simply call "life." You start with an endowment that has to be allocated across a portfolio of assets, and the goal is to cross a foggy minefield and reach the other side with a portfolio that has increased substantially in value. The assets in your portfolio differ in their characteristics. One, which simulates your health, decreases over time, but you can invest resources to reduce the speed of decrease. If this asset hits a specified value, you are out of the game (i.e., you die). The other assets are income-producing but differ in their rates of return and in how much you can invest. These variations are hard to predict—because of the fog. Some, for example, are more predictable than others (i.e., they are less affected by the fog). In the game, time is conceptually continuous but is represented by discrete periods: If you don't make a specific decision during a given period to manage a specific asset, the asset will remain under the influence of the last time you made a decision concerning it. (This assumption is quite realistic; we all know that there are many things in our lives that will not change unless we decide to act upon them. If we delay our decision to act, things simply remain "as usual"—that is, the same as they were the last time we decided to change them.) And, of course, there are potential dangers in the form of mines that can explode and destroy your assets. You can, however, spend part of your resources to get some (imperfect) information.

Clearly, there are many issues involved in setting up the parameters of foggy minefields, including not only the one just described but also technical matters pertaining to creation of the actual simulation. However, in my opinion, the most interesting issue to investigate is the question of which decision rules, or heuristics, work effectively in foggy-minefield situations, as well as in variations of the game. How would different operational versions of the "commit only as far as you can predict" heuristic perform, and how sensitive would these be to changes in the game's parameters? What other rules might experts in decision making suggest?

Finally, going beyond research, it would make sense to have such a game played systematically at schools (from kindergarten up to our elite universities). After all, and as we know too well, our children and grandchildren will also grow up facing the vagaries of foggy minefields and thus will need to know how to handle both subway and coconut uncertainty.

RECOMMENDED READING

Hogarth, R. M., and N. Karelaia (2007). "Heuristic and Linear Models of Judgment: Matching Rules and Environments." *Psychological Review* 114, no. 3: 733–758.

Makridakis, S., R. M. Hogarth, and A. Gaba (2009). *Dance with Chance: Making Luck Work for You*. Oxford: Oneworld Publications.

Savage, L. J. (1954). *The Foundations of Statistics*. New York: John Wiley & Sons.

Taleb, N. N. (2007). *The Black Swan: The Impact of the Highly Improbable*. New York: Random House.

Winter, S. G., G. Cattani, and A. Dorsch (2007). "The Value of Moderate Obsession: Insights from a New Model of Organizational Search." *Organization Science* 18, no. 3: 403–419.

4 The More Who Die, the Less We Care

PAUL SLOVIC

A defining element of catastrophes is the magnitude of their harmful conse-quences. To help society prevent or mitigate damage from catastrophes, im-mense effort and technological sophistication are often employed to assess and communicate the size and scope of potential or actual losses.[1] This effort assumes that people can understand the resulting numbers and act on them appropriately.

However, recent behavioral research casts doubt on this fundamental as-sumption. Many people do *not* understand large numbers. Indeed, large numbers have been found to lack meaning and to be underweighted in decisions unless they convey *affect* (feeling). As a result, there is a paradox that rational models of decision making fail to represent. On the one hand, we respond strongly to aid a single individual in need. On the other hand, we often fail to prevent mass tragedies such as genocide or take appropriate measures to reduce potential losses from natural disasters. I think this occurs, in part, because as numbers get larger and larger, we become insensitive; numbers fail to trigger the emotion or feeling necessary to motivate action.

I shall address this problem of insensitivity to mass tragedy by identifying certain circumstances in which it compromises the rationality of our actions and by pointing briefly to strategies that might lessen or overcome this problem.

BACKGROUND AND THEORY: THE IMPORTANCE OF AFFECT

Risk management in the modern world relies upon two forms of thinking. *Risk as feelings* refers to our instinctive and intuitive reactions to danger. *Risk*

as analysis brings logic, reason, quantification, and deliberation to bear on hazard management. Compared to analysis, reliance on feelings tends to be a
quicker, easier, and more efficient way to navigate in a complex, uncertain,
and dangerous world. Hence, it is essential to rational behavior. Yet it sometimes misleads us. In such circumstances we need to ensure that reason and
analysis also are employed.

Although the visceral emotion of fear certainly plays a role in risk as feelings, I shall focus here on the "faint whisper of emotion" called *affect*. As used
here, *affect* refers to specific feelings of "goodness" or "badness" experienced
with or without conscious awareness. Positive and negative feelings occur rapidly and automatically; note how quickly you sense the feelings associated
with the word *joy* or the word *hate*. A large research literature in psychology
documents the importance of affect in conveying meaning upon information
and motivating behavior. Without affect, information lacks meaning and will
not be used in judgment and decision making.

FACING CATASTROPHIC LOSS OF LIFE

Risk as feelings is clearly rational, employing imagery and affect in remarkably
accurate and efficient ways; but this way of responding to risk has a darker,
nonrational side. Affect may misguide us in important ways. Particularly problematic is the difficulty of comprehending the meaning of catastrophic losses
of life when relying on feelings. Research reviewed below shows that disaster
statistics, no matter how large the numbers, lack emotion or feeling. As a result, they fail to convey the true meaning of such calamities and they fail to
motivate proper action to prevent them.

The psychological factors underlying insensitivity to large-scale losses of
human lives apply to catastrophic harm resulting from human malevolence,
natural disasters, and technological accidents. In particular, the psychological
account described here can explain, in part, our failure to respond to the diffuse and seemingly distant threat posed by global warming as well as the threat
posed by the presence of nuclear weaponry. Similar insensitivity may also un-
derlie our failure to respond adequately to problems of famine, poverty, and
disease afflicting large numbers of people around the world and even in our
own backyard.

THE DARFUR GENOCIDE

Since February 2003, hundreds of thousands of people in the Darfur region of western Sudan, Africa, have been murdered by government-supported militias, and millions have been forced to flee their burned-out villages for the dubious safety of refugee camps. This has been well documented. And yet the world looks away. The events in Darfur are the latest in a long list of mass murders since World War II to which powerful nations and their citizens have responded with indifference. In her Pulitzer Prize–winning book *A Problem from Hell: America and the Age of Genocide*, Samantha Power documents in meticulous detail many of the numerous genocides that occurred during the past century. In every instance, American response was inadequate. She concludes: "No U.S. president has ever made genocide prevention a priority, and no U.S. president has ever suffered politically for his indifference to its occurrence. It is thus no coincidence that genocide rages on" (Power, 2003, p. xxi).

The UN general assembly adopted the Convention on the Prevention and Punishment of the Crime of Genocide in 1948 in the hope that "never again" would there be such odious crimes against humanity as occurred during the Holocaust of World War II. Eventually some 140 states would ratify the Genocide Convention, yet it has never been invoked to prevent a potential attack or halt an ongoing massacre. Darfur has shone a particularly harsh light on the failures to intervene in genocide. As Richard Just (2008) has observed, "we are awash in information about Darfur. . . . [N]o genocide has ever been so thoroughly documented while it was taking place . . . but the genocide continues. We document what we do not stop. The truth does not set anybody free. (p. 36) . . . [H]ow could we have known so much and done so little?" (p. 38).

AFFECT, ANALYSIS, AND THE VALUE OF HUMAN LIVES

This brings us to a crucial question: How *should* we value the saving of human lives? An analytic answer would look to basic principles or fundamental values for guidance. For example, Article 1 of the UN Universal Declaration of Human Rights asserts that "[a]ll human beings are born free and equal in dignity and rights." We might infer from this the conclusion that every

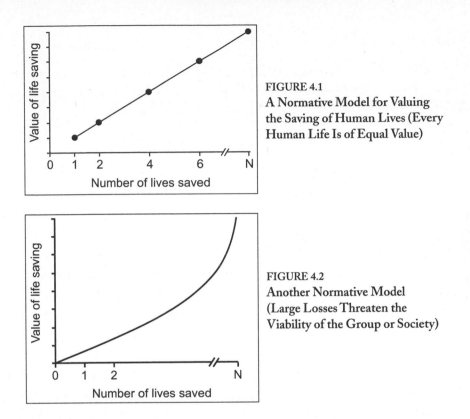

FIGURE 4.1
A Normative Model for Valuing
the Saving of Human Lives (Every
Human Life Is of Equal Value)

FIGURE 4.2
Another Normative Model
(Large Losses Threaten the
Viability of the Group or Society)

human life is of equal value. If so, then—applying a rational calculation—
the value of saving N lives is N times the value of saving one life, as represented by the linear function in Figure 4.1.

An argument can also be made for judging large losses of life to be disproportionately more serious because they threaten the social fabric and viability of a group or community (see Figure 4.2). Debate can be had at the
margins over whether one should assign greater value to younger people versus the elderly, or whether governments have a duty to give more weight to
the lives of their own people, and so on, but a perspective approximating
the equality of human lives is rather uncontroversial.

How *do* we actually value human lives? Research provides evidence in support of two descriptive models linked to affect and intuitive thinking that reflect values for lifesaving profoundly different from those depicted in the
normative (rational) models shown in Figures 4.1 and 4.2. Both of these descriptive models demonstrate responses that are insensitive to large losses of
human life, consistent with apathy toward genocide.

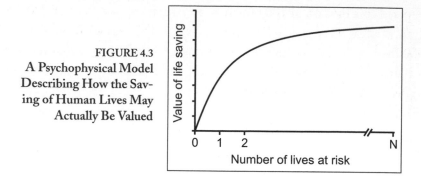

FIGURE 4.3
A Psychophysical Model
Describing How the Sav-
ing of Human Lives May
Actually Be Valued

THE PSYCHOPHYSICAL MODEL

There is considerable evidence that our affective responses and the resulting value we place on saving human lives follow the same sort of "psychophysical function" that characterizes our diminished sensitivity to changes in a wide range of perceptual and cognitive entities—brightness, loudness, heaviness, and wealth—as their underlying magnitudes increase.

As psychophysical research indicates, constant increases in the magnitude of a stimulus typically evoke smaller and smaller changes in response. Applying this principle to the valuing of human life suggests that a form of *psychophysical numbing* may result from our inability to appreciate losses of life as they become larger. The function in Figure 4.3 represents a value structure in which the importance of saving one life is great when it is the first, or only, life saved but diminishes as the total number of lives at risk increases. Thus, psychologically, the importance of saving one life pales against the background of a larger threat: We may not "feel" much difference, nor value the difference, between saving 87 lives and saving 88.

My colleagues David Fetherstonhaugh, Steven Johnson, James Friedrich, and I demonstrated this potential for psychophysical numbing in the context of evaluating people's willingness to fund various lifesaving interventions. In a study involving a hypothetical grant-funding agency, respondents were asked to indicate the number of lives a medical research institute would have to save to merit receipt of a $10 million grant. Nearly two-thirds of the respondents raised their minimum benefit requirements to warrant funding when there was a larger at-risk population, with a median value of 9,000 lives needing to be saved when 15,000 were at risk (implicitly valuing each life saved at $1,111), compared to a median of 100,000 lives needing to be saved out of 290,000 at risk (implicitly valuing each life saved at $100). Thus respondents saw saving 9,000 lives in the smaller population as more valuable than saving more than ten times as many lives in the larger population. The same study also found that people were less willing to send aid that would save 4,500 lives in Rwandan refugee camps as the size of the camps' at-risk population increased.

In recent years, vivid images of natural disasters in South Asia and the American Gulf Coast, and stories of individual victims there, brought to us through relentless, courageous, and intimate news coverage, unleashed an outpouring of compassion and humanitarian aid from all over the world. Perhaps there is hope here that vivid, personalized media coverage featuring victims could also motivate intervention to prevent mass murder and genocide.

Perhaps. Research demonstrates that people are much more willing to aid identified individuals than unidentified or statistical victims. But a cautionary note comes from a study in which my colleagues and I gave people who had just participated in a paid psychological experiment the opportunity to contribute up to $5 of their earnings to the charity Save the Children. In one condition, respondents were asked to donate money to feed an identified victim, a 7-year-old African girl named Rokia, of whom they were shown a picture. They contributed more than twice the amount given by a second group who were asked to donate to the same organization working to save millions of Africans (statistical lives) from hunger. Respondents in a third group were asked to donate to Rokia, but were also shown the larger statistical problem (millions in need) shown to the second group. Unfortunately, coupling the large-scale statistical realities with Rokia's story significantly *reduced* contributions to Rokia (see Figure 4.4).

Why did this occur? Perhaps the presence of statistics reduced the attention to Rokia essential for establishing the emotional connection necessary to motivate donations. Alternatively, recognition of the millions who would not be helped by one's small donation may have produced negative feelings that inhibited donations. Note the similarity here at the individual level to the failure to help 4,500 people in the larger refugee camp. The rationality of these responses can be questioned. We should not be deterred from helping 1 person, or 4,500, just because there are many others we cannot save!

In sum, research on psychophysical numbing is important because it demonstrates that feelings necessary for motivating lifesaving actions are not

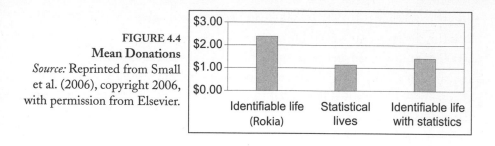

congruent with the normative/rational models in Figures 4.1 and 4.2. The nonlinearity displayed in Figure 4.3 is consistent with the devaluing of incremental loss of life against the background of a large tragedy. It can thus explain why we don't feel any different upon learning that the death toll in Darfur is closer to 400,000 than to 200,000. What it does not fully explain, however, is apathy toward genocide, inasmuch as it implies that the response to initial loss of life will be strong and maintained, albeit with diminished sensitivity, as the losses increase. Evidence for a second descriptive model, better suited to explain apathy toward large losses of lives, follows.

THE COLLAPSE OF COMPASSION

American writer Annie Dillard reads in her newspaper the headline "Head Spinning Numbers Cause Mind to Go Slack." She writes of "compassion fatigue" and asks, "At what number do other individuals blur for me?"[2]

An answer to Dillard's question is beginning to emerge from behavioral research. Studies by social psychologists find that a single individual, unlike a group, is viewed as a psychologically coherent unit. This leads to more extensive processing of information and stronger impressions about individuals than about groups. Consistent with this, a study in Israel found that people tend to feel more distress and compassion and to provide more aid when considering a single victim than when considering a group of eight victims.[3] A follow-up study in Sweden found that people felt less compassion and donated less aid toward a pair of victims than to either individual alone.[4] Perhaps the blurring that Annie Dillard asked about begins for groups as small as two people.

The insensitivity to lifesaving portrayed by the psychophysical-numbing model is unsettling. But the studies just described suggest an even more disturbing psychological tendency. Our capacity to feel is limited. To the extent

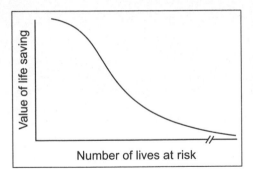

FIGURE 4.5
A Model Depicting
Psychic Numbing:
The Collapse of
Compassion—When
Valuing the Saving of Lives

that valuation of lifesaving depends on feelings driven by attention or imagery, it might follow the function shown in Figure 4.5, where the emotion or affective feeling is greatest at $N = 1$ but begins to decline at $N = 2$ and collapses at some higher value of N that becomes simply "a statistic." Whereas Robert J. Lifton coined the term *psychic numbing* to describe the "turning off" of feeling that enabled rescue workers to function during the horrific aftermath of the Hiroshima bombing,[5] Figure 4.5 depicts a form of psychic numbing that is not beneficial. Rather, it leads to apathy and inaction, consistent with what is seen repeatedly in response to mass murder and genocide.

THE FAILURE OF MORAL INTUITION

Thoughtful deliberation takes effort. Fortunately evolution has equipped us with sophisticated cognitive and perceptual mechanisms that can guide us through our daily lives efficiently, with minimal need for "deep thinking."

Consider how we typically deal with risk. Long before we had invented probability theory, risk assessment, and decision analysis, there were such faculties as intuition, instinct, and gut feeling, honed by experience, to tell us whether an animal was safe to approach or water was safe to drink. As life became more complex and humans gained more control over their environment, analytic ways of thinking evolved to boost the rationality of our experiential reactions. Beyond the question of how water looks and tastes, we now can look to toxicology and analytic chemistry to tell us whether it is safe to drink. But we can still use our feelings as well, an easier path.

As with risk, the natural and easy way to deal with moral issues is to rely on our intuitions: "How bad is it?" Well, how bad does it feel? We can also apply reason and logical analysis to determine right and wrong, as our legal system attempts to do. But, as Jonathan Haidt, a psychologist at the University of Virginia, has demonstrated, moral *intuition* comes first and usually dominates moral *judgment* unless we make an effort to critique and, if necessary, override our intuitive feelings.[6]

Unfortunately, moral intuition fails us in the face of genocide and other disasters that threaten human lives and the environment on a large scale. We cannot trust it. It depends upon attention and feelings that may be hard to arouse and sustain over time for large numbers of victims, not to mention numbers as small as two. Left to its own devices, moral intuition will likely favor individual victims and sensational stories that are close to home and easy to imagine. Our sizable capacity to care for others may be demotivated by negative feelings resulting from thinking about those we cannot help. Or it may be overridden by pressing personal and local interests. Compassion for others has been characterized by social psychologist Daniel Batson as "a fragile flower, easily crushed by self-concern."[7] Faced with genocide and other mass tragedies, we cannot rely on our intuitions alone to guide us to act properly.

WHAT TO DO?

Behavioral research, supported by common observation and the record of repeated failures to arouse citizens and leaders to halt the scourge of genocide and to prevent thousands from perishing in natural disasters, sends a strong and important message. Our moral intuitions often fail us. They seduce us into calmly turning away from massive losses of human lives, when we should be driven by outrage to act. This is no small weakness in our moral compass.

Fortunately, we have evolved a second mechanism, moral judgment, to address such problems, based on reason and argument. In the case of genocides and other mass crimes against humanity, we must focus now on engaging this mechanism by strengthening international legal and political structures that pre-commit states to respond to these tragedies rather than being silent witnesses. The United Nations is the institution that was created in part to deal with such issues, but structural problems built into its very charter have made it ineffective. Appreciation of the failures of moral intuition makes development of new institutional arrangements even more urgent and critical. For it may only be laws and institutions that can keep us on course, forcing us to doggedly pursue the hard measures needed to combat genocide when our attention strays and our feelings lull us into complacency.

Elsewhere, David Zionts and I have proposed that international and domestic law should require officials to publicly deliberate and proffer reasons to justify action or inaction in response to genocide;[8] that is an aspect of the notion of legitimation discussed in this book by Paul Kleindorfer. If enforced, a requirement for public justification would likely heighten pressure to act to save lives rather than allowing people to die.

The stakes are high. Failure to understand how our minds become insensitive to catastrophic losses of human life and failure to act on this knowledge may condemn us to passively witness yet another century of genocide and mass abuses of innocent people. It may also increase the likelihood that we will fail to take appropriate action to reduce the damages from other catastrophic events.

RECOMMENDED READING

Batson, C. D., K. O'Quin, J. Fultz, M. Vanderplas, and A. Isen (1983). "Self-Reported Distress and Empathy and Egoistic Versus Altruistic Motivation for Helping." *Journal of Personality and Social Psychology* 45: 706–718.

Dillard, A. (1999). *For the Time Being*. New York: Alfred A. Knopf.

Fetherstonhaugh, D., P. Slovic, S. M. Johnson, and J. Friedrich (1997). "Insensitivity to the Value of Human Life: A Study of Psychophysical Numbing." *Journal of Risk and Uncertainty* 14, no. 3: 283–300.

Haidt, J. (2001). "The Emotional Dog and Its Rational Tail: A Social Intuitionist Approach to Moral Judgment." *Psychological Review* 108: 814–834.

Just, R. (2008). "The Truth Will Not Set You Free: Everything We Know About Darfur, and Everything We're Not Doing About It." *The New Republic* (August 27), pp. 36–47.

Kahneman, D. (2003). "A Perspective on Judgment and Choice: Mapping Bounded Rationality." *American Psychologist* 58: 697–720.

Kogut, T., and I. Ritov (2005). "The Singularity of Identified Victims in Separate and Joint Evaluations." *Organizational Behavior and Human Decision Processes* 97: 106–116.

Lifton, R. J. (1967). *Death in life: Survivors of Hiroshima*. New York: Random House.

Power, S. (2003). *A Problem from Hell: America and the Age of Genocide*. New York: Harper Perennial.

Slovic, P. (2009). "How Do We Stop Genocide When Our Moral Intuitions Fail Us?" In E. Shafir, ed., *Behavior and Policy*. [Submitted.]

Slovic, P., M. L. Finucane, E. Peters, and D. G. MacGregor (2004). "Risk as Analysis and Risk as Feelings: Some Thoughts About Affect, Reason, Risk, and Rationality." *Risk Analysis* 24: 1–12.

Västfjäll, D., E. Peters, and P. Slovic (in preparation). *Compassion Fatigue: Donations and Affect Are Greatest for a Single Child in Need*. Eugene, OR: Decision Research.

5 Haven't You Switched to Risk Management 2.0 Yet?

Moving Toward a New Risk Architecture

ERWANN MICHEL-KERJAN

Interdependency is the defining element of the 21st century.

—Tony Blair, former British prime minister

The general surprise that came with the series of catastrophes and crises that have unfolded one after another over the past few years—terrorist attacks, natural disasters, financial crises, to name a few—reminded me of excerpts of *The Plague*, the famous novel written some sixty years ago by French author, journalist, and Nobel Laureate Albert Camus: "There have been as many plagues as wars in history, yet always plagues and wars take people equally by surprise."

This is mainly because, in addition to the human behaviors introduced in previous chapters, there is another one that seriously challenges the traditional economic view of rationality: most of us are myopic. We all focus on what is likely to happen tomorrow, not necessarily on how our actions today can have long-term consequences several years from now. So we don't see the seeds of disasters that are being sown until it is too late. The 2008–2009 financial crisis is just the latest—and perhaps most devastating—economic illustration of the stunning consequences of myopic behaviors.

Until recently, few world leaders or thinkers would have pegged the accelerating rhythm of large-scale catastrophes as one of the biggest economic and social challenges in the foreseeable future. But the evidence is now telling: If you consider the twenty-five most costly insured catastrophes in the world between 1970 and 2008 (all adjusted to 2008 prices), all of them occurred after 1987. Furthermore, of these twenty-five events, more than half have occurred since 2001, twelve of them in the United States. This new era of catastrophes poses a major challenge for decision making: Dealing with an average of one or two such catastrophes every twenty years is one thing; dealing frequently with five or ten on many different fronts, as is currently the case, is quite different.

And I predict that this trend toward more catastrophes will continue, in large part because of hyper-concentration of population/value in high-risk areas and also, as Paul Slovic and I discuss in the Introduction to this book, because globalization is making the world much more interconnected than ever before, such that risks are becoming fundamentally more interdependent.

To learn how people will/should behave in this new risk environment, we must increase our comprehension of it.

MANAGING AND FINANCING EXTREME EVENTS: A NEW ERA CALLS FOR A NEW MODEL

The catastrophe risk management field is actually at a crossroads today, as we are faced with extreme events of a totally new nature and scale. Although considerable research has been done to better understand disasters, recent events have seriously challenged the established paradigm.

Not very long ago, disasters were considered to be low-probability events because they did not occur often. That assumption was very reassuring for the economist: The *expected loss* of these events (understood here as the potential loss associated with a disaster multiplied by the probability of that event occurring) was often relatively low. Furthermore, it was often possible to establish a list of risks that one organization could face and determine the probability of each one of these based on occurrences in the past. In a sense, that was Risk Management–Version 1.0.

But in the first few years of the twenty-first century, the world has faced a string of catastrophes of a totally new dimension. In fact, there has not been a six-month period in the past few years without a major crisis that simultaneously affected several countries or industry sectors. In the terrorist attacks of September 11, 2001, a superpower was challenged on its own soil in an unprecedented way. After 9/11, the reality of international terrorism became clear, and national security became a top priority on the agenda of the United States and many other countries. The event has had an enduring impact on the rest of the world as well. Hurricane Katrina, a violent but long-anticipated hurricane, overwhelmed a vulnerable coastline, met an unprepared government, inflicting historic economic damage and lasting social impacts.[1] The massive failure of the electric power distribution system—a ten-second event in August 2003 that resulted in a massive United States–Canada blackout, demonstrated how human error and short-term competitive pressure can result in poor risk management that, in turn, jeopardizes our critical infrastructures. The December 2004 tsunami was responsible for the deaths of nearly 300,000 people in just a few hours due to lack of an alert system. And more recently, in May 2008, a major earthquake in the Sichuan province in China killed nearly 50,000 people, just a few weeks after a major cyclone killed over 100,000 in Myanmar.

The severity of these events demonstrates that the world is changing, and that we have entered a new era. On many critical points relating to extreme-event preparedness, the conventional economic thinking has been wrong. Conventional thinking holds that risks are mainly local and routine—that it is possible to list all untoward events that could happen, determine their probability based on past experience, measure the costs and benefits of specific risk protection measures, and implement these measures for each risk. Many organizations and governments are making decisions using risk and crisis management tools based on these outdated assumptions. As a result, they do not have the agility needed to move quickly to respond to unplanned events and global risks that are arising at an increasing rate. This failure to prepare adequately impacts not only the organizations and governments themselves but also a number of others with which they are interconnected.

A NEW RISK ARCHITECTURE IS STILL TO BE DEFINED

The aforementioned extreme events seem quite varied in terms of the types of catastrophes involved, the countries affected, and the impacts on the rest of the world. But if we look closely it is possible to see that these events are related in the sense that they define a new pattern. And this is why there is a need for

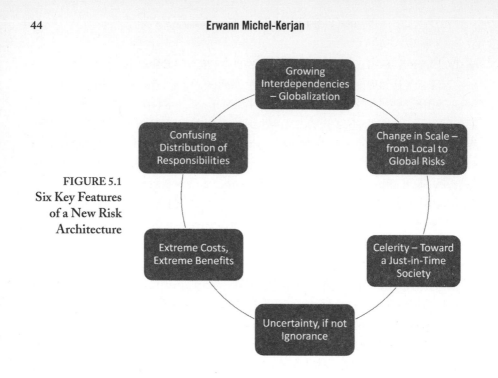

FIGURE 5.1
Six Key Features
of a New Risk
Architecture

a new risk management architecture. Below I offer a view of six defining features of this new architecture, as summarized in Figure 5.1.

Feature 1: Extreme Costs, Extreme Benefits

This new risk architecture is first and foremost characterized by a much wider variance in possible losses and gains than ever seen before. The recent events in the United States have had unprecedented economic consequences. Given the hundreds of billions of dollars of economic losses due to catastrophes that have occurred in the United States since 2001, it might be difficult to remember that when Hurricane Hugo hit the country in 1989, it was the first catastrophe to inflict more than $1 billion of insured losses. But times have changed. Hurricane Katrina in 2005 killed 1,300 people and forced 1.5 million people to evacuate—a historic record for the nation. Economic damages totaled nearly $150 billion, a third of which was covered by private insurance (for wind damage, about $45 billion) and public insurance (for flood damage, $18 billion paid by the Federal National Flood Insurance Program—another historic record). Federal relief to the victims and for local reconstruction amounted to over $125 billion (yet another historic record).

With increasing urbanization and the concentration of social and economic activities in high-risk areas, costs of catastrophes will continue to increase. The development of Florida highlights this point. According to the U.S. Bureau of the Census, the population of Florida has increased significantly over the past fifty years: 2.8 million inhabitants in 1950, 6.8 million in 1970, 13 million in 1990, and more than 19 million projected for 2010 (a 600 percent increase since 1950). The likelihood of severe economic and insured losses will escalate as well, unless cost-effective mitigation measures are implemented. Today, insured assets worth no less than $2.4 trillion are located on the coasts of Florida alone; if one takes into account the coasts ranging from Texas to Maine, the figure jumps to more than $8 trillion. We are sitting on a ticking bomb. The question is not *whether* other large-scale catastrophes will occur but *when* and *how frequently* they will strike, and how extensive will be the damage they cause.

This wider variance in level of risk also creates new business opportunities. Catastrophe bonds, also known as "cat bonds"—financial instruments that transfer catastrophe exposure to investors on the financial markets—quickly developed in the aftermath of the 2005 hurricane season in the United States. For instance, it is possible for a company not to use insurance itself but to sell $100 million of exposure to an earthquake of magnitude 6.0 or above to investors on the markets. If nothing happens or the earthquake is below this threshold, investors keep the premiums paid by the company; if an earthquake of higher magnitude occurs, investors have to indemnify the company. Doing so allows diversification of the risk beyond the traditional insurance and reinsurance markets. Between 1996 and 2008, over 100 cat bonds were issued—57 between 2005 and 2007 alone, as a response to increases in reinsurance prices in the aftermath of Hurricane Katrina. The take-away here is that as catastrophes unfold, businesses should start thinking about not only how to protect their assets but also what new products and services could be developed in this new environment.

Feature 2: Confusing Distribution of the Roles and Responsibilities of the Public and Private Sectors

In considering almost all of the catastrophes that have occurred during the past decade, we find it nearly impossible to dissociate the economics of catastrophe management from politics. One measure of this confusing distribution of roles lies in the lack of pre-established and publicly known rules as to who should

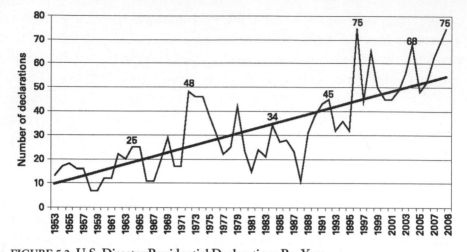

FIGURE 5.2 U.S. Disaster Presidential Declarations Per Year
Sources: Author's calculation with data for the U.S. Department of Homeland Security.
Note: Peak values on the graph correspond to some presidential election years in the United States.

pay what amount to victims of disasters: Insurance? State government? Federal government? The upward trend in the number of U.S. presidential disaster declarations between 1953 and 2008 (as depicted in Figure 5.2) is illustrative. This trend raises the obvious question as to what are the key drivers of such presidential decisions and whether some states are more likely to benefit than others.

It is interesting to note that many of the peak disaster years correspond to presidential election years. This is consistent with recent research showing that election years are very active times for disaster assistance (all other things being equal). Four salient examples are the Alaska earthquake in 1964, Tropical Storm Agnes in June 1972, Hurricane Andrew in September 1992, and the series of four hurricanes in 2004. Then, during 2008, another election year, no fewer than seventy-five disaster declarations were issued—the historical high point. In other words, with catastrophes come very visible political responses, often based on discretion rather than on pre-established rules.

This contributes to a fuzzy distribution of the roles in preparing against future disasters and recovering from them. If one asks people on the street, "Who do you think is in charge of preparing the country against future crises?" the most cited response will likely be state and federal governments (whether as regulators or first responders). However, although government entities certainly play a crucial role, a large portion of the critical services that allow our country to operate is owned or operated by the private sector (85 percent in the United States). Indeed, we must look specifically at how private actions affect public vulnerability so that we can be better prepared.

Feature 3: Growing Interdependencies—Globalization

An understanding of this third feature is critical to the new risk architecture being proposed here: As a result of growing globalization of social and economic activities, we have reached a degree of interdependence never before experienced. What happens on one continent today can affect those on another continent tomorrow.

For economists, this means that in a more dangerous world we are now seeing the emergence of *security externalities*. This concept implies that failures of a weak link in a connected system could have devastating impacts on all its parts, and that as a result there may be suboptimal investment in the individual components. An illustrative example is the Pan Am 103 catastrophe in 1988, when an uninspected bag containing a bomb was placed on Malta Airlines at a small unsecured airport in Malta, transferred in Frankfurt to a Pan Am feeder line, and then loaded onto Pan Am 103 in London's Heathrow Airport. The bomb was designed to explode above 28,000 feet, a height normally first attained on this route over the Atlantic Ocean. The plane exploded over Lockerbie, Scotland, killing all 243 passengers, 16 crew members, and 11 people on the ground. The only thing Pan Am could have done to prevent the crash would have been to inspect all transferred bags, a costly practice followed only by El Al airlines at that time.

With respect to the 2008–2009 financial crisis, the collapse of the American International Group (AIG), one of the world's largest insurers, was mainly caused by the operation of AIG Financial Products, a 377-person London unit that was run with almost complete autonomy from the parent company. The fall of the consulting company Arthur Andersen, due in part to its Houston branch's ties to Enron, is another corporate example.

What is fundamentally at stake here is summed up by the following question, which economists Geoffrey Heal and Howard Kunreuther have researched extensively in the past few years: What is the incentive for one country, organization, or division, or an individual employee in your organization, to invest in costly mitigation/prevention measures if that country, organization, or individual employee knows that others, upon which their activities and future might depend, are not investing (in order to be more competitive in the short run) and that their failure to do so could affect the entire system? Such interdependencies also have a critical impact on good crisis management. Indeed, each organization often rushes to protect its own interests without any consideration as to how *its* specific choices will *affect others* or whether a global concerted approach would be more beneficial for several organizations at the same time.

What can be done? In some cases a change of strategy by one agent or a small set of agents within an organization (or industry or country) can shift the equilibrium radically. This change can be referred as *tipping* (a term first introduced by Nobel Laureate economist Thomas Schelling in the 1970s). Tipping requires an initial mover or group of movers who begin the process.

What are the policy and strategy implications of tipping in the context of large-scale global risks? Perhaps the most important of these is that it is possible to move from a state of nature where there is no investment in self-protection to one with full investment by persuading a subset of individuals or companies to change their behaviors—the tipping subset. This can be done through proper economic incentives or some type of requirements. Sometimes it may be in their interest to do so. In other cases, they may need an outside incentive to change strategy. Leadership, either through trade associations or through a small group of influential organizations, may convince others of the need to adopt adequate risk management measures. They have to persuade only the members of the tipping subset to change, rather than everyone. This was done in the aftermath of the Anthrax crisis with the creation of a global information sharing platform among more than twenty countries. It was launched so that executives could exchange information about the solutions each country was implementing and work out a concerted strategy to deal with future global threats (see Lagadec, Michel-Kerjan, and Ellis, 2006).

Feature 4: Change in Scale from Local to Global Risks

One consequence of these increasing interdependencies is that disasters and crises are likely to affect greater and greater numbers of people. Dealing with large-scale disasters is much more challenging than dealing with a series of local small accidents. Many do not appreciate the radical difference. The resources and simultaneous collaborative efforts required are not simply cumulative but exponential. Critical to these efforts are global response, global reaction capacity, and multinational coordination. Another important consideration is the fact that information is shared on a larger scale and among a greater number of stakeholders whose actions are ultimately likely to affect the output. Finally, psychological factors make it difficult to appreciate large-scale threats and damages, as Paul Slovic explained in the previous chapter.

Feature 5: Celerity—Toward a Just-in-Time Society

The development of rapid transportation and cheap communication has created a "just-in-time" society. People and products are moving faster and faster from one part of the globe to the other. While this trend provides a wide range of positive returns, there is also a flip side: Risks are more likely to spread very rapidly. Thanks to jet travel, for instance, a pandemic starting in Asia today can quickly spread worldwide. The just-in-time society also puts pressure on us to make decisions more quickly than before, without necessarily taking the time to adequately measure the possible effects these actions will have on others in the long run.

Feature 6: Uncertainty, If Not Ignorance

A lot of research has been devoted in past decades to decision making under uncertainty; many of the pioneers in this field are contributors to this book. The question of uncertainty will likely become even more central in the near future. Indeed, this feature and the five detailed above create an environment in which assessing risks becomes more difficult than ever before. Most of us were trained to solve problems with clear questions and clear scientific knowledge. Knowing the risk profile, we made investment decisions. But historic data do not shape the future anymore, given how rapidly the world is changing. We move from risk to uncertainty, if not to dynamic uncertainty or even pure ignorance.

WHY BEING SELFISH TODAY MEANS TAKING CARE OF OTHERS . . .

Although the framework represented by these six complementary features is somewhat simplified, it can be used to further discussion of a large number of recent untoward events witnessed in various industries and parts of the world. Understanding this framework should also help clarify avenues for finding remedies to disasters and crises as they continue to unfold at an accelerating rate.

How we will behave as individuals in this new era is still to be seen. But history has shown that new world leaders emerge from crises when they have ideas that can (and will) reshape the future. A world with many more catastrophes and crises simply requires a different type of leaders, a different policy agenda, and different markets. It might also require a different type of economists.

As we discussed in the Introduction, the world is becoming more and more like a small interdependent village: Crises that are ignored because they are occurring 5,000 miles away are increasingly likely to have important, and very rapid, second-order effects. Given this, we might reflect on an irony: Being selfish today means taking care of others. Without a doubt, this is a different picture for how to represent economic rationality based on self-interest.

Or, if you prefer, in Albert Camus' own words: "Until now I always felt a stranger in this town, and that I'd no concern with you people. But now that I've seen what I have seen, I know that I belong here whether I want it or not. This business is everybody's business."

Welcome to Risk Management–Version 2.0.

RECOMMENDED READING

Auerswald, P., L. Branscomb, T. LaPorte. and E. Michel-Kerjan, eds. (2006). *Seeds of Disaster, Roots of Response: How Private Action Can Reduce Public Vulnerability*. New York: Cambridge University Press.

Dacy, D., and H. Kunreuther (1969). *The Economics of Natural Disaster: Implications for Federal Policy*. New York: The Free Press.

Froot, K., ed. (1999). *The Financing of Catastrophe Risk*. Chicago: University of Chicago Press.

Gladwell, M. (2000). *The Tipping Point*. New York: Little Brown.

Kunreuther, H., and G. Heal (2003). "Interdependent Security." *Journal of Risk and Uncertainty* 26, nos. 2/3: 231–249.

Kunreuther, H., and E. Michel-Kerjan (2009). *At War with the Weather: Managing Large-Scale Risks in a New Era of Catastrophes*. Cambridge, MA: MIT Press.

Lagadec, P., E. Michel-Kerjan, and R. Ellis (2006). "Disaster via Airmail: The Launching of a Global Reaction Capacity After the 2001 Anthrax Attacks." *Innovations* 1, no. 2: 99–117.

PART TWO

ARE WE ASKING THE RIGHT QUESTIONS? ECONOMIC MODELS AND RATIONALITY

PART TWO (CHAPTERS 6 TO 10) provides a framework of ideas and concepts that is essential to understanding and appreciating the notion of rationality (at least as it is studied in the social sciences). These chapters, necessarily, are somewhat more technical than other parts of the book.

The first three offer an overview of how the debate about the use of models of rationality has evolved over time, what the different schools of thought are, how our approaches to decision making have changed over the past few decades, and why the notion of rationality itself is in constant flux. They also show how decision analysts are now using such models to contribute to a better world—for instance, by creating youth programs where teenagers are taught to apply decision-making tools so they are equipped to improve their own future. Along the way, we learn that people often make better decisions if they know that they will be required to explain or justify their choices to others after the fact—possibly a critical new process for the future of decision making.

Part Two also reveals some of the most recent technologies at our disposal to better measure decision processes. During the past ten years, many economists have teamed up with neurologists and brain scientists. This improbable marriage has proven to be a happy one and has led to the birth of a new discipline: neuroeconomics. Potential applications include areas as diverse as marketing, finance, national security, and health care—all of which make neuroeconomics an exciting focal point for the future.

6 A Two-Edged Sword

Implications of Decision Psychology for Decision Analysis

PAUL J. H. SCHOEMAKER

Decision analysis (DA) is an analytic discipline used to help people make better decisions by first structuring the problem carefully, then generating a good range of potential actions, assessing possible outcomes, and finally ranking actions by calculating expected values or utilities.[1] Typical tools used include decision trees, probability estimation, risk attitude analyses, portfolio perspectives, sensitivity analyses, simulation, and value of information calculations. The basic philosophy is to break a problem into smaller pieces, address each, and then combine them.

For example, if a senior in high school has to decide which college to attend after having been accepted at five schools, the first step in decision analysis would be to systematically list the pros and cons of each school. Then the student would have to think deeply about key tradeoffs, such as tuition cost versus the quality of the school, proximity to home versus exposure to new experiences, or, say, academic challenge versus time for social activities. Next, the student would link the pros and cons of each school to these personal values in order to produce a ranking. If the schools at the top of this ranking are close, the decision analyst might recommend getting more information or perhaps ask the student to rethink the tradeoffs or other subjective inputs. And if none of the schools turn out to be very attractive, the analyst might suggest that other alternatives be explored.

Decision analysts prefer this kind of disciplined approach because it is very systematic. They are generally distrustful of relying solely on intuition or casual analyses of problems that entail conflicting goals, complexity or uncertainty, and empirical data. Decision analysts believe that problem decomposition, thoughtful tradeoff analysis, probability assessments, and sensitivity analysis in general will help people to both gain insights and, ultimately, make better decisions. Indeed, this is how they define a good decision, at the risk of becoming tautological (i.e., that an optimal choice is one that follows the dictates of decision analysis). They may also cite descriptive research from the psychology of judgment and decision making to support their belief that people, when left to their own devices, tend to act inconsistently, make elementary mistakes of logic, or fall victim to a long list of potential decision traps. And indeed, the field of decision psychology—also known as behavioral decision theory—has catalogued a depressingly long list of traps, from myopic framing and overconfidence to anchoring and wishful thinking.[2]

At first glance, the case for decision analysis seems very strong and in many cases it can really help reveal the best course of action. But there are some concerns as well. Intuition can in some cases outperform analytical approaches. Although humans may seem like bumblers in psychological experiments, they can be very smart in the real world (see Gigerenzer, 2002). Just as rats may look stupid in maze learning experiments, they may outsmart their human masters in the kitchen when it comes to finding food. Another important consideration is that decision analysis is not easy to master, may not fit a person's preferred thinking style, and may be hard to apply in practical domains, which explains why its impact has been modest on the whole.

WHAT IS EXPECTED UTILITY?

To appreciate these issues fully, we first need to introduce some of the basic ideas of both decision analysis and behavioral decision theory. Suppose the student in the above example is left with two top schools to choose between. To simplify, assume further that all relevant considerations have been mapped into a single overall attractiveness measure, called *utility*. Since there is uncertainty about how much utility either school will actually yield after four years, a decision analyst might express this risk in terms of three levels of utility (High, Medium, and Low) with subjective probabilities attached to each.

School A entails the following profile (45 percent, H; 30 percent, M; 25 percent, L), meaning that there is 45 percent chance of scoring High eventually, a 30 percent chance of Medium, and a 25 percent chance of Low. If we now assign the following utility values on a scale from zero to ten, H = 10, M = 5, and L = 0, we can compute the expected utility score for school A as: .45*10 + .3*5 + .25*0 = 6. Next, assume that School B has a different profile, namely (60 percent, H; 10 percent, M; 30 percent, L). Which school is better for our student, do you think? Decision analysts would simply calculate the expected utility of B, namely .6*10 + .1*5 + .3*0 = .65, and recommend this option as best since it scores higher than school A.

Of course, this is a rather simple example and the recommendation for School B includes several important caveats. It assumes, first, that all conjectures and estimates are indeed correct and, second, that the person's risk attitude is measured in addition to just tradeoffs under certainty.[3] Third, our basic analysis above ignores the value of collecting additional information on key features of each school (e.g., social life, academic rigor, job access), as well as the very important option of switching schools if not happy. This latter thought introduces a dynamic element into the decision and is referred to as *real options analysis*. To do this justice would require building a decision tree, in which the student can switch schools after the first, second, or perhaps even third year (if allowed), so as to assess the value of future information that may arise. This will help assess the value of keeping your options open by making flexible versus rigid decisions.

NORMATIVE DEBATES

As this simple example shows, decisions can get complicated fast in real-world settings. But the field of *decision theory* initially focused on more abstract problems, such as what it means to make a rational decision under risk rather than in a setting characterized by real-world messiness. Early theorists conveniently assumed that all good options were already identified (so, little need for creativity) and that all possible states of nature and their consequences would be well defined (an exceedingly unrealistic assumption). The focus in those first few years of decision theory (i.e., in the 1960s) was mostly on the underlying decision principles that should govern a rational choice, akin to studying Newtonian physics in an idealized world of no friction, conservation of energy, and no quantum mechanical effects. Although many papers were written about the-oretical issues, two major problems stood out. They concerned normative questions about preferences and beliefs, respectively, as explained next.

On the preference side, one serious problem was that quite a few smart people would knowingly and willingly violate a key assumption of the rational model, as shown by French economist and Nobel Laureate Maurice Allais. To illustrate, which would you prefer: option A, which offers $3,000 for sure, or option B, which entails a gamble offering an 80 percent chance of getting $4,000 and a 20 percent chance of getting zero? Even though the expected value of the gamble is $3,200, most people would prefer $3,000 for sure (option A) since they want to play it safe. But when these two options are em-bedded in two new gambles C and D, such that C offers a 25 percent chance of option A and D offers a 25 percent chance of option B, many people switch their preference. To most of us, a 25 percent of getting $3,000 (which is op-tion C when worked out) is less attractive than a 20 percent of getting $4,000 (which is option D when calculated through). This switch of preference vio-lates a key tenet of expected utility theory known as the *independence axiom*.

Also, there were problems on the probability side. One famous debate con-cerned a paradox posed by Daniel Ellsberg (of later fame due to publishing the Pentagon Papers). It involved multiple urns, some with known and some with unknown odds of drawing a winning ball. Instead of estimating the expected value of the unknown probability, and sticking with that estimate, most peo-ple exhibit strong aversion to ambiguity in violation of basic probability prin-ciples. A simpler version of the paradox would be as follows. You can choose one of two urns, each containing red and white balls. If you draw red you win $100 and nothing otherwise. You know that urn A has exactly a 50–50 ratio of red and white balls. In urn B, the ratio is unknown. From which urn do you wish to draw? Most people say A since they prefer the known chance over the unknown, especially since some suspect that urn B is perhaps stacked against them. But even if people can choose the color on which to bet, they still prefer A. Rationally, you should be indifferent, or if you think you can guess the color ratios, choose the urn with the better perceived odds of win-ning. Yet, smart people would knowingly violate this logical advice.

The vigorous debates about how widely accepted various "self-evident" principles of rational choice theory are raised two challenges for decision analysis. First, if not everyone buys into them, how rational can they really be? Second, if decision analysts use their authority, intellect, and confidence to persuade clients to revise their basic preferences and beliefs to comply with the dictates of their model, what do these revised opinions represent? Do such artificially constructed measures really capture people's true values and beliefs about risk and return? Indeed, do they measure anything at all, other than compliance? For example, we can counsel people not to pay attention to feelings of regret, either before or after a decision, because it is irrational to worry about things you can't control. But if these sentiments run deep, they cannot and should not be ignored. As Pascal warned, the mind can never fully know what stirs the heart, and yet disregarding this advice is precisely what decision analysis seeks to do. Telling a child not to be afraid after seeing a scary movie does not always work, however rational the advice may be. A better, more psychologically rooted approach would be to tell the child a happy story so as to shift attention away from the scary one. Overly rational models do not always offer the best solution.

WHAT IS BEHAVIORAL DECISION THEORY?

Behavioral decision research is the study of how people make decisions in actuality, be it in controlled laboratory settings or in the messiness of the real world. This descriptive research draws mostly on cognitive psychology and suggests that people have the greatest trouble making good decisions when dealing with losses and/or ambiguous probabilities.[4] Howard Kunreuther was a pioneer in showing that we often make suboptimal decisions about insurance, especially when they involve very low probabilities. For example, many people in high-risk areas decline flood and earthquake insurance, even when such policies are heavily subsidized by the federal government. And yet, these same people will gladly buy very expensive air-accident insurance (from machines placed at airports) or opt for costly medical insurance policies with low deductibles. How can people be saved from their own folly? Is it really just a matter of sitting down with a decision analyst (in the form of either a person or a software package), constructing a utility function, and calculating expected utilities? Unfortunately, it is not quite that simple. For the rational model to work its magic, decision makers must be able to articulate their basic taste and preferences and make sure they do not violate basic axioms of rational choice. As noted above, that is a real problem.

Decision analysis and other forms of decision support try to help overcome people's inherent information processing limitations. However, behavioral research very much undermines some core premises of the prescriptive model, namely that people have coherent beliefs and preferences (and wish to obey the axioms). Also, the behavioral research calls into question the validity of various methods used to assess utilities as well as probabilities. This "double-edged sword" has not been as fully appreciated in the decision theory literature as it should be, especially among decision analysts.

LIMITS OF THE RATIONAL MODEL

I briefly address here why and where behavioral perspectives need more consideration in decision analysis, starting with the fundamental *decomposition* and *aggregation* assumptions underlying the classic normative model. Decomposing a decision into components is behaviorally problematic if humans can do so only to a limited extent. Consider the most basic assumption of decision analysis—namely, separating beliefs from values.

Beliefs refer to the external world and include misconceptions and predictions, such as believing that Zurich is the capital of Switzerland (which is *not* true, it happens to be Bern) or that it will rain tomorrow (which will be proved right or wrong tomorrow). *Values* refer to inherently subjective statements about personal likes and dislikes, such as saying that one likes beer over wine, or that when buying a car, safety is more important than style. The normative theory holds that values and beliefs must be independent of each other. For example, my subjective estimate as to the probability that it will rain tomorrow should not be influenced by whether I wish for rain or not. But behaviorally it very much does (just ask football fans what the odds are that their team will win). Most people suffer at times from wishful thinking or perhaps undue concern or worry (see Tom Schelling's chapter in this book), and admonishing them not to do so is a weak remedy.

Deep down, human beings exhibit a wide array of foibles, twitches, and quirks that interfere with the rational model. Consider extreme cases, such as trying to get a person suffering from attention deficit disorder to engage in a utility elicitation exercise, or to get an autistic child to express subjective beliefs, or to get a drunken person to choose rationally by ordering a taxi—good luck. Although well intentioned, classic rationality is a very demanding discipline, even for healthy, sober people, and therefore may run into the very human obstacles it seeks to overcome, namely those associated with bounded rationality and the underlying sea of emotions. In some sense, we all suffer a bit from attention deficit disorder, autism, and inebriation, and therefore decision analysis needs to adapt more to us rather than vice versa. Much research is being conducted on the role of affect and mood, which can influence our perceptions and values far more than heretofore acknowledged. But there is little guidance in classical decision analysis on how to deal with this. We need prescriptive approaches that better balance the rational ideals we strive for with our cognitive and emotional limitations.

But suppose we actually manage to separate beliefs from values; the next step, then, is to measure each component further, via subjective probability and utility assessment. This seems rationally straightforward (a simple matter of asking people some questions and clearing up the inconsistencies), but is behaviorally far more complex. Decades ago, researchers enumerated important biases that complicate probability encoding in real-world settings, from anchoring effects (whereby you focus too much on a specific number or threshold) and availability biases to wishful thinking and overconfidence. Researchers did the same for utility encoding, which likewise suffers from distinct traps and biases (see Kleindorfer et al., 1993). Decision analysts would not have known about such biases without the benefit of behavioral decision research. Decision analysts then proposed various antidotes to such biases, such as asking questions in a variety of ways, in an effort to make their analysis more robust and valid. However, the effectiveness of such procedures remains in doubt since subsequent research has shown that such de-biasing seldom works well.

A PRACTICAL CASE FOR TEENAGERS: DECISION EDUCATION FOUNDATION

The Decision Education Foundation (DEF) based in Palo Alto, California, is a philanthropic organization that aims to improve decision making among adolescents and adults (see www.decisioneducation.org). DEF was founded in 1996 by Professor Ron Howard from Stanford University with two of his former doctoral students, Eric Horvitz and David Heckerman from the Decision Theory Group at Microsoft Research, and several other decision experts from the Strategic Decisions Group, including Tom Keelin, Jim Matheson, and

Carl Spetzler. I was invited to join DEF's board a few years ago to help reflect the behavioral perspective. DEF conducts summer programs for high school teachers across the country. During a two-week program, we train these teachers—most of whom represent charter schools—in the basic principles of decision analysis and behavioral decision theory, while we learn more about the challenges and opportunities of their particular schools.

Our aim is to make these teachers partners in providing high school students with the decision skills needed to live happy and productive lives. Each teacher can adopt key elements in his or her curriculum as appropriate. Thus, for instance, algebra or statistics can be taught using expected value/utility or decision tree ideas, and the importance of mental frames or decision biases can easily be woven into English or history courses.

Our belief is that American high schools today do not equip students sufficiently to deal with the challenging world that surrounds them, as evidenced by high dropout rates, violence, teen pregnancy, and drug abuse. Rather than preach to these students to "just say no" to drugs, violence, and other destructive temptations, we encourage them to think through the issues they face for themselves and offer them the tools to do so (see Keelin et al., 2008).

To do this well, we must meet three challenges. First, we need to understand more deeply when, where, and why teenagers go astray in daily life. Clearly, this issue varies according to social class, problem context, presence of adult role models, culture, and individual characteristics such as age, IQ, temperament, and personality. Second, we need to cultivate deep knowledge about developmental psychology, since the adolescent's brain is still forming. Young people seem not to integrate emotion and reason as effectively as adults. Imaging studies suggest that the brain of older adults shows less evidence of fear, anger, and hatred than that of young adults, who tend to be more impulsive and to dwell on negative feelings. Third, we need to decide what the focus of our efforts is: the person or the environment in which he or she makes a decision. Especially for adolescents, viewing decisions as vehicles to learn more about themselves and the world at large may be more important than optimizing any single decision in isolation, such as what summer job to take, whom to invite to prom, or what car to buy.

Figure 6.1 shows the elements of a good decision as defined by DEF. It represents a broad, well-tested view of what constitutes good decision analysis, including various behavioral components.

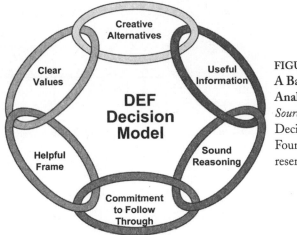

Figure 6.2 provides a snapshot of the quality of the decision at a given point in time, in order to judge whether more work is needed. The practical challenge is to select decision-making methods that move the cursor in each link to the right efficiently, while periodically taking stock of the overall profile, without overshooting the optimal target. This is essentially a heuristic and iterative process, guided by intuition and decision coaching, in order to find the optimal position for each link. It is important to recognize that in the rational components of the model lie judgments and values that are behaviorally rooted and, thus, that deep biases may never fully surface or be completely eliminated. This is a key challenge for the aggregation assumption alluded to earlier.

The DEF approach, illustrated in Figure 6.3, is a well-founded, proven, and practical way to integrate traditional decision analysis with behavioral insights about the psychology and sociology of choice. The basic approach is "divide and conquer," since the model breaks a complex decision down into separate components. Its formal part seeks to personalize the analysis by capturing attitudes and values that are specific to the decision maker (such as subjective beliefs, value tradeoffs, and risk aversion). Once the component pieces are sufficiently examined, they are combined using normative integration principles, such as expected utility theory, probability axioms, and predicate logic (or other types). Importantly, some form of sensitivity analysis is usually conducted to assess which assumptions and other inputs are most in need of revalidation or more precise estimates. How well "divide and conquer" works in practice often hinges on behavioral issues.

1
Helpful Frame
2
Clear Values
3
Creative Alternatives
4
Useful Information
5
Sound Reasoning
6
Commitment To Follow Through
0%
50%
100%
A decision is only as good as its weakest link.
100% is the point at which additional effort is not worth it.

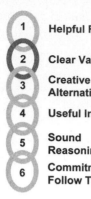

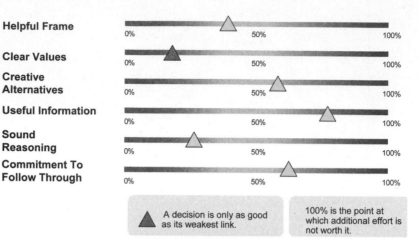

FIGURE 6.2 Profile of a Decision's Quality
Source: Copyright 2008, Decision Education Foundation. All rights reserved.

Other Academic & Applied Fields:
Developmental Psychology; Neuroscience; Education Theory; Counseling; Organization Theory, Politics; Sociology; Anthropology; Humanities; Law
Decision Education Foundation
Classical Decision Analysis
Decision Trees
Value & Utility Theory
Probability Estimation
Sensitivity Analysis
Behavioral Decision Theory
Heuristics & Biases
Framing; Group Judgment;
Emotion; Intuition;
Creativity

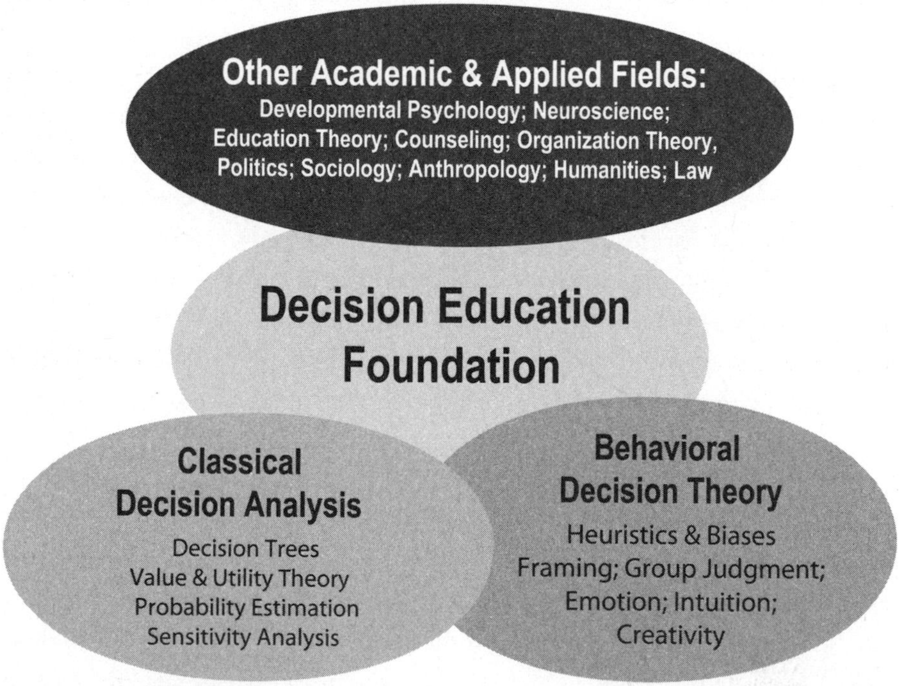

FIGURE 6.3 DEF Approach

At some point the rational model encounters the problem of aggregation, namely how to put the pieces together again. Here we need to judge periodically how far to improve any one link before knowing the costs and benefits of this effort. The challenge is to balance wasted effort due to incremental myopia against waste stemming from overshooting on any one link. This meta-decision, about how best to approach the original decision, is itself complex and uncertain. It calls on feeling and intuition that transcend the rational model.

IN CLOSING: A SPORTS ANALOGY

How do we move forward at DEF and elsewhere in improving decision making in the real world? The prescriptive side of decision making can be approached in at least three distinct ways. Using a sports analogy, we can improve our tennis or golf game by (1) studying how the game ideally should be played, (2) focusing on our own characteristic weaknesses, and (3) changing the environment in which we play or practice to counter our natural biases. Let's examine each.

Classical rationality follows approach 1 in that we teach people how a decision should ideally be made. In the context of a golf lesson, this means spending considerable time on achieving the textbook ideal in terms of grip, stance, and swing. And in more advanced golf classes it means understanding the physiology of our body, the physics of the club swing, and the ball's trajectory as well as its behavior on the green (i.e., reading the grain or slope).

Approach 2 would go much lighter on the general theory at first and focus much more on common as well as idiosyncratic mistakes of beginners (see Russo and Schoemaker, 2002). The golf coach might say, forget all the theory and just hit a hundred balls so that we can see where your greatest weaknesses lie. For some this might suggest focusing on improving their stance; for others, on improving their grip; and for yet others, on keeping their head still or having their weight shift sooner during the swing. The key distinction is that approach 2 starts with careful behavioral observations, not general normative theory, as well as with strong tailoring to a the specific person (rather than assuming that one size fits all).

Lastly, there is the approach of changing the environment through decision architecting, as emphasized by Richard Thaler and Cass Sunstein in their book *Nudge*. Once we know that people are prone to certain biases, we might change the decision environment such that it counters these tendencies. In golf, we might discourage beginning players from tacking difficult courses or teeing off the black tees, so that they don't overreach and develop bad habits. For adolescents, we might disable the radio in the first year of driving, add a video recorder in the back of the car, or install a tamper-proof black box that records engine speeds and unusual brake pressures. In high school cafeterias, food managers might place the salads and other healthy foods within easier reach than the desserts. There are many creative ways to change the decision environment to mitigate the adverse effects of our common decision biases.

To really improve decision making in the real world, all three approaches need to be pursued and integrated as much as possible.

RECOMMENDED READING

Gigerenzer, Gerd (2002). *Adaptive Thinking: Rationality in the Real World* (Evolution and Cognition Series). Oxford: Oxford University Press.

Keelin, Tom, Paul J.H. Schoemaker, and Carl Spetzler (2008). *The Fundamentals of Making Good Decisions*. Palo Alto, CA: Decision Education Foundation.

Kleindorfer, Paul, Howard Kunreuther, and Paul J.H. Schoemaker (1993). *Decision Sciences: An Integrative Perspective*. Cambridge: Cambridge University Press.

Russo, J. Edward, and Paul J.H. Schoemaker (2002). *Winning Decisions: Getting It Right the First Time*. New York: Doubleday.

Thaler, Richard H., and Cass R. Sunstein (2007). *Nudge*. New Haven, CT: Yale University Press.

7 Constructed Preference and the Quest for Rationality

DAVID H. KRANTZ

WHAT CHOICES ARE WISE?

This question has been discussed for millennia. Many proposed answers share a common theme, eloquently expressed by Plato in *The Protagoras*:

> What measure is there of the relations of pleasure to pain other than excess and defect, which means that they become greater and smaller, and more and fewer, and differ in degree? For if any one says: "Yes, Socrates, but immediate pleasure differs widely from future pleasure and pain"—to that I should reply: And do they differ in anything but pleasure and pain? There can be no other measure of them. And do you, like a skillful weigher, put into the balance the pleasures and the pains, and their nearness and distance, and weigh them, and then say which outweighs the other.

Behavioral research has shown that Plato was wrong: The tradeoffs among different pleasures and pains depend heavily on context. "Skillful weighing" has to take account of how weights vary with context. A more flexible definition of rationality must be sought, one that acknowledges a variety of ways of solving decision problems.

Much behavioral research suggests that decision makers are often unwise. One can scarcely disagree! Yet arguments about what is wise must be delicate, because behavioral research also suggests that standards of wisdom need to be set with great care.

CONSTRUCTED CHOICE

Some choices are indeed based on preferences. A person choosing strawberry rather than chocolate ice cream might anticipate the taste of each flavor, and then choose the greater anticipated pleasure. The outcome of weighing strawberry versus chocolate may be transient ("Today I feel like strawberry") or stable ("I always prefer strawberry over chocolate"), but in either case the choice reveals the preference at that point in time.

In many choice settings, however, a decision maker may not have a "preference." Disparate goals do not project onto a common scale of pleasure and pain, so the metaphor of "weighing" in a balance does not apply. Rather, the choice settings, including the particular options available, influence the degree to which various goals are activated and/or valued; a setting may sometimes even lead to adoption of goals not previously considered at all. For example, even in a familiar tradeoff, such as saving time versus saving money, the valuation of each dimension varies with context. If a person is asked how much money he would pay to save one hour, the very task highlights and enhances the value of money; if asked how much time would need to be saved to justify the expenditure of $20, the task itself highlights and enhances the value of time. Thus, the tradeoff is not fixed. Moreover, the availability of a new labor-saving device may lead a decision maker to adopt goals not considered at the start of the time/money tradeoff, such as trying out the device, or capitalizing on a low introductory price.

Thus, "preference" among alternative plans is often *constructed* in the given setting. Often, people go beyond the options given, constructing new feasible plans and then selecting one of them, perhaps on the basis of newly activated goals.

RATIONALITY IN THE CONTEXT OF CONSTRUCTED CHOICE

Activation of additional goals and construction of choice cannot be viewed as irrational. Rationality should *not* demand that every possible goal be considered in advance, valued, and incorporated into a utility function. Abandoning the common currency of "utility" leads to a key question: *Given that choices are constructed, what standards of rationality can be applied, to aid decision makers and to improve decisions?*

Thinking about choice in terms of plans designed to achieve multiple goals (see the analogy with foggy minefields in the chapter by Hogarth in this book) leads the analyst to consider the relevance of some broad classes of goals that might be hard to cement into a definite utility function governing tradeoffs—in particular, *emotion* goals, *social* goals, and *intergenerational* goals. It also leads to a series of new descriptive/normative questions. For example, how does "pure time preference" (discounting the future because of impatience: "What I can consume today matters much more than what I would be able to consume two years from now because this seems too far from me to matter") vary among different goal categories? To what extent *should* observed variation in impatience for different goals be taken into account in economic projections concerning the *present value* of future income, achievements, health, and so on? Similarly, how are different goals downweighted in the face of uncertainty? *Should* observed differences in risk acceptance for different goal categories be taken into account in assessing "expectations" relative to a proposed plan? Finally, are goals themselves subject to criticism? Traditional utility theory permits any tastes whatever; but actual prescriptive advice sometimes criticizes bad taste or even the wisdom or the morality of some goals.

Emotion Goals

Consider individual choices to buy insurance. People frequently justify insuring even against small losses by saying that they are "buying peace of mind." Reduction of acute and chronic anxiety and avoidance of regret (e.g., "I should have bought insurance") are prominent examples of emotion goals. While such goals may be viewed as rational, decision making may be flawed either because decision makers momentarily assign very high values to an emotion goal (e.g., purchasing flight insurance at the airport even though such insurance is typically very much overpriced given the very small probability of a crash) or because they overlook less expensive ways of achieving the goal (e.g., purchasing general accident insurance).

Decisions could be aided by *re-valuing emotion goals in a different frame* and by *making more salient alternative plans* for dealing with strong emotion. Advertisers often evoke strong emotion in order to sell their products; therefore, standards for consumer-friendly advertising could also be helpful.

Social Goals

People form a multitude of affiliations, including ones that endure (devotion to friends, to family, to colleagues, to religion, to country, to social or professional organizations, etc.) and ones that are quite transient (a brief sexual fling or an even briefer conversation in a hotel elevator). The human tendency to form numerous affiliations, varying greatly in strength as well as duration, sets our species apart from other social animals.

Social goals are goals that connect closely with some particular affiliation. Examples include (a) goals connected directly with affiliation, (b) role and/or status aspirations within a group, (c) role and/or status obligations arising when one has achieved a desired role or status goal, and (d) goals held on behalf of others.[1]

Social goals have powerful effects on decision making. I believe that it is futile to analyze reciprocation or cooperation without taking into account social rewards and punishments in addition to economic payoffs. Some theories attempt to deal with social goals in terms of a personality variable ("altruism" or "social value orientation"). Such approaches do not take into account the relation between social goals and affiliation. People have many different affiliations, with different strengths, and with specific social goals, such as status aspirations or role obligations, derived from each affiliation. "Personality" is even less fixed than preference.

Within the complex panoply of social goals, I'd like to focus on one subtype: *adherence to standards*.[2] In thinking about our socioeconomic system, I am amazed not by defection from standards—betrayal, greed, theft, carelessness, or laziness—but by the contrary, by the fact that all these ills are still infrequent enough to draw strong negative comment when they occur, and infrequent enough to allow social and economic relationships to be mainly fruitful. In America, we have done much to undermine standards, through complex ownership schemes, exploitation schemes, misleading advertising, emphasis on financial rewards and glorification of greed; yet the system of affiliations and social norms has proved astonishingly resilient. How much more stress this network can take is a good question. Here is some prescriptive advice: Let's not find out!

In thinking about freedom versus regulation, we need to recognize the importance of standards, and to prescribe by law or regulation only those rule systems that will abet the development of internalized standards. Unless most players adhere to a relevant standard, enforcement will be costly and impracticable; and in any case, the variety of possible deviations cannot be foreseen and proscribed. Yet law and regulation can promote or reinforce standards. We seem, as this book is written, to be at a critical juncture in history, where standards supported by broad-based affiliations can emerge and grow stronger, or can disappear into a web of inter-group conflict.

Intergenerational Goals

From the present viewpoint, having environmental goals, including ones that may have a major impact on future generations (e.g., limiting the quantity of greenhouse gas that we are emitting today because we now know they will remain in the atmosphere even after we die and after negatively affecting subsequent generations), is just as rational as any other goal category. One advantage of considering multiple goal categories is the ability to recognize multiple relationships of goals to time. From an intuitive standpoint, some goals have intrinsic short time horizons—today's lunch or dinner. Some have intermediate or long horizons, and some of the latter are acute (remodeling a kitchen, once achieved, is over) while some are chronic (maintaining a friendship). Still other goals are repeated, with various desired temporal frequencies. Many environmental goals have psychological time stamps only for their initial achievement, not for later consumption. Clearing pollution in a given place may happen in a month or in ten years, but after that, it is timeless.

Economic analysis of environmental change requires a standard of rationality that takes account of these inter-temporal complications. Rationality demands that the evaluation of alternative plans take account of the multiple goals across time, their time stamps or timelessness, and the differences in impatience across goal categories.

Criticizing Goals

In traditional utility theory, specific endgoals are not to be challenged. Wanting to climb the Matterhorn mountain, one of the highest peaks in the Alps, or to collect yogurt containers for every brand sold worldwide could be seen as totally irrational by others who have different goals in their life. Constructed

choice leaves two doors at least a bit ajar, through which criticism can enter:
(1) People do give each other prescriptive advice about goals; and (2) research
shows that goals differ in the extent to which people who pursue them are
happy. Before starting to criticize the goals of others, however, we might do
well to gain some understanding of the origin of various goals. One of the
most basic questions is, Do people *choose* goals voluntarily? Or do people adopt
goals without any choice process, perhaps only gradually becoming conscious
of pursuing a goal? Furthermore, how are goals abandoned? Goal abandon-
ment is one of the central phenomena of human aging, and successful aban-
donment of infeasible goals may be a key element of rationality.

RATIONALITY IN FLUX

Economic analyses have been based on Plato's notion of a skillful weigher:
To evaluate a plan, one first assigns utilities to every type of pain or pleasure
that may result from the plan, at every point in time; then weights the utilities
by probabilities to take account of uncertainty; and, finally, evaluates the plan
in terms of such a weighted sum. My arguments indicate the need for a
broader standard of rationality. Why should the standard not change? Even
standards of mathematical proof changed in the millennia separating Euclid
from Hilbert, and they are still not quite settled. I see no reason why Plato's
standard of rationality—or its modern economic versions, for that matter—
should not also change in the face of increased knowledge of decision making,
especially knowledge about choice construction and context-dependent social goals.

In the twentieth century, American philosophers Nelson Goodman and
John Rawls developed the concept of *reflective equilibrium*: Intuitions about
correct inductive reasoning (Goodman) or about justice (Rawls) are part of
the raw material from which philosophical analyses are built. A philosophical
principle that negates strongly held intuitions about correct induction or about
justice should be modified; yet an intuition that conflicts with a compelling
principle must also be modified. The principles and the intuitions end up in
equilibrium. Similarly, principles of rational choice should be in equilibrium
with intuitions about how wise choices are made.

Designs for decision do change. Probability came into decision making in
the seventeenth century; geographical information systems, in the twentieth.

Maximization of subjective expected utility is not the standard of rationality, but it is nonetheless an extremely useful tool. When and how best to use it are still subject to advances in knowledge.

RECOMMENDED READING

Carlson, K., C. Janiszewski, R. Keeney, D. H. Krantz, H. Kunreuther, M. F. Luce, J. E. Russo, S. Osselaer, and D. Winterfeldt (2008). "A Theoretical Framework for Goal-Based Choice and for Prescriptive Analysis. *Marketing Letters* 19: 241–254.

Goodman, N. (1955/1983). *Fact, Fiction, and Forecast.* Cambridge, MA: Harvard University Press.

Krantz, D. H., and H. C. Kunreuther (2007). "Goals and Plans in Decision Making." *Judgment and Decision Making* 2: 137–168.

Krantz, D. H., N. D. Peterson, P. Arora, K. Milch, and B. S. Orlove (2008). "Individual Values and Social Goals in Environmental Decision Making." In T. Kugler, J. C. Smith, T. Connelly, and Y.-J. Son, eds., *Decision Modeling and Behavior in Uncertain and Complex Environments.* New York: Springer.

Nickerson, C., N. Schwarz, E. Diener, and D. Kahneman (2003). "Zeroing In on the Dark Side of the American Dream: A Closer Look at the Negative Consequences of the Goal for Financial Success." *Psychological Science* 14: 531–536.

8 What If You Know You Will Have to Explain Your Choices to Others Afterwards?

Legitimation in Decision Making

PAUL R. KLEINDORFER

Legitimation refers to the process and consequences of explaining our choices to others. The anticipation that one may be required to explain or justify decisions after the fact might be expected to affect the decisions that are made.[1] A short summary of the descriptive theory of legitimation could be stated as follows: If a decision maker knows he or she is being observed while making a decision, this will have predictable effects on the process and outcomes of decision making. The parallel prescriptive theory of legitimation supports the notion that it is both sensible and desirable to subject some aspects of decision making to *ex post* review, both to justify outcomes of choice and to provide affected stakeholders with assurance that their interests have been considered. In this chapter, I examine a few of the underlying strands of research that have addressed descriptive and prescriptive theories of legitimation and then briefly note the challenges of legitimating policies related to climate change.

INDIVIDUAL DECISION MAKING AND LEGITIMATION

The idea that being observed in the act of decision making could affect decisions is a very old one. One need only consider the importance of mother-child relationships to see its critical importance. Being observed by one's mother clearly awakens, even in adulthood, many memories about what it means to engage in "proper behavior." In social settings, one can think of the basic process at work in legitimation as the imposition of sanctions on a decision maker if social norms are violated in the decision process or in the outcomes resulting from decisions. Social norms serve as jointly recognized reference points that define and reinforce acceptable behavior among members of a group. Hence actions, and/or outcomes, that an actor anticipates will be observed by group members could be affected by social norms held by the group members even when no one in the observing group can formally sanction noncompliance.

This line of thinking has been the subject of a considerable body of experimental work by psychologists and sociologists over the years. For example, psychologists have designed several studies to analyze whether accountability ("anticipation of required justification") would affect decision making, and they found that it does. Indeed, this whole body of experimental research suggests that observability of behavior, together with expected valuation and social norms, acts to alter reasoning processes and decision outcomes. Environmental cues that draw attention to norms and to norm compliance by others in the reference group are a further factor affecting behavior.

Individual psychology, following Freud and the development of self-knowledge, has also addressed the issue of legitimation. Freud developed the concept of "ego-ideal," which is a child's conception of what its parents consider to be morally appropriate and an important element for the child's developed super-ego. In the psychology of decision making, this idea of evoked ideals is captured by the set of role models, some actual and some constructed, that are triggered in particular contexts, and that act to condition our decisions. We are at one and the same time our mother's child, parent, grandparent, spouse, professor, ordinary citizen, and so on, and each of these roles may be played off against a different background of learned behaviors and social norms that condition us in these respective roles and provide legitimation for our actions.

An intriguing examination of this nexus between action, reflection, and conditioning role models to legitimate choice is the theory of "possible selves" developed by Hazel Markus and Paula Nurius. They advance a cognitive framework that envisages each individual as having not just a set of "now selves" but also a set of "future possible selves," which collectively serve to embody the individual's ambitions, concerns, and legitimation reference points in much the same way as does Freud's psychoanalytic ego-ideal. Which of these possible selves is evoked as the image of desirable behavior/selves and undesirable behavior/selves is interesting in evaluating an individual's decisions as well as a focus for psychotherapeutic intervention to ensure that these evoked selves are aligned with a healthy working self.

The point of all these studies is that the nature of anticipated legitimation—that is, "I know in advance that I will have to justify to others after the fact the choices I made, and why I made them"—can have significant effects on the decision process and outcomes of choice. These effects appear to be the result of incentives for the decision maker to align behavior with norms that are viewed as applicable to the decision context. They appear to be strengthened when the decision maker knows that the decision process is being observed or that it will have to be explained afterwards.

LEGITIMATION AND DECISION MAKING

The process of legitimation may begin before outcomes are fully observed, as in the current climate change debate, for which outcomes may not be known for decades or even centuries. The basic argument is that legitimation leads us to use "accepted models" or particular data that are routinely used for particular types of decisions. In this way, if a negative outcome occurs, one can take shelter in the company of fellow travelers. Howard Kunreuther's research on homeowners' reliance on the behavior of friends and neighbors when considering whether to buy earthquake insurance in California was an early example of the importance of this kind of thinking.[2] Since then, decision scientists have come to rely on notions of fairness and justifiability based on "what others are observed as doing, giving, or getting" as fundamental to everything from tax systems to labor agreements to executive compensation.

An interesting example of the consequences of legitimation is evident in Howard Kunreuther's extensive work on siting of hazardous facilities.[3] This research found that technical decision analytic models of experts were often eschewed in favor of more qualitative and participative models. While these participative processes might rely on technical support in the background, the foreground was entirely devoted to understanding the concerns of affected parties in terms that were meaningful to these parties.[4]

In the siting of hazardous facilities, the use of qualitative and participative processes rather than purely technical approaches represents the anticipated difficulty of justifying experts' estimates of risk to nonexpert stakeholders. When these stakeholders are powerful (as is often the case at the local-community level in many countries with hazardous facility siting problems), then acceptance and understanding in their terms becomes more important to being able to implement a project than compliance with some objective benchmark of risk. However, legitimation in this context gives rise to a tension between playing to the crowd in a manner that might gain acceptance for a project, on the one hand, and, on the other, providing well-intentioned guidance based on solid science, which may be more difficult for some stakeholders to swallow.

A CONTEMPORARY CHALLENGE: CLIMATE CHANGE AND SUSTAINABILITY

A topic likely to be center stage in the policy and research agenda for some time to come is climate change and sustainability. The difficulties in legitimating public policy in this area are well illustrated in the controversy among economists triggered by the Stern Report, written by British economist Nicholas Stern and published in 2006.[5] This report analyzes the potential consequences of inaction in the face of climate change and recommends a strong precautionary program to reduce greenhouse gases that are believed to be the likely culprit driving global warming and associated sea-level rise. The controversy that developed following the publication of the Stern Report was focused on how to deal with the tradeoff of the cost of investments to mitigate climate change effects against the still very uncertain benefits associated with these investments. The debate here is clouded by huge uncertainties, large time lags between actions and effects, and massive complexities and knowledge gaps in the underlying science.

With respect to legitimation, these characteristics imply difficulties both for validation of policy actions as well as for individual choices of citizens about where they will live, how much energy they should consume, and many other decisions that until now have largely been dealt with by the market or the government. Let me note a few of the major difficulties for legitimation surrounding this issue.

1. *Aggregate valuation of alternative options:* As the problems in this context are very long term and beyond the temporal reach of market-based instruments, political choices will be fundamental in determining policies. The whole edifice of science in support of political choices is the centerpiece of hermeneutics and legitimation. In this sense, climate change policy is a prime example of the legitimation crisis formulated by Habermas.

2. *Individual valuation of alternative options:* How should the views of citizens, as participants in the democratic processes underlying political choices, be informed and represented in the political process? In terms of representing citizens' values and preferences in this process, direct methods such as surveys are likely to be impractical because of the very characteristics of the climate change problem (i.e., uncertainty, complexity, and large delays between action and outcome). How to shape, inform, and represent individual preferences in this context remains a largely open question.

3. *Intergenerational equity, irreversibility, and intertemporal choice:* Legitimation problems are particularly difficult in these areas because it is impossible to bring all the affected parties into the decision context at the time policy choices are made. The special problems of intergenerational equity (meaning all the future generations who will be affected by our actions today but who are not yet born) and irreversibility have been at the heart of the climate change debate, just as they were for disputes about radioactive waste. More generally, the "precautionary principle" and the sustainability debate overall has been focused on the central question of what it actually means for present generations to live in such a manner as to not disadvantage future generations.

4. *Low-probability, high-consequence events:* Added to the above are the continuing perplexities of risk management and mitigation associated with the low-probability, very high-consequence outcomes of climate change. Howard Kunreuther's primary contributions to the social sciences have been in this area, and several other chapters in this volume examine these. Suffice it to say that from a legitimation perspective, the lack of easily interpretable feedback on climate change policies contributes to the ease of misinterpretation and denial of the noisy signals that arise from climate change.

WHAT TO DO?

What guidance can research on legitimation theory provide us to inform this discussion? According to Habermas, we should engage in open discourse and attempt to promote communicative rationality, rather than holing up in our disciplines and attempting to legitimate the goodness of one or another policy by decorating our ideas with the plumage of intellectual certifications. At first glance, Habermas's call for a more democratic approach would appear to be an impossible recipe to follow, given the complexities of this problem. However, on reflection, are the ideas so difficult that individual citizens cannot be brought into the discussion? Can they be made aware, in meaningful terms, of the stakes—and of the tradeoffs for themselves and their grandchildren? And rather than speaking about the potential cost of various policies for addressing climate change in terms of a net present value of $800 billion or 3 percent of global GDP in the year 2050 (the types of economic numbers attached to the Stern Report to summarize the cost of climate change policies), can we express the consequences of these alternatives in terms that are meaningful to individuals in various parts of the world? I think the answer to both of these questions is most definitely yes. Moreover, given the magnitude of the stakes in this problem, it seems to me critical to bring the citizens of the planet into a meaningful and urgent debate of these policies, which have the potential to significantly affect their lives and those of many generations to come.

Research on legitimation provides some guidance regarding the ways in which decision processes will be affected by alternative approaches to accountability, justification, and observability. However, the characteristics of the climate change problem pose a particularly difficult problem with respect to legitimation. Truth and validation of theories, and the associated recommendations derived from them, are ultimately based on well-intentioned inquiry. However, from epistemology and Thomas Kuhn's work on the history of the philosophy of science we know that models of such inquiry, and the guarantors of truth in these models, take many forms. They range from simple consensus among affected parties to deductive coherence, to correspondence with corroborative evidence, to survival against explicit rebuttal challenges. In the realm of climate change policy, we urgently need to recognize these alternative modes of inquiry, open them to public scrutiny, and expose the fundamental limits of our knowledge as we take action.

CONCLUSION

A broad search for optimal solutions seems not to be the first impulse of human decision makers. Rather, it is to use models and data that have worked passably well in the past, and that seem to be supported by many fellow travelers. If the models we use have been crowned with some formal dignity by academic or professional credentials or practices, so much the better. As researchers we might ask, "What is resolved by recognizing the key role of legitimation in management, in public policy, and in our research lives?" In my view, the main benefit is to promote a broader understanding of the context and of the stakeholders affected by our research, including their different frames of reference and values (see Part Five in this book). As researchers, we are good at anticipating objections and favorable responses from our peers from a methodological point of view. However, in many areas of management and policy, certainly including climate change and sustainability, it is crucial to adopt a broader frame for legitimation that anticipates and encourages our confrontation with the real stakeholders of our research.

RECOMMENDED READING

Easterling, Douglas, and Howard C. Kunreuther (1995). *The Dilemma of Siting a High-Level Nuclear Waste Repository.* Boston: Kluwer Academic Publishers.

Habermas, Jürgen (1973). *The Legitimation Crisis.* Boston: Beacon Press.

Kleindorfer, Paul R., Howard Kunreuther, and Paul J.H. Schoemaker (1993). *Decision Sciences: An Integrative Perspective.* New York: Cambridge University Press.

Kuhn, Thomas S. (1996). *The Structure of Scientific Revolutions*, 3rd ed. Chicago: University of Chicago Press.

Markus, Hazel, and Paula Nurius (1986). "Possible Selves." *American Psychologist* 41, no. 9: 954–969.

Simon, Herbert A. (1976). "From Substantive to Procedural Rationality." In S. J. Latsis, ed. *Method and Appraisal in Economics.* Cambridge: Cambridge University Press.

9 Neuroeconomics

Measuring Cognition and Brain Activity During Economic Decision Making

COLIN F. CAMERER

Americans are accustomed to driving cars on the right-hand side of the road and, hence, to first looking to the left when crossing a two-way street. In London, however, people drive on the left-hand side so you should first look to the right (and Londoners do). When Americans visit London they often "forget" and look left, not right. Some accidents result.

Psychology has a substantial understanding of this phenomenon: It is called a Stroop task. *Stroop task* is the generic term for tasks that pit a highly automated (sometimes called "overlearned") response against the need to adjust the response. The classic original example involves naming the color of the ink that a word is printed in. If a word is printed in green ink, and the word is *RED*, people often say "red" by mistake because reading words is much more automatic than naming ink colors.

Perhaps the best that economists have done on the Americans-in-London problem is to conclude that the habit of looking left is a "subjective constraint on feasible strategies," akin to having a neck brace that makes it difficult to look to the right. But given that the constraint is *in the brain*, it would be useful to add some psychological or neural detail to economic theory to explain cases like this.

Ever since the rise of the revealed preference paradigm in economics, constructs like utilities of goods, beliefs about event likelihoods, processing of information, and temporal discount rates have been treated as impractical—and perhaps unnecessary—to observe directly. Recently, however, a few econo-mists interested in better understanding and modeling individual behavior have begun to use tools developed in psychology and neuroscience (which studies the nervous system) to observe neural and cognitive correlates of these "unobservables" more directly than ever before. The tools and language of cognitive neuroscience make it easy to explain the Americans-in-London phe-nomenon through the concept of Stroop tasks and an understanding of which brain regions are active during those tasks, such as the cingulate cortex. The cingulate (Latin for "collar") wraps around the corpus collosum in the center of the brain (a thick band of fibers that connect the left and right hemi-spheres). It is a large region and the anterior (front) part is known from hun-dreds of studies to be active during conflict, "executive function," and the overriding of natural responses.

This approach has revealed some new predictions. One of these pertains to the cingulate cortex, which is activated not only by Stroop tasks but also by tasks that require "executive function," attention, and resolving conflict. If the cingulate is busy doing another task, then less attention will be paid to cor-recting the Stroop mistake. This explanation is likely to predict that Ameri-cans talking on cell phones, or trying to remember the name of the spouse of an acquaintance they've just spotted, will have more accidents crossing Lon-don streets. Admittedly, one could get this prediction from an economic model, but only if scarce attention is built in, along with some facts about what kinds of tasks "spend" attention, whether attention can be consciously directed, and so forth. These details are best supplied by cognitive neuro-science rather than by casual intuition.

Behavioral economics is the use of psychological methods and constructs to introduce limits on computation, willpower, and self-interest into economic analysis. *Neuroeconomics* extends upon behavioral economics by including neu-ral data for the purpose of creating a mathematical approach to the micro-foundation of economics that is neurally measurable (Rangel, Camerer, and Montague, 2008). The types of models that are likely to emerge from neu-roeconomics will be computational models that are very much in keeping with famous American psychologist Herbert Simon's idea of using algorithms to express cognitive processes. Below I will briefly describe the long-run goal of this "neuroeconomic" approach, give an extended example, and mention some caveats.

THE GOAL OF NEUROECONOMICS

Neuroscientists use a number of different tools, including animal studies, analysis of the behavior of patients with neurological lesions or psychiatric disorders, response times, tracking of eye movements to measure information acquisition, psychophysiological measures (e.g., skin conductance, pupil dilation), pharmacological interventions, and computational modeling as well as scans from functional magnetic resolution imaging (fMRI)[1] and other devices providing brain images. Each tool has some limitations that can be overcome by the advantages of a complementary tool; thus, combinations of studies often have remarkable scientific power.

The case for using neuroscience to explain economic decisions (hence the notion of neuroeconomics) rests on three principles:

1. Economists are interested in individual choices.
2. The brain is the organ that makes choices.
3. More will eventually be known about the brain due to technological advances.

These principles, if accepted, logically imply that economists should be interested in what technological advances tell us about the brain.

Of course, there are some ways to wriggle out of this implication. You could say that economics is *not* the study of choices but is instead—and should only ever be—the use of a particular type of theory that is inherently agnostic about brain mechanisms (i.e., rational choice theory). I think that this claim is provably false because many economists have used other approaches than rational choice theory when it has proved interesting or useful to do so (e.g., learning and evolutionary theories applied to strategic choices). It is also reasonable to figure out where preferences come from by rooting them in processes like parental socialization of children and early childhood development, whereby the details of how those processes work will be informed by developmental neuropsychology.

This implication raises another question about the division of labor. My view is that some degree of collaboration with neuroscientists by *some economists* is necessary to create good technology transfer from neuroscience to economics (much as a company importing goods from another country should have bilingual workers who actually travel back and forth). If economists simply settle for whatever neuroscientists have to offer, economists will not get the ideas and studies they most want. Through collaborations they might.

AN APPLICATION: EYE-TRACKING AND BACKWARD INDUCTION IN BARGAINING GAMES

The example I would like to discuss is based on studies of alternating-offer bargaining games (Johnson et al., 2002). It is not an example of neuroeconomics per se, because the only variable measured is indirect—namely, which information people look for on a computer screen. However, the hope is that in future studies such measures of cognitive process will be linked directly to brain activity and other psycho-physiological correlates to form a tentative picture of the mechanisms and behavioral outputs involved.

Alternating-offer bargaining games are fashionable to study as models of how bargaining could be studied noncooperatively with mathematically precise results (and later linked to cooperative approaches). In the games we study, bargaining occurs over three stages, between two players. At each of the three stages, the first player offers a division of a known sum of money to a second player. If the offer is accepted by this second player, the game ends. If the offer is rejected, the proposed amount is divided by two and the second player who rejected the offer can make the next offer (offering rights alternate).

Thus, in the first stage, player 1 offers a division of $5 to player 2. If rejected, player 2 offers a division of $2.50 to player 1. If rejected, player 1 offers a division of $1.25 to player 1. If that final offer is rejected they earn zero. (Note that the last round is an ultimatum.)

If both players have mutual knowledge that the players are self-interested and rational, the unique sub-game perfect equilibrium is that the first player should offer around $1.25 to player 2, who should accept it because if s/he does not, s/he will have only $1.25 at the next round to divide, thus the maximum alternative amount.

In the 1980s a controversy emerged from a series of experiments using variants of this game.[2] The controversy revolved around three distinct issues: What would happen to the results in subsequent rounds after the players learned by experience, and what were the "suitable learning conditions"? (2) Did the subjects have a taste for fairness or some kind of social preference involving distaste for inequality? (3) Were the subjects looking all the way ahead or not?

Eric Johnson had earlier developed a computer mouse–based technology to measure the acquisition of information. In a study published in 2002, he as well as Sankar Sen, Talia Rymon, and I used this technology to hide the dollar amounts available at the three stages in boxes that could be "opened," revealing the dollar amount, by moving a cursor into the box. (The box amounts varied across trials to limit memory.)

The behavioral result was similar to that found in most earlier studies in this field: Players offered an average of $2.11, and offers of less than $1.80 were rejected about half the time. The question, however, is whether they were reasoning strategically (in "equilibrium") but adjusting for fairness, or failing to fully compute an ideal strategy.

Measuring what subjects are looking at on the computer screen is potentially a way for economists to distinguish between these two different interpretations. In fact, on about 10 percent of the trials, players did not even open up the third box to see how much was available. In a boundedly rational way, their lazy pattern of looking made some sense because only 8 percent of the games went into the third stage. We concluded that while fairness preferences might be part of the story (as the simpler ultimatum game strongly suggested), limited look-ahead was too. Such a clear conclusion could not be reached so quickly without knowing what subjects were looking at.

Another thing researchers can do with attentional data is try to predict from what people look at what they are likely to do. We did this in the 2002 paper, which summarizes the results in a series of "icon graphs" and associated histograms showing the frequency of various offer amounts. We sorted trials into four groups based on lookup patterns. One group ("Zero") looked at the first stage (labeled 1) the most often. The rightmost group ("Trained") looked at the third stage the most often; at the second stage, the second most often; and at the first stage, the least often. Looking more and more at future stages yields offer distributions that slide from the equal split of $2.50 toward the perfect equilibrium of $1.25.

Two other groups of economists have published eye-tracking results since our 2002 study.[3] Nonetheless, I am a little surprised that this tool has not been used more often. Many rational choice and behavioral theories make predictions about sets of information that either must be attended to or could be ignored. This is especially true in game theory.

Sometimes these debates about why naïve choices are being made can be resolved much more rapidly by a series of carefully designed studies with eye-tracking (and response times as well) than with a much longer series of studies that use only choice data.

Economists have often wondered about decisions involving uncertainty versus risk and the distinction between the implications of evidence and the weight of evidence. American economist Daniel Ellsberg drew attention to the difficulty of modeling ambiguity (his term) using subjective probability with an elegant paradox.

In one version (Hsu et al., 2005), subjects were asked whether they would rather have $3 for sure or choose to bet $10 that the temperature was *above* 55 degrees or *below* 55 degrees in New York on a particular day (i.e., they would win $10 if they were right). Other subjects were asked a similar question, but about the temperature in Dushanbe, Tajikistan. More subjects chose to bet on New York rather than on Tajikistan.

Call the New York bet "risky" and the Dushanbe bet "ambiguous." Subjects generally preferred to bet on either side of the New York bet (i.e., above or below) and to avoid the Dushanbe bet. This was a paradox[4] because if they didn't want to bet that Dushanbe was low, and their beliefs about *Probability* (low in Dushanbe) + *Probability* (high in Dushanbe) add to 1, they should logically have been eager to bet that Dushanbe was high.

In the same 2005 study, subjects made a long series of bets while their brains were being scanned using fMRI. The researchers found that there was more activity in the lateral orbitofrontal cortex (LOFC) and the amygdala when the subjects were making ambiguous choices than when they were making risky ones (see Figure 9.1).

The amygdala is known to be involved in very rapid reactions to potential threat (hence its role as a "vigilance" area of the brain) as well as in emotional learning and reward evaluation. The heightened activity it exhibits in response to ambiguity is consistent with the idea that the reluctance to bet on either side of a proposition under ambiguity is similar to a fear or freezing response, as if ambiguity-aversion were a fear of the economic unknown.

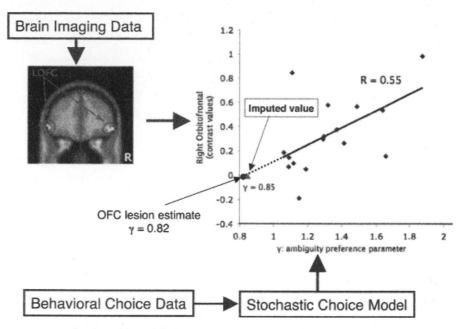

FIGURE 9.1 Linking Neural, Behavioral, and Lesion Data
Differential bold signal brain activity in the amygdala and the lateral orbitofrontal cortex
(LOFC) in response to ambiguous versus risky choices. Right panels show time courses of
activity in left (L) and right (R) areas after onset of stimulus (gamble requiring evaluation).
Source: Reprinted from *Science* with permission.

A subject-specific choice parameter expressing the degree of ambiguity
aversion was inferred from the subjects' choices for money. Those parameter
estimates were modestly correlated (across subjects) with the activity in the
right LOFC observed in fMRI brain imaging; that is, the brains of subjects
with low parametric ambiguity aversion showed less activity in the LOFC.
Furthermore, by extrapolating the correlation between the choice parameter
and the brain imaging activity to patients with no activity in the relevant area
(LOFC), the researchers theorized that patients with lesions in that area
would behave as if they had a particular numerical parameter—namely, 0.85.
Later experiments involving patients with damage in the same area, as revealed by fMRI, yielded a numerical estimate of 0.82 based on their choices.
In short, the fMRI measurement used activity in a region to predict a choice
parameter value for lesion patients that actually predicted the later choices of
a separate group of subjects.

WHAT CAN NEUROECONOMICS DO FOR ECONOMICS?

I am optimistic about the potential of neuroeconomics in the long run. Why? For one thing, a variety of methods can be used in research in this area, and many of these can be combined. For example, psychophysiological measurements (e.g., skin conductance), eye-tracking, electroencephalography, fMRI, tools for studying brain connectivity, and tools for causally influencing behavior (e.g., temporarily disrupting function using transcranial magnetic stimulation, analyzing pharmacological changes) are strongly complementary. The variety of approaches usually means that an obvious limit of one method can be overcome by another method.

Another reason for my optimism is that successful collaborations between neuroscientists and economists are already flourishing across remarkable boundaries. Many neuroscientists are interested in economic paradigms as models of higher-order cognition and social interaction, and as tools for studying pathology and disorder. The editorial process in neuroscience also encourages exploration and tends to be rapid and effective. (In contrast, publishing in economics journals seems to be slower and is often more frustrating.)

My optimism is also fueled by the fact that skeptical reactions are either expressions of perceived boundaries between fields (as defined by their traditional tools) or claims about what cannot be done that will eventually be overcome by empirical results and theory development.

I should add, however, that several elements of economic valuation and exchange, while clearly important, have been left aside because they do not fit the preferences-information-constraint framework. These topics include attention, emotion, conceptual association (as in advertising) and categorization, personal interaction in service purchases, fear and panic in insurance, health, and macroeconomic activity. Knowing more about these basic processes from a cognitive neuroscience perspective could inspire interesting extensions of economic theory.

Howard Kunreuther during his career has led by example in using a variety of tools, including surveys, naturalistic studies of business practice (surprisingly rare in economics), and experiments—whatever it takes to learn something. Neuroscience is similarly opportunistic.

RECOMMENDED READING

Camerer, C. F. (2003). *Behavioral Game Theory: Experiments on Strategic Interaction.* Princeton: Princeton University Press.

Crawford, V. P. (2008). "Look-Ups as the Windows of the Strategic Soul: Studying Cognition via Information Search in Game Experiments." In A. Caplin and A. Schotter, eds. *Perspectives on the Future of Economics: Positive and Normative Foundations.* Oxford: Oxford University Press.

Hsu, Ming, Meghana Bhatt, Ralph Adolphs, Daniel Tranel, and Colin F. Camerer (2005). "Neural Systems Responding to Degrees of Uncertainty in Human Decision-Making." *Science* 9 (December): 1680–1683.

Johnson, Eric, Colin F. Camerer, Sankar Sen, and Talia Rymon (2002). "Detecting Failures of Backward Induction: Monitoring Information Search in Sequential Bargaining." *Journal of Economic Theory* 104, no. 1: 16–47.

Rangel, A., C. Camerer, and P. R. Montague (2008). "A Framework for Studying the Neurobiology of Value-Based Decision Making." *Nature Reviews Neuroscience* 9: 545–556.

10 The Useful Brain

How Neuroeconomics Might Change Our Views on Rationality and a Couple of Other Things

OLIVIER OULLIER

Humans love *boxes*.

By boxes, I mean anything from a folder to a mental category that is supposed to facilitate our lives.

Think about the hard drive of your computer. Don't you have a bunch of folders for personal items—where you store digital photos of people you love and work-related documents? Or a "to-do list" with an "urgent things to be taken care of" column and a "not so urgent" one next to it?

In addition to the physical (and electronic) ones, there are all these mental boxes we rely on.[1] We use them to categorize and classify our thoughts (important, or not), emotions (happiness, sadness), opinions (interesting, boring), and even people we know (relative, friends, colleagues).

Whether we admit it or not, we are box-dependent.

But there is a downside to this habit. Whenever categorization enters the game, the ghost of simplification rears its head and dichotomies that are not supposed to exist are artificially created. And science has always constituted a fertile ground for artificial dichotomies to emerge and persist, sometimes forever.

Think about the rationality versus emotion debate that motivates this book (two quite time-resistant boxes, as discussed in the Introduction). As stimulating and interesting as this debate can be, we have been walking in circles for ages and some fresh insights could definitely come handy.

But what if there were no such things as emotion on the one hand and rationality on the other?

SHAKING THE (IR)RATIONALITY TREE: WELCOME TO "EMO-RATIONALITY"

Given our current state of knowledge in the behavioral and brain sciences, I tend to favor the following proposition, not as an economist but as a neuroscientist:

> The dichotomy between *rational* and *affective decision making* may be an *artificial* construction of our minds to help us categorize our choice behavior. From what we know so far, our brain does *not* seem to generate emotions and rationality in an independent fashion. Rather, it might be dealing with a complementary pair, a kind of "emo-rationality."

This perspective, which has recently gained acceptance in the brain sciences,[2] still remains bizarre for (too) many economists. If confirmed, however, it could have a major impact on economics, markets, and public policy. This is why, over the past decade, I—and a number of colleagues[3]—have become increasingly interested in the following question: *How can the joint study of behavior and brain dynamics help economics and other social sciences take a more realistic approach to understanding decision-making processes?*

THE CURIOUS CASE OF PHINEAS GAGE

The emo-rationality idea—although to my knowledge never before formulated this way—has a history.

It might have started in the middle of the nineteenth century, when Phineas Gage, a railroad construction worker, suffered a terrible accident that would change forever not only his life but also our understanding of the way emotions affect social behavior.

On September 13, 1848, somewhere near Cavendish, Vermont, Gage was the leader of a team of men who were blasting rocks with powder in preparation for the Rutland and Burlington Railroad. Suddenly, an uncontrolled explosion sent a three-foot, seven-inch, thirteen-and-a-half-pound, quarter-inch-diameter iron rod through his forebrain. Literally. The rod not only penetrated the skull under the left cheekbone but went all the way up through his brain before landing some thirty yards away.

Phineas Gage survived despite the fact that a large portion of his forebrain was missing (or at least severely damaged)—an injury that would have disrupted the dense reciprocal information exchange between the frontal lobe and deeper areas of his brain. Dr. John Martyn Harlow, a local physician thanks to whom we know so much about the case since he wrote daily reports on Gage's condition,[4] took good care of him.

Despite the hole in his skull, the survivor returned home ten weeks after the accident. He even tried to resume work less than a year later. But as his co-workers mentioned, something had changed: "Gage was no longer Gage!"

Before the accident, he was a respectful and polite person, in addition to being a dedicated and efficient employee mostly held in high esteem. Afterward, his behavior changed dramatically. He became prone to intemperate outbursts, spiteful to others, and impatient. His inability to hold to a plan for future actions and his overall lack of "emotional control" ended up costing him his job.

Gage's case, later popularized by neurologist Antonio Damasio in his best-selling book *Descartes' Error*,[5] is one of the first-known demonstrations that the frontal areas of the brain play a key role in rational behavior by "controlling" emotional reactions.[6] But one can wonder if, reciprocally, emotions participate in rational behavior.

This is where *neuroeconomics*[7] comes into play.

WHAT CAN WE LEARN FROM THE MARRIAGE OF ECONOMICS AND NEUROSCIENCE?

Today, this multidisciplinary field—which brings together economics, neuroscience, psychology, philosophy, sociology, and physics—is offering new empirical and theoretical insights on how emotions and rationality interdependently sha(r)p(en) our decisions. Among the most striking examples are a couple of neuroscientific studies of a familiar experimental economic setting, the Ultimatum Game (UG). The first of these was conducted by scientists at Princeton University in 2003.[8] Alan Sanfey, Jonathan Cohen, and

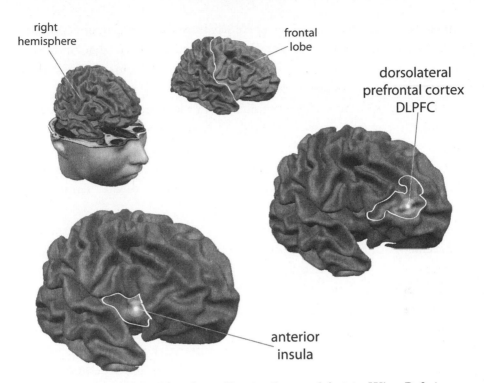

right hemisphere

frontal lobe

dorsolateral prefrontal cortex DLPFC

anterior insula

FIGURE 10.1 Some of the Brain Areas Showing Increased Activity When Refusing an Unfair Offer in the Ultimatum Game
Note: These are not actual experimental data but 3D reconstructions generated courtesy of Brain Voyager© for illustrative purposes.

colleagues used functional magnetic resonance imaging (fMRI)[9] in order to estimate the brain activity that occurs when people decide to accept (or not) an unfair share of money in the UG.[10] From a purely rational view, whether a proposition is unfair or not should not make any difference to their decision— they would get more money by accepting than by rejecting it. Still, these UG experiments have shown repeatedly that many of us prefer what we consider a "fair" offer that earns us less money over an "unfair" one with a higher outcome. This setting constitutes a good illustration of an "irrational" economic decision.

Functional magnetic resonance imaging reveals a significantly higher brain activity in the dorsolateral prefrontal cortex, or DLPFC (considered one of the "rational" parts of the brain), the anterior insula (considered one of the emotional parts), and the anterior cingulate cortex (a kind of mediator between emotion and cognition) when the decision to *refuse* an *unfair* offer is made, as opposed to accepting it (see Figure 10.1). Thus it appears that both parts of the brain, respectively identified as rational and emotional, are involved in the final decision—corroborating the emo-rational hypothesis.

However, only the evolution of activity in the more "emotional" part of the brain (the insula) allows us to predict whether an unfair offer will be accepted or not. One could therefore be tempted to conclude that the "emotional brain" somewhat prevails over the more "rational brain" when such decisions are being made. In fact, reality is a bit more complex than this, as a second experiment has revealed.

Neuroscientists are capable of imaging the brain while it thinks, calculates, and decides. But they can also alter brain functioning by simulating lesions.[11] Daria Knoch, Ernst Fehr, and their colleagues at the University of Zurich recently investigated whether decisions in the UG would be affected if one of the so-called—or so-believed, I should say—rational parts of the brain (the DLPFC) were "asleep" for a little while. If rationality is temporarily in the "off mode," one would logically expect emotions to take over, irrational behavior to dominate, and—in the UG—unfair proposals to be rejected more often.

In fact, what the experimenters discovered was precisely the opposite. In this study, recently published by the prestigious magazine *Science*,[12] people actually *accepted* more unfair offers![13] In short, when the so-believed rational part of the brain is deactivated, people tend to favor rational choices.[14]

These results force us to confront our tendency to build artificial boxes and create conceptual dichotomies. This trend is a by-product of our desire to categorize things such that each has a unique and specific function. We may think of emotions and rationality as two separate things, but the brain, a complex dynamical system, seems not to work this way.

Neuroscience can certainly bring us to a better understanding of decision-making processes. The two UG experiments described earlier provide information that could never have been obtained without the union of neuroscience and economics; the former brought the methods, while the latter provided the framework. I also believe that we have embarked on a new scientific path that could lead us to a serious rethinking of the ways we have conceptualized emotion and rationality for decades—a rethinking that could seriously impact our daily lives.

FROM LABORATORY EXPERIMENTS TO DECISIONS IN EVERYDAY LIFE

One way to ensure the scientific and social development of neuroeconomics is to move from laboratory experiments to field studies of decision making in everyday life. Indeed, most neuroeconomics experiments have thus far been performed in isolation from the real world, where people—usually college students—are stuck in fMRI scanners and have to make very simple decisions. Furthermore, in most of these experiments, they are making decisions about money they cannot lose; because university rules do not allow students to lose their own money during experiments, the only money they can lose is the amount that we researchers give them to participate in our experiments. Anyone watching our work from outside the scientific perspective might wonder about its practical relevance.

I share this concern to a certain extent because I am aware that, for all neuroscience's usefulness in furthering an understanding of individual human behavior and decision making, the brain, on its own, is rather useless. After all, people are not solely their brains. And their behavior is not just the output of their brains in action. Rather, they are made up of brains encased in bodies that are evolving in a physical environment, interacting with confederates, constrained by their past, and driven by the goals they have set that could become their future, not to mention the more or less explicit social demands they have to cope with.[15] Indeed, an individual's personality, behavior, and decisions emerge from countless interactions and coordination patterns occurring at myriad levels ranging from brain cells discharging to people talking to each other. And experiments performed in labs simply cannot account for all these parameters.

Cognizant of these limitations, some scientists are now moving beyond the laboratory to perform exciting new experiments. This has been made possible by the development of alternatives to existing brain imaging techniques, which are very expensive. In fact, the brain has many ways of letting us know how it reacts to or processes a situation. Eye movements, pupil dilations, heartbeats, skin-conductance data, and facial expressions are among the many "external" signs that can be used to accurately assess brain dynamics as people interact with the environments of their daily lives.

In situ neuroeconomics has actually already happened. In 2007, John Coates, a former Wall Street trader turned neurophysiologist at Cambridge

University, ran live experiments on the trading floor of a bank located in London. Analyzing the hormonal levels of traders during their day of work, he determined over a period of several days how these levels fluctuated with the traders' financial performance and the volatility of the market. Hormones in the blood are a means by which the brain "talks and listens" to distant organs; as such, they represent yet another form of information regarding how the brain is (re)acting in a certain context.

In the London trading floor experiment, the operators were in their "natural" work environment and thus could either make or lose money in what was clearly a real-life situation for them. The study revealed that *testosterone* (a hormone involved not only in sexuality but also in impulsive and risky behaviors) and *cortisol* (a hormone whose level increases under stress) are strongly influenced by the volatility of the market. One major finding was that these two hormones—one favoring impulsivity and the other one accompanying stress—play "hot and cold" in the sense that they have to remain within a certain concentration range in order for a trader to perform well on the market. One can see here a hint that emo-rationality is "in our blood" as well.

NEUROECONOMICS AND BEYOND

The aforementioned study poses an additional question to neuroeconomics, inasmuch as economists study more than one individual at a time: *What can we learn from a single brain (or a dozen) that can be generalized so as to advance our understanding of the complexity of markets?* This question of how to scale-up results from the very micro to the very macro is of interest to both neuroscience and economics.[16] Neuroscientists wonder about the parallels between the activity of an individual neuron and the integration of billions of neurons in the brain of any individual. And economists wonder about those between local individual behavior (micro-economics) and national or international aggregate behaviors (macro-economics).[17]

As a brain scientist, I am tempted to ask: *Can we make any progress in understanding complex interactions by studying electrical activity or metabolic estimation of a few cubic millimeters of brain matter?* The answer is: It depends. This information will never be sufficient to explain, predict, or decode human behavior and measure economic decision per se. But as we saw in the examples discussed above, neuroeconomics is clearly capable of giving information that other fields might have guessed at but never provided evidence for. And by liberating neuroeconomics from its laboratory constraints, we ensure that the best is certainly to come.

All in all, whether one is a neuro-aficionado, a neuro-opportunist, or a neuroskeptic, it can hardly be denied that we are currently witnessing a true paradigm shift whereby neuroscience might help refine, for better or worse, fundamental concepts that we take for granted, such as genuine notions of human behavior, (ir)rationality, conscience, or free will. These advances are already having major implications in our lives. For example, programs have been launched to evaluate how neuroscience might impact public policy.[18] Applications range from justice (*What would happen if one day we found reliable ways to distinguish a true statement from a lie? Can we measure emo-rationality, and could we use those findings to screen or select judges or witnesses?*) to new strategies for informing customers and fighting against addictions and obesity, for example. A better understanding of the decision-making processes of people who suffer from the latter pathologies could save a lot of money being spent on health care. It could also save lives.

Clearly emo-rationality is an in-between world that challenges the belief that rationality and emotion are separate. As I have argued in this chapter, they might be united in a more complex interdependent way than that represented by the two simple boxes we are used to. A lot of people are going to be nostalgic for the "good old days" when decision making was either rational or not.

My way of looking at it is to consider ourselves extremely lucky. If our brains were not so complex (structurally and functionally), and our environments so rich (informationally speaking), we would not be asking ourselves these questions today.

And we would certainly not be able to make those boxes we enjoy so much.

RECOMMENDED READING

Akerlof, G. A., and R. J. Shiller (2009). *Animal Spirits: How Human Psychology Drives the Economy, and Why It Matters for Global Capitalism.* Princeton: Princeton University Press.

Edelman, G. (2004). *Wider Than the Sky: The Phenomenal Gift of Consciousness.* New Haven, CT: Yale University Press.

Hayek, F. A. (1952). *The Sensory Order: An Inquiry into the Foundations of Theoretical Psychology.* Chicago: University of Chicago Press.

Kelso, J.A.S. (1995). *Dynamic Patterns: The Self-Organization of Brain and Behavior.* Cambridge, MA: MIT Press.

Oullier, O., A. P. Kirman, J.A.S. Kelso, eds. (2010). *The State of Mind in Economics.* Cambridge: Cambridge University Press.

Schrödinger, E. (1974). *What Is Life? Mind and Matter—Autobiographical Sketches.* Cambridge: Cambridge University Press.

PART THREE

INDIVIDUAL DECISIONS IN A DANGEROUS AND UNCERTAIN WORLD

IN PARTS ONE AND TWO we learned a great deal about how our behavior, even in common situations, often deviates from models of rationality used by economists. We also learned why having the necessary tools is essential for making the right decisions when we are faced with risk and uncertainty.

In Part Three, we confront a world that is not only uncertain but dangerous. The first three chapters in this section (11, 12, and 14) address the question of how humans behave when faced with the possibility of truly catastrophic risks. How do we react in situations involving risk and ambiguity? In what ways are those reactions likely to change depending on how much experience we have? And is it rational that we feel less threatened by events that will take place far in the future?

Whether ambiguous or not, dreadful possibilities stimulate strong emotional responses, such as fear and anxiety. In such instances, many people focus on the emotionally perceived severity of the outcome rather than on its likelihood: Probabilities are neglected. Knowing this, we should not be surprised that public figures and activists often describe tragic outcomes. Rarely do we hear them quote probabilities. The latter, even if reasonably large, would have little resonance in the public debate.

Part Three ends with three chapters (15 to 17) in which knowledge of decision sciences is applied specifically to the case of natural disasters. Why is it that people fail to learn from disasters, only to make the same mistakes again and again? And why, when it comes to insuring against such catastrophes, does our behavior, as individuals or politicians, rarely follow the path of what the "economic man" (described in the introduction of the book) would do? As these chapters demonstrate vividly, the reason is that other things matter more to us. Unfortunately, this propensity is of great consequence to society in that it leads us to collectively mismanage disasters (a hint of what's to come in Part Four).

But a question remains before we close this introduction to Part Three: Have you noticed something unusual in the chapter numbering? Yes, you are right; there is no Chapter 13. Well, given what we learned about superstition in Part One, we decided not to take that risk. One never knows.

11 Virgin Versus Experienced Risks

CAROLYN KOUSKY, JOHN PRATT, AND RICHARD ZECKHAUSER

INTRODUCTION

Every day we face a multitude of risks. Some we have experienced before; some we have not. Some we have contemplated; others have never crossed our minds. We define four types of risk based on these two dichotomies, as shown in Figure 11.1: virgin risks, contemplated risks, experienced risks, and neglected risks. Individual, institutional, and societal responses to these four types of risk vary in predictable ways.

	Out of Mind	Recognized
No Occurrences	Virgin Risks	Contemplated Risks
Past Occurrences	Neglected Risks	Experienced Risks

FIGURE 11.1 Typology of Risks

Virgin risks are those we have neither experienced nor considered. For an individual, a car crashing into her living room is surely a virgin risk. For society, the meltdown in securities markets of 2008–2009, and its aftermath, was similarly a virgin risk. Of course, if risks are unlikely enough to be virgin risks, we should be concerned with them only if they are of high consequence.

Contemplated risks are those that have not occurred but are recognized. For an individual who has never had a heart attack, the possibility of one may fall into this category. For the United States, the chance of an avian flu pandemic is a contemplated risk: A massive outbreak has not yet happened, but newspapers have discussed this possibility and public and private officials are preparing for it.

Experienced risks, our third category, are risks we both think about and have experienced before. The flu, a fender bender, or a computer crash is an experienced risk for most individuals.

Neglected risks, the last category, have occurred but are not currently contemplated. For example, a century ago an asteroid exploded over Tunguska, Siberia, with 1,000 times the power of the atomic bomb on Hiroshima; it toppled 80 million trees. But the risk of an asteroid explosion has drifted out of public consciousness into the category of neglected risk (leaving aside, of course, NASA's Asteroid and Comet Impact Hazards Group).

This chapter focuses on learning from the occurrence of an extreme event. For many risks, the probability of an occurrence is unknown and may be changing over time. In these cases, even experts must rely on conjectural or subjective assessments of the risk, as we see with climate change. When new information comes to light, such as the occurrence of an extreme event, individuals, institutions, and society must update their assessment of the risk. New information from other sources, such as scientific studies, will also lead to learning. For example, we learned about climate risks from a 2-mile-long ice core from Antarctica that extended the climate record back an additional 210,000 years.

In theory, a rational observer, following the receipt of new information, would update her assessment of the risk given new information. The theoretical model for rational updating, a mathematical formula called Bayes' Rule, is discussed in the next section. Unfortunately, most people are not equipped—mentally or mathematically—to be so ideally rational. Therefore, individuals and society will alter their expectations about extreme events in a nonscientific and often biased fashion. This chapter explores a two-part conjecture: (1) After the occurrence of a virgin risk, people will overestimate the probability of another occurrence in the near future; (2) by contrast, after an experienced risk occurs, people will under-update their assessment of another event occurring soon.

THE INABILITY TO USE BAYESIAN UPDATING IN EVERYDAY PRACTICE

Risks are often posited to have an unknown true probability. The textbook model for how to proceed employs Bayes' Rule (after eighteenth-century

British mathematician Thomas Bayes), which shows mathematically how people should rationally change their existing beliefs about something in light of new evidence. Individuals use information available beforehand to form a so-called prior belief about the probability that an event will occur in a given period. New evidence about the risk is captured in something called a likelihood function, which expresses how plausible the evidence is given each possible value of the probability. The prior belief and the likelihood function are then combined to produce what is called a posterior distribution, which is simply the updated version of the prior probability. This requires thinking about a probability model and all its important parameters, and assessing precisely what their distribution was before the occurrence.

While this process might work well in theory, it is rarely used in a complete way in everyday practice, even by those with training in decision analysis. We mention a few prominent explanations among many. Individuals and policy makers are unlikely to have prior beliefs in their heads, especially for virgin risks, and not thinking about every possible risk before it occurs is a perfectly sensible way to organize one's life. However, people often neglect risks that they should consider. For example, in the late 1970s, Howard Kunreuther undertook what would become an important study on flood and earthquake insurance purchases in California. He discovered that people in flood- and earthquake-prone areas often neglected the risk, failing to purchase insurance even when it was subsidized. By doing so, these individuals were ignoring not a 1 in 100,000 possibility but perhaps a 1 in 100 or even a 1 in 50 possibility with grave consequences that could have been alleviated affordably. It is somewhat striking to realize that even today, although information about the risk of earthquakes is well known in California, fewer than 1 in 5 households are insured.

One might think that the prior probability of a virgin risk is zero. Once the event in question occurs, however, it can happen again. A rational person confronted with the occurrence of a virgin-risk event would surely reconsider what his prior assessment of the risk should have been had he thought about the possibility. Although Carl Glatfelter Jr. of McSherrystown, Pennsylvania, never imagined that a car would crash through the front wall of his home, pushing him out a back window,[1] if he'd been forced to place a probability on it he might have given it a 1 in 100 million chance per year. At least until it happened.

It is notoriously difficult, however, to assess what one's prior assessment of the risk would have been had one thought of the event before it actually occurred. Most Americans had never contemplated the possibility of a terrorist attack in this country at the level of 9/11. After it occurred, an attack of that magnitude—or much worse—was not beyond belief, and indeed was thought to have a positive probability of happening again. Thus, most Americans' subjective assessment of terrorism risk should have been far higher after 9/11 than before, despite measures taken to lower such risks after 9/11, since the near-zero prior probability should overwhelm any subsequent response that may have lowered the objective risk. A survey of law school students published in 2003 by economists Kip Viscusi and Richard Zeckhauser in the *Journal of Risk and Uncertainty*, however, found that around 40 percent of respondents believed their personal risk assessment was higher before the attacks than currently.[2] In another study of professional-school students and undergraduate business students in 2005, they showed that over two-thirds of respondents exhibited the same phenomenon.[3] These respondents experienced a recollection bias, whereby after the occurrence of a low-probability event, one thinks that one's prior risk assessment was much higher than it actually was. This could be due to an attempt to reduce cognitive dissonance, for self-justification, or simply to misremembering.

It may also be a variant of hindsight bias, in which knowing the outcome alters an individual's assessment of how likely it was to have occurred. For example, in a 1975 study by psychologist Baruch Fischhoff, who is also a contributor to this book, subjects were given passages to read about the Gurkha raids on the British in the early 1800s. Some were told how the conflict ended, and others were not. When asked what the probability of occurrence of each outcome was, those who knew the outcome gave it a much higher probability. With such "secondary hindsight bias," individuals are unaware that the occurrence of an event influences what they believe *ex post* that they would have estimated *ex ante*. This bias prevents individuals from accurately reconstructing after an event what their prior assessment of the likelihood of that event really was before it happened, making Bayesian updating especially problematical for virgin risks.

What if individuals could accurately assess the prior probability they would have attached to an event had they thought about it? Fully proper prediction of the future risk requires more—namely a probability distribution over a hypothesized true probability p, which is updated once an event happens. Consider the difficulty. An event occurs. An individual concludes that beforehand she would have thought its probability was $\bar{p}$. Now she has to go one step deeper and assess how likely she would have thought the various values of the true p were that were averaged to produce $\bar{p}$. This strikes us as almost beyond the bounds of human capability, even for those trained in decision analysis, let alone for those who are not.

The individual may also need to define how much new information the event provides. It is often convenient to think of such situations in terms of binomial trials. Although there are some cases in which an event occurs and knowledge of the number of trials in the data can be taken as given, such as an adverse reaction to a drug in a defined group of patients, often it is unclear how many "trials" have occurred. It is difficult to determine how many people have been exposed to a particular chemical, or how many potential terrorist attacks have been prevented, especially if one is not privy to proprietary or classified information. For all these reasons, then, Bayesian updating is unlikely to be used. How, then, do individuals incorporate new information from the occurrence of an event?

UPDATING AS A FUNCTION OF PREVIOUS EXPERIENCE AND PREVIOUS CONTEMPLATION

We conjecture that individuals will excessively update their assessment of virgin risks after one occurs, and fail to (or barely) update their assessment of experienced risks, even when significant updating is warranted. Some experienced risks are well-understood systems with a large amount of frequency data, justifying little updating. For others, however, we have far fewer observations than we think and/or the risk is changing over time. Then, we suspect, individuals update their risk assessments less than they should.

For example, Carolyn Kousky recently examined the changes in property sales prices in St. Louis County, Missouri, before and after the devastating 1993 flood involving the Missouri and Mississippi rivers, both in and out of the floodplain, to determine how homeowners' assessment of the risk changed after the occurrence of an extreme event.[4] During this flood, 100-year floodplains were inundated, as were many 500-year floodplains, particularly those behind failed levees. In our classification, 100-year floodplains represent experienced risks: Floods have previously occurred in these areas and the flood hazard is widely recognized, with national regulations requiring disclosure of the flood risk to homeowners and those with a mortgage required to purchase a flood insurance policy. By contrast, 500-year floodplains represent virgin risks: They had not been recently flooded, and the risk in these areas was also out-of-mind, with no information-disclosure or insurance requirements. After the 1993 flood, property values in the 500-year floodplains declined 2 to 5 percent on average (whether or not they had been flooded in 1993). All property values in municipalities located on one of the flooded rivers declined 6 to 10 percent compared with property in the interior of the county. (These declines were statistically significant.) This finding suggests dramatic updating of the risk. However, there was almost no change in property values in the 100-year floodplains, many of which were flooded, suggesting little to no updating of this experienced risk.

And here is the paradox. Homeowners in the 100-year floodplains should have updated their risk assessments, for three reasons. First, there is insufficient experience to know the probability of a flood with any precision. While there are data on flood events in St. Louis going back to the Lewis and Clark expedition in the early 1800s, this time series is not nearly long enough to provide a tight estimate on the likelihood of an event thought to occur perhaps once a century. Second, the risk is evolving over time. Flood risk has been shown to be increasing over time in the St. Louis area due to structural changes to the Missouri and Mississippi rivers, increased development in the watershed, and possibly climate change. Third, the expected consequence of an event represents a combination of its likelihood and its severity. The floods in 1993 were much more severe than anything previously experienced. There should have been an update in the belief of residents there about the severity of future floods, a factor that would certainly affect housing values.[5]

Two subject areas in behavioral economics, prospect theory and the availability heuristic, help explain the over-updating of virgin risks and the under-updating of experienced risks after an extreme event. A finding of prospect theory is that individuals place excess weight on zero. The Russian Roulette problem illustrates this phenomenon. Most people are willing to pay more to remove one bullet from a six-cylinder gun when it is the only bullet than if there are two (or more) bullets in the gun. That is, a reduction in risk from 1/6 to zero is worth more to them than a reduction from 2/6 to 1/6, even though they are equal reductions in the probability of death, and money is less valuable in the two-bullet case since they are 1/6 likely to die anyway.

Similarly, people perceive an increase in risk from, say, 0 percent to 0.1 percent as large but an equal absolute increase from say 5 percent to 5.1 percent as small. This tendency leads to excessive updating for a previously virgin risk and to barely any updating for an experienced risk. Suppose, for example, an uncontemplated event occurs and fully rational updating would change the risk from 0.01 percent to 1 percent, a 100-fold increase. We conjecture that individuals might instead produce a posterior risk assessment of say 5 percent, a value 5 times too high.

The enormous change in perception when a probability goes from 0 to positive is consistent with evidence from other areas. The theory of just noticeable differences explores such phenomena. For instance, as a noise gets louder, a greater change in volume is needed to make the change perceptible. This is similar to our argument that as base probabilities get larger, small changes in probability are not perceived as well.

The availability heuristic also supports our conjecture. It asserts that individuals assess the probability of an event as higher when examples come to mind more readily. Once an event has occurred, it is much more salient, leading individuals to overestimate its probability. While the first occurrence of a risk makes it suddenly salient, the third occurrence, say, does not add much to its availability. This would explain the substantial updating for virgin risks and the relatively little updating for previously experienced risks.

When dealing with experienced risks, people may suffer from heuristic confusion, assuming, even if incorrect, that they are in a situation where data are extensive and the system is well understood. In such situations, another occurrence of the event in question does not add much information. Many times, however, we act as though we have more information than we do. For instance, in areas where floods occur on average once every 100 years, even if the process were unchanging, thousands of years of data would be needed to accurately assess the probability of a flood in a given year. Such a long time series of data is rarely available.

The bottom line is that with most of the low-probability experienced risks of great interest that affect society as a whole, we have relatively little experience. This means that the updating of our assessments should often be substantial. Indeed, when the probability distribution of a risk is changing over time, the occurrence of an extreme event should lead to even greater updating.

CONCLUSION

We have made two conjectures about human failures when extrapolating from the observance of low-probability, high-consequence events to predictions about future events. First, we tend to overreact when virgin risks occur. The particular danger, now both available and salient, is likely to be overestimated in the future. Second, and by contrast, we tend to raise our probability estimate insufficiently when an experienced risk occurs.

Follow-up research should document these tendencies with many more examples, and in laboratory settings. If improved predictions are our goal, it should also provide rigorous statistical models of effective updating of virgin and experienced risks. Future inquiry should consider resembled risks as well. Evidence from both terrorist incidents and financial markets suggests that we have difficulty extrapolating from risks that, though varied, bear strong similarities.

Behavioral biases such as these are difficult to counteract, but awareness of them is the first step. Requiring careful analysis of all available data could help decision makers to make better risk assessments. History has shown, however, that it is difficult to not overreact to virgin events and to downplay new evidence on experienced risks. Moving from awareness to behavioral change will be challenging, but given the importance of the decisions affected, change is essential.

RECOMMENDED READING

Fischhoff, B. (1975). "Hindsight ≠ Foresight: The Effect of Outcome Knowledge on Judgment Under Uncertainty." *Journal of Experimental Psychology: Human Perception and Performance* 1, no. 3: 288–299.

Kahneman, D., and A. Tversky (1979). "Prospect Theory: An Analysis of Decision Under Risk." *Econometrica* 47, no. 2: 263–292.

Kousky, C. (2010). "Learning from Extreme Events: Risk Perceptions After the Flood." *Land Economics*, forthcoming.

Kunreuther, H. C., ed. (1978). *Disaster Insurance Protection: Public Policy Lessons*. New York: John Wiley and Sons.

Pratt, J. W., and R. J. Zeckhauser (1982). "Inferences from Alarming Events." *Journal of Policy Analysis and Management* 1, no. 3: 371–385.

12 How Do We Manage an Uncertain Future?

Ambiguity Today Is Not Ambiguity Tomorrow

AYSE ÖNCÜLER

AMBIGUOUS CHOICES

The Gallup Investor Optimism index, an indicator that measures individual investors' outlook of the current investment climate, dropped from a peak value of 178 in January 2000 to a low of minus 49 in December 2008. This dramatic drop in investors' confidence was partly due to ambiguity (or uncertainty) aversion: With the sharp decline and growing uncertainty in the markets in 2008, many investors became pessimistic and decided to make only conservative choices. Except for very sophisticated investors, many of us do not sufficiently diversify our portfolios, preferring to hold only familiar (less ambiguous) stocks such as well-known national companies' stocks or those of their own employer. Ambiguity about what the future looks like also explains why banks stopped lending money altogether following the crash of the subprime mortgage market.

What contributes to this ambiguity avoidance, and how do we deal with it, particularly when it concerns future events? Are we as averse to ambiguity in the future as we are ambiguity today? Not necessarily, suggests behavioral evidence. We tolerate future uncertainty more easily, and sometimes we even ignore or deny it completely.

Most decisions in life involve some degree of uncertainty about the chances of an event happening or its possible consequences: What is the probability of an earthquake in my region? Should I be concerned about the health risks associated with cell phone usage? What is the dollar amount of risk exposure I have in my retirement fund? These kinds of questions are difficult to answer.

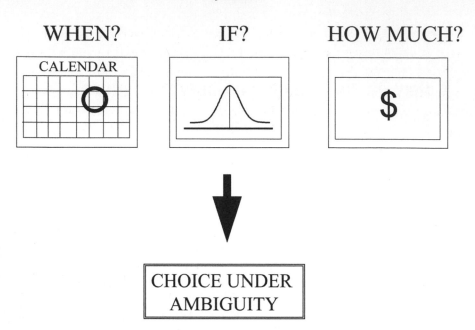

FIGURE 12.1 Uncertainties in Choice Under Ambiguity

In particular, potential losses from natural or man-made hazards (e.g., market crashes, terrorism attacks, natural disasters, global warming) are more difficult to assess than well-defined probability examples (e.g., playing the roulette at a casino, buying a lottery ticket). This is because missing information about probabilities and outcomes causes uncertainty about one's uncertainty. Global warming is an example: There is no unanimous agreement among scientists and policy makers about the likelihood or the economic and environmental impact of climate change at a local level. In short, it is very difficult to choose among highly uncertain policy options and to tackle the problem in an efficient manner.

In a decision context, ambiguity can be present in three ways, as pictured in Figure 12.1 and as summarized below:

1. unknown timing: ambiguity about *when* the event will happen
2. unknown probabilities: ambiguity about *if and how often* the event will happen
3. unknown stakes: ambiguity about *how much* will be at stake if the event happens

In the early 1960s, Daniel Ellsberg demonstrated aversion to the second type of ambiguity (unknown probabilities) in a simple experiment with two urns containing red and black balls.[1] Indeed, people usually avoid options with unreliable information about probabilities. Maybe this is why bankers find comfort in highly sophisticated mathematical models; using such models they can assure themselves that they know precisely the risk they are taking when investing in mortgage-based securities, credit derivatives, and other alternative risk transfer mechanisms.

In many situations, ambiguity aversion is governed not only by unknown probabilities but also by unknown outcomes. For instance, we cannot put an exact dollar amount on the potential damage from a major quake in a particular region. In the case of global warming, we have only a vague idea about the chain of reactions it can cause, such as extreme weather conditions, rising sea levels, and so on. And, as this book is being written, the size of the global loss from the economic crisis is yet to be determined. (Of course, ten years from now history books will specify this loss, but for now nobody can describe it with any degree of confidence.)

At this point, we should note the difference between ambiguity aversion and risk aversion. *Risk aversion* is a preference for certainty over risk, whereas *ambiguity aversion* is a dislike of gaps and inconsistencies in information regarding probabilities or outcomes. For instance, a person may be willing to take risks in domains that she feels confident about (playing poker, participating in extreme sports, investing in volatile markets) but may be averse to situations where these risks are not accurately defined or are debatable (using cell phones, eating genetically modified food). Brain studies also confirm this distinction. Ambiguity lights up regions in our brain that are associated with negative feelings, such as fear, disgust, and displeasure, whereas these regions are not activated when we are faced with a risky choice.

Aside from Ellsberg's classic urn problem, most cases of ambiguity have a dynamic component: The uncertainty is not resolved immediately upon the making of a decision. In fact, in many cases we do not even know when (if ever) the uncertainty will be resolved. Consider the following hypothetical earthquake scenario. Let's say that seismic experts suggest there's a 10 percent chance a major earthquake will occur in a particular region in the next twenty years, causing a loss of approximately $50 billion. First of all, the likelihood and loss figures themselves (i.e., ambiguous probabilities and outcomes) may be disputable. Second, it is very unlikely that the ambiguity will resolve today or tomorrow. Third, it is not clear whether one's own house will be affected by this earthquake. When making a decision about buying earthquake insurance or investing in mitigation measures, a homeowner will need to evaluate costs and benefits for the next twenty years and beyond, not just for the present time. We know that people are generally uncomfortable with missing information about a current event. But how will they react when this uncertainty is prolonged into the future? Will those people who expect to live in their houses for the next twenty years be more or less tolerant of ambiguity? Will those who put their money into long-term investments be more or less concerned about ambiguity? Interestingly, as I will discuss later on, many people become more tolerant of future uncertainty. This means that our homeowner will feel less threatened by an earthquake the longer she plans to live in the area. The same is true of our investor: The longer he plans to hold his portfolio, the less he will be concerned about market uncertainties.

As noted earlier, another source of uncertainty is ambiguity about the particular time of an event: We do not know exactly when during the next twenty years the earthquake will occur. Seismic studies may provide a probabilistic estimate about when it is likely to happen, but there is still doubt about the exact timing—it can happen anytime within the next twenty years or even later. How would our homeowner react to this imprecise information about the timing of the catastrophic event? Behavioral evidence suggests that she prefers to know exactly when the event will occur and is even willing to pay for acquiring this information.

ATTITUDES TOWARD AMBIGUITY

Ambiguity can be defined as "the subjective experience of missing information" whereby the incomplete information prevents us from making a safe prediction. Mainstream economic analysis assumes that probabilities either are precisely known (as in roulette) or can be inferred from objective judgments (as in weather forecasts). From a behavioral standpoint, this is not necessarily true. Risk (known probabilities) and uncertainty (unknown or incompletely known probabilities) may lead to different behaviors. As Ellsberg demonstrated, individuals are generally averse to events with ambiguous probabilities (i.e., those for which the probability distribution is not known precisely). For example, given a choice between a gamble where I can get $100 with a 50 percent chance of success and one where I can get $100 but with unknown odds, I will most likely choose the first one. In short, ambiguity aversion is quite common for unknown probabilities.

Most of the research on ambiguity focuses on vague probabilities. However, in some situations, uncertainty can also exist with respect to outcomes (i.e., whether the outcome is precisely known or not). Table 12.1 presents some stylized examples of this taxonomy of precise/imprecise probabilities and outcomes. For instance, on a roulette table, the chances of winning or losing and the amount at stake are well specified; hence this example falls into the category of precise probabilities/precise outcomes. The outcome of an airplane crash is almost always certain, whereas the probability of having such an accident is not—a case of ambiguous probabilities/precise outcomes. We could estimate (more or less) our chances of getting a tax audit depending on our income bracket, but it is difficult to foresee any possible penalties—a case of precise probabilities/ambiguous outcomes. And, finally, if we do not have a clear prediction about the probability and the magnitude of damage from an earthquake, we are looking at a case of ambiguous probabilities/ambiguous outcomes.

		Probabilities	
		Precise	**Ambiguous**
Outcomes	**Precise**	Playing roulette	Plane crash
	Ambiguous	Tax audit	Earthquake

TABLE 12.1 **Examples for Different Sources of Ambiguity**

Behavioral studies show that many people are averse to ambiguity for both probabilities and outcomes. Thus we don't like to leave things to total chance (ambiguous probabilities). We also do not like the vagueness associated with possible consequences (ambiguous outcomes). For instance, we prefer to know the exact possibility of a financial crash or an earthquake and also whether a market crash or an earthquake will destroy none, half, or all of our endowments. Some studies have shown that we are even willing to pay a premium to decrease the uncertainty surrounding probabilities and consequences of adverse events. What is the implication of this aversion for future events? The following section tackles this question and shows that we are not all that uncomfortable with future uncertainty.

AMBIGUITY AND THE FUTURE

Up to now, I've said little about how timing affects our reaction to uncertainty. For many decision problems we do not know when the event will be realized; examples include natural disasters such as earthquakes and hurricanes, health problems as a result of prolonged exposure to radiation, and life expectancy itself. How do we behave when faced with such uncertainty? Economic theory assumes that individuals discount the future in a constant manner—that they would prefer risky timing to the equivalent sure timing. Thus, for instance, if an online bookstore announces that it can deliver my order in one to three weeks, I should be unconcerned about the difference between this option and receiving the book in exactly two weeks. However, in reality, people are averse to timing uncertainty—we prefer to know for sure when an event will happen.

How does time affect ambiguity preferences, especially with respect to the two sources of ambiguity—probabilities and outcomes? One framework that may be useful in answering this question is construal level theory, developed by two Israeli psychologists, Nira Liberman and Yaacov Trope. They propose that the mental representations of events in the near future are fundamentally different from those of events in the far future and that this difference can affect our choices. Specifically, we tend to focus on the desirability of an event when it is in the far future and to switch to feasibility concerns when it is imminent. For instance, when planning our summer vacation, we focus on the desirable aspects such as going to a nice location, seeing our friends, and so on. But when the date approaches, we start focusing on the feasibility dimension: reserving the hotel, packing our bags, and so on. In the context of risky choice, then, probabilities are subordinate to outcomes: The possible outcomes (i.e., desirability) are more salient in the long run, but as time passes the probability of an event happening (i.e., feasibility) becomes more important. This would imply the following.

1. People prefer to seek information about the desirability of future prospects (i.e., outcomes) before seeking information about the feasibility of attaining them (i.e., probabilities): If there is a possibility that

I will receive some money in the future, I would initially like to know how much I may get, rather than what my chances of receiving it might be.

2. The probability dimension becomes more salient as time passes: As the date approaches, I would focus more on my chances of receiving the money.

Following these observations, we can conjecture that time has an impact not only on risk preferences but also on preferences for ambiguous events. Regarding events that are currently happening we are averse to uncertain probabilities and somewhat more tolerant of uncertain outcomes. If probabilities become less salient over time and outcomes become more salient, the negative influence of uncertain probabilities would decrease; that is, individuals would become less ambiguity-averse for future events. In short, in cases where both probabilities and outcomes are highly unknown—as with global warming—individuals would be more tolerant of missing information when the event takes place in the future. Postponing a vague event causes less anxiety than an immediate one.

My colleagues Dolchai La-ornual and Selcuk Onay and I recently conducted an experiment in a European business school. Preliminary results from our experiment supported our prediction. In some of the scenarios, we gave the participants full information about the risk involved, such as receiving $10,000 with a probability of 50 percent. In others, there was missing information about outcomes (receiving an amount between $5,000 and $15,000) and/or probabilities (with a probability of 25 percent to 75 percent). The results consistently showed that ambiguity attitudes change over time. Both for positive outcomes (e.g., winning the lottery, getting a tax rebate) and negative ones (e.g., paying a traffic ticket, losing in the stock market), ambiguity aversion decreases with time. More people choose the scenario "Winning between $5,000 and $15,000 with a chance of 25–75 percent" than the scenario "Winning $10,000 with a chance of 50 percent" when both options occur within three months from the day they are asked to make this choice. In short, we are more likely to take on unknown risks or costs when these pertain to the future than when they are current. The implication is that we tend not to seek out sufficient information about future uncertainty and, indeed, prefer to ignore it completely.

CONCLUSION

Results from the behavioral experiments my colleagues and I have performed suggest that people become less threatened by ambiguity when it concerns events that are to take place far in the future, perhaps because we make most of our decisions for the short term, and because a long horizon is much less salient to many. This finding has important policy implications in many do-mains, including investment decisions, attempts to reduce global warming, mitigation strategies against natural disasters, and health risks that are not well identified. If individuals are less ambiguity-averse for such future prospects, we would expect to see underinvestment in reducing or managing these risks today.

How can we properly handle future uncertainty? Designing policies and regulations that properly deal with our myopia (i.e., our strong focus on what can happen tomorrow rather than what can happen in ten years) would po-tentially help us make better choices about our future. Here's a good example from the financial markets: As a way of encouraging bankers to consider the long-term implications of their actions, the executive compensation system could be redesigned so that it promotes a risk-adjusted reward mechanism where bonuses are a function not only of short-term market performance but also of sound risk profiles. This would align the interests of executives with the general public in managing financial risks more efficiently.

The foregoing suggests that in order to be in better shape to endure diffi-cult times—whether in the form of financial crises, natural disasters, or any other large-scale risks—we need to rethink our way of dealing with ambigu-ity and to understand the future consequences of our immediate actions. Ig-noring the sources of ambiguity or postponing actions against them will only result in bigger problems in the future. The natural disasters of the last decade, the economic crisis of 2008, and the data on global warming all serve as an important wake-up call for implementing sound risk management policies that can reduce our myopia in managing long-term uncertainties.

RECOMMENDED READING

Ellsberg, D. (1961). "Risk, Ambiguity and the Savage Axioms." *Quarterly Journal of Economics* 75: 643–669.

Hogarth, R. M., and H. Kunreuther (1995). "Decision Making Under Ignorance: Arguing with Yourself." *Journal of Risk and Uncertainty* 10: 15–36.

Kahneman D., P. Slovic, and A. Tversky (1982). *Judgment Under Uncertainty: Heuristics and Biases*. New York: Cambridge University Press.

Liberman, N., and Y. Trope (1998). "The Role of Feasibility and Desirability Considerations in Near and Distant Future Decisions: A Test of Temporal Construal Theory." *Journal of Personality and Social Psychology* 75: 5–18.

Onay, S., and A. Onculer (2007). "Intertemporal Choice Under Timing Risk: An Experimental Approach." *Journal of Risk and Uncertainty* 5, no. 34: 2.

14 Dreadful Possibilities, Neglected Probabilities

CASS R. SUNSTEIN AND RICHARD ZECKHAUSER

Dreadful possibilities stimulate strong emotional responses, such as fear and anxiety.[1] Fortunately, most high-consequence negative events have tiny probabilities, because life is no longer nasty, brutish, and short. But when emotions take charge, probabilities get neglected. Consequently, in the face of a fearsome risk, people often exaggerate the benefits of preventive, risk-reducing, or ameliorative measures. In both personal life and politics, the result is harmful overreactions to risks.

One salient manifestation of probability neglect is that in two situations involving the same dreadful possibility, one much more likely to unfold than the other, individuals may value risk elimination nearly equally even though probabilities may differ by a factor of 20 or more. People focus on the bad outcome itself, and are inattentive to how unlikely it is to occur—hence their overreaction when the risk is low.

In other words, those who suffer from probability neglect will give up too much to wipe out a low-probability risk (moving from 0.001 to 0.000). They will frequently take excessive preventive action.[2] Corporations and governments suffer equivalent fates, in part because they need to respond to individuals and in part because of their own natural tendencies. Anthony Patt and Richard Zeckhauser labeled such overreactions as *action bias* in a 2000 article in the *Journal of Risk and Uncertainty* (Patt and Zeckhauser, 2000). That bias is especially likely if the relevant actors are able to obtain credit from themselves or from the public for responding to the risk.

It is predictable that following a terrorist attack, the public will both alter its behavior and demand a substantial governmental response. That will be true even if the magnitude of the risk does not warrant such a response, and even if the danger is far less than that presented by other hazards that inspire less dread. Consider, for example, the possibility that extensive security precautions at airports will lead people to drive rather than to fly; because driving is much riskier than flying, such precautions might cost many lives on balance. Further, the monies spent in recent years on airplane security seem out of scale with the level of risk reduction produced, particularly since numerous tests have found that the screening routinely fails to find weapons.

Perhaps such screening, however low the risk or ineffective the preventive, does reassure the public. If so, it serves a positive function, not unlike the nighttime hoof clops of mounted police, which make a very peculiar and recognizable noise. Squad cars may be better at deterring or catching criminals, but hoof clops are superior for fear reduction. The same points apply, of course, to many other purported forms of risk reduction, including measures to prevent financial crises, local steps to reduce greenhouse gas emissions, and regulation of abandoned hazardous waste dumps. Financial crises have a distinctive element: The fear itself may be a major stimulant for the crisis. As people sell in response, the downdraft accelerates, as we have seen in 2008 and 2009. Panics make reassurance that much more critical.

In the personal as opposed to social domain, we can find many analogues, as when people alter their travel plans to avoid slight risks of crime, restructure their portfolios to avoid small risks of big financial losses, or change their diets to avoid minimal health risks. Probability neglect promotes overreaction. The costs of overreaction may be reduced assets (restructuring the portfolio), increased risk (driving rather than flying), or sacrificed pleasure (children forgoing Halloween due to extremely rare razor-blade incidents).

DEMONSTRATING PROBABILITY NEGLECT

Prospect theory, developed by Daniel Kahneman and Amos Tversky in their seminal 1979 publication (Kahneman and Tversky, 1979), gives no indication that the ratio of weights would change dramatically with the nature or with the description of a risk.

Experiments on probability neglect seek to assess whether attention to probability could be overshadowed by attention to the emotional impact of the outcome, quite contrary to what leading theories of decision making posit. Emotional activity appears to dampen cognitive activity. Loewenstein and Lerner (2003, p. 636) observe that "[a]s the intensity of immediate emotions intensifies, they progressively take control of decision making and override rational decision making." We would expand this assertion to include overriding well-documented behavioral patterns in decision making, such as those described by prospect theory. This suggests that a dreaded scenario could swamp or at least temper the importance assigned to dramatic probability differences.

Electric Shocks

Some of the relevant experiments explore whether varying the probability of harm would matter less in settings that trigger strong emotions than in those that are relatively emotionally neutral. One such study, in an effort to test the relevance of variations in probability to "strong-emotion" decisions, explored people's willingness to pay (WTP) to avoid electric shocks (Rottenstreich and Hsee, 2001). In the "strong-emotion" setting, participants were asked to imagine taking part in an experiment involving some chance of a "short, painful, but not dangerous electric shock." In the relatively "low-emotion" setting, they were told that the experiment entailed some chance of a $20 penalty. When asked to say how much they would be willing to pay to avoid participating in the relevant experiment, some participants were told that there was a 1 percent chance of receiving the bad outcome (either the $20 loss or the electric shock); others were told that the chance was 99 percent. The central result was that variations in probability affected those facing the relatively emotion-free injury, namely the $20 penalty, far more than they affected people facing the more emotionally evocative outcome of an electric shock. The electric shock results revealed substantial probability neglect. The median subject was willing to pay $7 to avoid a 1 percent chance, but only $10 to avoid a 99 percent chance—a mere 1.43 times as much despite a 99 times increase in risk. (For the $20 penalty, the corresponding ratio was 18 times as much.)

The researchers' concluded that when a hazard stirs strong emotions, most people will pay an amount to avoid it that varies little even with extreme differences in the starting probability. What we are stressing here is that when the probability of loss is very low, people will tilt toward excess action. They will favor precautionary steps even if those steps are not justified by any plausible analysis of expected utility.

For either social or personal risks, the implication is clear. When the potential loss is likely to trigger strong emotions, overreaction occurs, as it does when the loss is an economic meltdown, environmental catastrophe, terrorist attack, cancer death, or getting killed in a plane crash. Even if the likelihood of a terrible outcome were extremely low, people would be willing to pay a great deal to avoid it, whether through public or private action. Once a risk is in people's minds, their willingness to pay to avoid it will often be relatively impervious to significant changes in probability. The significant and often expensive precautions taken against possible sniper attacks by citizens of the Washington D.C. area in October 2002 provide a dramatic example; they attest to the phenomenon of probability neglect in the face of a vivid threat. Indeed, some of these precautions, such as driving great distances to gas stations in Virginia, almost certainly increased mortality risks on balance.[3]

Arsenic in Drinking Water

To investigate the possibility that values for eliminating low-probability fearsome risks get overblown, we asked law students to state their maximum willingness to pay to reduce levels of arsenic in drinking water. The questions they responded to were drawn from real life. They were based on actual choices confronting the U.S. Environmental Protection Agency, involving cost and benefit information approximating actual figures used by the agency itself.

Participants were randomly sorted into four groups representing the four conditions in a 2x2 experiment, where both the probability and the description of the risk varied. In the first condition, people were asked to state their maximum willingness to pay to eliminate a cancer risk of 1 in 1,000,000. In the second condition, people were asked to state their maximum willingness to pay to eliminate a cancer risk of 1 in 100,000. In the third condition, people were asked the first question, but the cancer was described in vivid terms as "very gruesome and intensely painful, as the cancer eats away at the internal organs of the body." In the fourth condition, people were asked the second question, but the cancer was described in the same vivid terms as in the third condition. In each condition, participants were asked to check off

TABLE 14.1 Willingness to Pay in Dollars for Elimination of Cancer Risk: Harvard Law
School Results, 2008

Probability	Unemotional description	Emotional description
1/100,000	241 (100) [20]	250 (100) [13]
1/1,000,000	59.21 (25) [19]	211 (200) [15]

Key: Mean (Median); [Number of subjects].

their willingness to pay among the following options: $0, $25, $50, $100,
$200, $400, and $800 or more. Notice that the description of the cancer in the
"emotional description" conditions added little information, since many cancer deaths bear these characteristics. Indeed, finding a significant difference
between the two descriptions would be telling, since the word *cancer* in general elicits dread. The results are shown in Table 14.1.

This study was conducted in two law school venues, the University of
Chicago (Sunstein, 2002) and Harvard Law School. At Chicago, the medians
were 100 and 25 for the "unemotional description" and 100 and 200 for the
"emotional description." While the sample size was too small to permit firm
conclusions, the qualitative results pointed in the hypothesized direction. The
emotional description drove out responses to the quantitative difference in
the risk.

At Harvard, both as shown in the table and as hypothesized, the valuations for the more emotional description hardly differed even though probabilities differed by a factor of 10. Indeed, median WTP was actually higher for
the 1/1,000,000 probability given the emotional description, though far from
significantly so. By contrast, for the unemotional description WTP for the
1/100,000 probability was far higher.

It is important to note that the difference in WTP, even for the unemotional description, was far below the 10 to 1 odds ratio; for the ratio of the
odds it was roughly 4 to 1. Both hypotheses were therefore supported. First,
varying the probability had an effect on WTP that was much less than rational decision theory would predict. (Future research should assess whether
even mentioning the word *cancer* induces sufficient emotion to reduce a ratio
of 10 to 1 to one of 4 to 1.) When the cancer was described in affectively gripping terms, people were insensitive to probability variations.[4]

Implications of the Results

These findings have two implications for overreactions. They suggest, first, that when extremely low-probability risks give rise to dread, they are likely to trigger a larger behavioral response than statistically identical comparisons involving less fearsome possibilities. Here, as in the experiment, there will be a kind of "emotion premium." The findings further suggest that probability neglect will play a role in the private and public reactions to emotionally gripping dangers, and that many people will focus, much of the time, on the emotionally perceived severity of the outcome, rather than on its likelihood.

In this light, it should not be surprising that our public figures and our cause advocates often describe tragic outcomes. Rarely do we hear them quote probabilities. The latter, even if reasonably large, would have little salience in the public debate.

Emotions beyond fear also may drive probability neglect. Consider outrage, an emotion stirred when low-probability risks are created from the outside, as they are with nuclear waste radiation. A similar risk from radon exposure comes from one's own basement but generates little outrage. Outrage can overshadow probabilities in much the same way as fear can, reinforcing our finding that emotional activity dampens cognitive activity. A central finding of relevant empirical work is consistent with that stressed here: A large difference in probability had no effect in the "high-outrage" condition, involving nuclear waste, but a significant effect was shown in the "low-outrage" condition, involving radon. People responded the same way to a high-outrage risk of 1 in 100,000 as to a risk of 1 in 1,000,000 (Sandman, Weinstein, and Hallman, 1998). Even when both the statistical risk and the ultimate consequences were identical in the high-outrage (nuclear waste) and low-outrage (radon) cases, people in the nuclear waste case reported a much greater perceived threat and a much higher intention to act to reduce that threat. Indeed, "the effect of outrage was practically as large as the effect of the 4,000-fold difference in risk between the high-risk and low-risk conditions" (Sandman, Weinstein, and Hallman, 1998, p. 106).[5]

In this light, it is not surprising that visualization or imagery matters a great deal to people's reactions to risks. Vivid images can produce palpable overreactions, as Paul Slovic and co-authors show in their work on the affect heuristic (Slovic et al., 2002). When an image of a bad outcome is easily accessible, people will become greatly concerned about a risk (Loewenstein et al., 2001). An interesting anomaly is that when people are asked how much they will pay for flight insurance for losses resulting from "terrorism," they will pay more than if they are asked how much they will pay for flight insurance from all causes (which by definition includes terrorism) (Johnson et al., 1993).[6] The likely explanation for this peculiar result is that the word *terrorism* evokes vivid images of disaster, outrage, or both, thus inhibiting judgments about probability differences. Note also that when people discuss a low-probability risk, their concern rises even when the discussion consists mostly of apparently trustworthy assurances that the likelihood of harm is infinitesimal (Alhakami and Slovic, 1994). The discussion helps them to visualize the risk, thus making it more frightening. The most sensible conclusion is that with respect to risks of injury or harm, graphic images of disaster can overwhelm the cognitive activity required to conclude that the probability of disaster is actually small.

CONCLUSION

Dreadful possibilities activate emotions and make people insensitive to the probabilities of harm.[7] Terrible outcomes that are easy to visualize trigger large-scale changes in thought and behavior even if the statistical risk is dramatically lower than those associated with many other activities with equivalent stakes that do not arouse public concern. Probability neglect helps to explain public overreaction to highly publicized, low-probability risks, including those posed by sniper attacks, abandoned hazardous waste dumps, anthrax, and, perhaps more generally, terrorism.

RECOMMENDED READING

Alhakami, A. S., and P. Slovic (1994). "A Psychological Study of the Inverse Relationship Between Perceived Risk and Perceived Benefit." *Risk Analysis* 14: 1085–1096.

Johnson, E. J., J. Hershey, J. Meszaros, and H. Kunreuther (1993). "Framing, Probability Distortions, and Insurance Decisions." *Journal of Risk and Uncertainty* 7, no. 1: 35–51.

Kahneman, D., and A. Tversky (1979). "Prospect Theory: An Analysis of Decision Under Risk." *Econometrica* 47: 263–291.

Loewenstein, G., and J. S. Lerner (2003). "The Role of Affect in Decision Making," in R. Davidson, K. Scherer, and H. Goldsmith, eds. *Handbook of Affective Sciences*. Oxford: Oxford University Press.

Loewenstein, G. F., E. U. Weber, C. K. Hsee, and E. S. Welch (2001). "Risk as Feelings." *Psychological Bulletin* 127: 267–286.

Patt, A., and Richard Zeckhauser (2000). "Action Bias and Environmental Decisions." *Journal of Risk and Uncertainty* 21, no. 1: 45–72.

Rottenstreich, Y., and C. Hsee (2001). "Money, Kisses, and Electric Shocks: On the Affective Psychology of Risk." *Psychological Science* 12: 185–190.

Sandman, P., N. D. Weinstein, and W. K. Hallman (1998). "Communications to Reduce Risk Underestimation and Overestimation." *Risk Decision and Policy* 3, no. 2: 93–108.

Slovic, P., M. L. Finucane, E. Peters, and D. G. MacGregor (2002). "The Affect Heuristic." In T. Gilovich, D. Griffin, and D. Kahneman, eds. *Heuristics and Biases: The Psychology of Intuitive Judgment.* New York: Cambridge University Press.

Sunstein, C. (2002). "Probability Neglect: Emotions, Worst Cases, and Law." *Yale Law Journal* 112: 61–107.

15 Why We Still Fail to Learn from Disasters

ROBERT MEYER

It is often said that people are poor learners from experience about the value of investing in protection against natural hazards. When Galveston, Texas, was destroyed by the great 1900 hurricane, residents diligently invested in the construction of a protective seawall to prevent the reoccurrence of such a disaster. But as years passed without a major storm, the threat of hurricanes was seen to wane, such that years later when Texans began to settle on the Bolivar Peninsula just to the north of Galveston few felt the need to build a similar seawall there. The cost of this oversight became clear in the summer of 2008, when Hurricane Ike destroyed most of the residences on the peninsula. Likewise, in the quiet years that have elapsed since the Northridge earthquake in 1994, the state of California has witnessed a decline in the percentage of residents buying earthquake insurance (five residents out of six in California have no quake insurance), even as the odds of a repeat quake have been steadily increasing.

What explains these seeming failures to learn from the past? The problem is perplexing because it cannot be written off as a simple consequence of people having short memories. Residents along the Texas Gulf Coast, after all, are constantly reminded of the omnipresent threat of hurricanes by the ubiquitous media coverage that such storms receive during hurricane season, and few social conversations in California don't include some mention of earthquakes—concerning either damage that one suffered in the past or what one has heard about threats in the future. Likewise, our failure to optimally invest in protection cannot be attributed to the absence of incentives; as an example, consider that residents in the state of Florida can earn substantial reductions in their wind-storm insurance premiums if they undertake certain investments in mitigation—yet substantial numbers fail to take advantage of the program.

I contend that the reason we often fail to invest optimally in protection lies *not* in our inability to foresee the possibility of future losses but, rather, in our inability to foresee the consequences of *how we decide* to protect against these losses. In particular, we underinvest because of the combined effect of three forces: (1) an instinct to learn by trial and error that subconsciously rewards us for *not* mitigating more often than for mitigating; (2) a tendency to base decisions on poor mental models of the physical mechanics of hazards; and (3) a tendency to be lured to take risks by a misplaced confidence in our ability to survive hazards, no matter how severe. These natural psychological barriers to learning about mitigation are then compounded by a fourth, societal factor: a tendency to entrust decisions about how much (and when) to invest in mitigation to agents who are not likely to suffer the direct consequences of poor decisions.

WHEN GOOD DECISION PROCESSES PRODUCE BAD CONSEQUENCES

One of the more remarkable findings that has emerged from the study of complex problem solving over the years is that we do not need to be particularly smart to be able to make smart decisions. Good pool players, for example, manage to know how to direct a ball to a pocket without knowledge of the mechanics of force and relative motion. The explanation for this ability is that we can often get quite good at things if we are simply put in an environment that is favorable to learning by trial and error: one where we are offered repeated opportunities to learn, where the feedback it affords us is clear (e.g., we can see whether the ball drops in the pocket or not), and where mistakes, when we make them, are not fatal.

The problem, however, is that if we apply this same principle when deciding whether to invest in protection against low-probability hazards, the result may be a pattern of behavior that is transparently dysfunctional: an unending cycle of underinvestment in mitigation followed by short bursts of mitigation, followed by a return to underinvestment. The reason is straightforward: During periods when there are no hazards present—which will be most of the time—trial-and-error learners will see few tangible rewards to their decisions to invest. As time evolves, the continued absence of positive feedback will further dampen instincts to invest—until, of course, a disaster serves to reactivate the perceived need. Many such oscillating investments in mitigation could be cited. When Hurricane Betsy flooded much of New Orleans in 1965, for example, the federal government was motivated to invest millions in a flood protection program. But as years passed without major storms, the returns on these investments became increasingly harder for both residents and legislators to see—an outcome that resulted first in the scaling back of the scope of the levee project, then in the deferment of investments in its maintenance. It took, of course, the disastrous floods of Hurricane Katrina in 2005 to reawaken policy makers to the risk faced by residents and businesses in the area, and to the area's critical need for renewed investments in mitigation.

THE COMPOUNDING ROLE OF POOR MENTAL MODELS

While compelling in its simplicity, there is clearly more to the story of why we under invest in mitigation than the fact that we are often not directly rewarded for doing so. We might personally not see the direct benefits of mitigation on a day-to-day basis, but there is nothing, after all, that precludes personal learning from being supplanted by *social* learning. Communities might develop social norms for investing in protection, and foster "virtual memories" for catastrophic events through the retelling of history. A prominent sight along the Overseas Highway in the Florida Keys, for example, is a monument honoring the 500 residents and temporary workers who lost their lives during the great 1935 Labor Day Hurricane—a monument that doesn't just commemorate their loss but also reminds current residents of the omnipresent threat posed by such storms. Likewise, even societies that lack the means of formal record keeping often keep memories of past catastrophes alive through storytelling and folklore. For example, the folk mythologies of almost all cultures include stories of great deluges or floods—mythical descriptions of what caused them, how they were survived, and how they might be avoided in the future.

Yet, this ability to "virtually" learn the wisdom of mitigation is a good thing only to the degree that the knowledge conveyed in simulated memories is objectively helpful. If individuals and/or societies have poor mental models of how and why natural hazards arise, then processes that reinforce these models would be decidedly counterproductive. As perhaps an extreme example, for generations farmers in the Henan province of China avoided consuming steamed bean soup (a dietary staple) for five days at the start of each year in the belief that doing so would help prevent floods—a superstitious belief that managed to persist despite having no grounding in scientific fact (see Thomas Schelling's chapter in this book).

But the existence of misinformed mental models of hazards is hardly limited to developing societies. A good modern illustration is the lack of understanding among many residents in hurricane-prone areas about the role that storm shutters play in mitigating building damage. Their primary function is typically believed to be the reduction of damage resulting from broken glass—a relatively small impact that would seem to hardly justify their large cost. In reality, however, the true purpose of shutters is to protect the interior integrity of the house envelope, the rupture of which can amplify ceiling and roof damage—leading, in the extreme, to the complete collapse of the house itself. Residents who lack this knowledge would understandably be resistant to the installation of shutters; it would simply be hard to envision how the worst consequences of not having them would offset the large payment they'd need to make upfront.

A perhaps better-known example is the misperception that many have about how the probability of encounters with natural hazards varies over time. The likelihood that a specific location will be impacted by a natural disaster at a given point in time is usually independent of whether it was impacted by a disaster at a previous point—even for hazards that follow known cycles such as earthquakes. Yet, residents and communities are notorious for believing that low-probability events are highly temporally correlated, as when the survivors of a 1-in-100-year flood who quickly resettle in the flood plain claim that they are "safe" for another 99 years. But the opposite—and equally wrong—conjecture often arises as well; an obvious example is the insurance company that dramatically raises its premiums after a busy hurricane season (if allowed by regulation) in the belief that this signals a long-term trend.

THE COUNTERPRODUCTIVE EFFECTS OF KNOWLEDGE

The above accounts still leave us with one remaining puzzle. In principle, the better we are at recalling the past and the more advanced our scientific knowledge about hazards and mitigation, the lower our losses should be from them. But the reality seems to be the opposite. For example, while hurricanes have plagued communities along the United States' Atlantic and Gulf coasts for decades, the inflation-adjusted losses imposed by recent storms dwarf those imposed by past storms. The reason is simple: It is not necessarily because all the recent storms have been more intense than those in the past but, rather, because we have been increasingly willing to put valuable property at risk. Hence, we are presented with something of a paradox of knowledge: The more that we know about hazards and how to survive them, the more, it seems, we are willing to place ourselves and our property in harm's way. When it comes to protecting against natural hazards, more knowledge—perhaps because it makes us more comfortable—can be a dangerous thing.

A good example of this paradox of knowledge is the fate of the town of Indianola, Texas. In 1875, Indianola was a thriving Gulf Coast town of 5,000 that was home to the second-most important port in Texas, behind Galveston. In September of that year, however, Indianola was destroyed by a major hurricane and the accompanying tidal surge. The community rapidly recovered from this disaster and rebuilt—only to see the town destroyed yet again by a hurricane in 1886. Lacking any knowledge of hurricane climatology, and knowing little about how such a disaster might be prevented from happening yet again, the surviving residents reached the only sensible conclusion they could: They moved elsewhere.

In contrast, the far more advanced knowledge that we have today about hurricane risks and mitigation tends to produce something of the opposite reaction among communities and individuals: The belief that storms and other hazards are both survivable and predictable has induced aggregate risk taking, with the dominant migration pattern being to coastal zones that would have been deemed too unsafe for sensible development in earlier, less knowledgeable times.

What explains this effect? Past research on risk taking and learning in other domains suggests three complementary mechanisms. The first is that the tendency for knowledge to foster risk taking can be seen as the mirror image of the well-known tendency for individuals to *avoid* risky decisions when the odds of different outcomes are unknown or ambiguous—as Ayse Öncüler describes in this book. The more precisely that we know the odds of a gamble we are facing—such as the odds that our home will be hit by a hurricane or an earthquake in a given year—the more amenable we may be to the prospect of playing that gamble.

A second, complementary, mechanism is the effect of controllability: our willingness to be more open to taking on risks when we believe—however wrongly—that we have *control* over the outcome. Just as people are often willing to wager more in a dice game when they think they can control the roll, greater confidence in our ability to control losses from hazards by engineering risk reduction measures (even if we don't actually follow through) may contribute to an exaggerated willingness to take risks. Specifically, a homeowner who knows that she can make her home safer by investing in cost-effective risk reduction measures (such as storm shutters) might mentally commit to making the investment but perpetually defer its actual implementation—until, of course, a disaster actually arises and her roof is blown off.

There is another influence, too, which might be called the survivability effect: We are more inclined to engage in risk if we believe that the odds of a truly catastrophic outcome are negligible. It is just this underestimation of extreme outcomes that many have used to explain the widespread collapse of investment banks and lending institutions in 2008 in the United States: Banks undertook risky leveraging strategies in the belief that even the worst-possible default scenario would be survivable.

In the context of natural hazards, a dramatic comparative illustration of this effect is the curious difference one sees in the geographic distributions of settlement patterns in the world's two most cyclone-prone populated land masses: Northern Luzon in the Philippines and South Florida in the United States. Both display highly asymmetric geographic distributions of cities, but of opposite natures: Whereas the beaches along the southeast coast of Florida are lined with cities, those along the east coast of Luzon are largely unpopulated, with most residents living in the center or west coast of the island. While many historical causes can be posited to explain these two settlement patterns, the beneficial effect that Luzon enjoys by not having its major population centers located in the east cannot be overlooked: Because most severe typhoons that make landfall on Luzon arrive from the east, most of their damaging energy tends to be spent by the time major cities such as Manila are affected. Major cities in South Florida, in contrast, enjoy no such protective barrier; hurricanes arriving from the east land with full force, making the area prone to such catastrophes as the Great Hurricanes of 1926 and 1928 and Hurricane Andrew in 1992. Why do we see such different adaptations? One explanation has to do with timing and economics: Luzon was settled at a time when typhoon risks from the east could be neither predicted nor mitigated, and there was little economic benefit from locating ports and cities on the riskier windward side of the island. In contrast, settlement in South Florida was not only supported by a tourism economy for which beach locations held real value but, even more important, took place at a time when hurricanes were seen as predictable and their damage controllable (or at least recoverable). Hence, in addition to the paradox of increased scientific knowledge, we have the paradox of survivability: The greater the number of individuals who come to believe that our steps toward mitigation make even the worst storms survivable, the more inclined communities may be to put this survivability to the test.

THE AGENCY PROBLEM

While to this point we have focused on individuals' psychological impediments to mitigation, it is important to emphasize that in many situations the fault lies in what economists have referred to as the *agency problem*: the tendency for society to put the ultimate decision-making power in the hands of policy makers who are not at risk of suffering the consequences of mitigation-investment mistakes. After the great San Francisco earthquake and fire of 1906, for example, local authorities were initially moved to enact stronger building codes—but these were quickly removed from the books when contractors complained that they were slowing the pace of the city's reconstruction. Likewise, many of the homes and businesses along the Mississippi Gulf Coast that were destroyed by Hurricane Katrina were structures that were built in the same location—and to the same codes—as structures that had been destroyed by Hurricane Camille in 1969. The reason that homes were rebuilt to old codes was the same as that which drove the San Francisco rebuilding: As strong as a community's urge is to rebuild itself in a way that precludes future disasters, it has an even stronger urge to survive now—something that often cannot await the passage of new building codes.

POSTSCRIPT: CAN LEARNING BE IMPROVED?

This brings us to a final, natural, question: Can the above-described limits to effective learning be overcome? The answer is twofold. On the one hand, following the adage that knowledge of the cause is half the cure, the fact that we know something about the factors that impede learning presents opportunities for improving decisions through improved communication and incentive programs. To illustrate, the above discussion suggests that it is important not just to instruct residents as to what investments they should make in mitigation but also to accompany these instructions with education designed to equip them with accurate mental models of *why* these investments are necessary for safety. Whereas a resident who sees storms shutters simply as a way of protecting glass might be tempted to postpone the investment, one who sees them as essential to ensuring that the home's roof stays intact might feel a greater sense of urgency. Likewise, knowledge of the fact that long time intervals between disasters tends to extinguish instincts to invest in mitigation suggests the need for policies that encourage the persistence of long-term investments, such as imbedding investments in a home's mortgage plan.

On the other hand, the above discussion also suggests that improvements in education and the provision of incentives may be offset by factors that *impede* mitigation and are harder to overcome. The better able we are to predict natural hazards (such as with improved hurricane forecasting) and the more informed we are about how to mitigate against them, the less lethal they are likely to seem—and, hence, the lower our reluctance will be to take actions that put us in harm's way. In the 1800s, residents of Indianola, Texas, lacked warning advice by the National Hurricane Center, lacked building codes, and lacked an agency like FEMA to help with recovery after a storm. But they had one thing that modern coastal residents in the Bolivar Peninsula to the north lack: a fearful respect for Nature that caused them to move to where they did not have the *need* to mitigate.

RECOMMENDED READING

Meyer, Robert (2006). "Why We Under-Prepare for Hazards." In Ronald J. Daniels, Donald F. Kettl, and Howard Kunreuther, eds. *On Risk and Disaster: Lessons from Hurricane Katrina*. Philadelphia: University of Pennsylvania Press.

16 Dumb Decisions or as Smart as the Average Politician?

Economic and Behavioral Explanations for Insurance Demand

MARK V. PAULY

INTRODUCTION

Insurance is one of mankind's greatest inventions. I used to rank it just a little behind fractional reserve banking—a modern banking practice in which banks keep only a fraction of their deposits in reserve and lend out the remainder—which by its nature expands money supply beyond what it would otherwise be. But the recent turmoil in capital markets (with insurance not totally unaffected) suggests that the two financial instruments may now be even.

Several of the previous chapters in this book have already referred to insurance decisions as illustrative examples of a much broader set of decisions under risk, uncertainty, and even ambiguity. Here I would like to specifically discuss decision-making processes underlying the decision to purchase insurance coverage or not. And while most consumers buy some insurance and some investors make (or lose) fortunes at it, consumer behavior often fails to fit the usual models of expected utility maximization (see the description by Paul Schoemaker in his chapter). Faced with this phenomenon, Howard Kunreuther and I have collaborated over the years on research that tries to identify explanations for what happens as well as to suggest normative public policy strategies intended to evaluate and potentially modify consumer and insurer behavior. Our work largely deals with the broad question of *what to do when there is a fork in the intellectual road*: When confronted with behavior that appears to be inconsistent with a simple version of the traditional expected utility economic model, should one (a) posit different kinds of utility or choice function for consumers or (b) modify or amplify the traditional model by adding constraints on time, money, and information?

Here I will give some examples of insurance buyer behaviors that involve such inconsistencies, indicate the kinds of analysis associated with approaches (a) and (b), and use these to discuss more generally the methodological strategy that should be used in each of these circumstances.

AVERSION TO DEDUCTIBLES

Insurance firms never plan on paying back all of the premiums they collect in the form of policyholder benefits, because they have administrative costs and capital costs that they have to cover. These costs are termed *loading* and are usually described as a proportion of benefits paid out. For example, a premium of $130 might lead to payouts of $100 per insured person, in which case the loading proportion would be $30 or 30 percent. What kind of insurance does it make sense to buy when you know that some of your premium will go to cover costs in this way?

A well-known proposition in insurance theory established in 1953 by Nobel Laureate economist Ken Arrow (who has also contributed to this book) maintains that the optimal policy will be full coverage above a deductible, so above a predetermined deductible of, say, the first $1,000 of the claim, the insurance will pay 100 percent of the losses incurred.[1]

In many circumstances, however, consumers do not seem to be rational in this sense; they seem to prefer policies with low or no deductibles even when the higher premium to cover them is very large relative to the amount of additional money one would expect to collect: For auto insurance, individual health insurance, or homeowners insurance, even comfortably middle-class households tend to choose plans with deductibles of only a few hundred dollars, and they do so even in the face of high proportional loadings. This preference for a low-deductible policy by so many buyers seems too strong to square with reasonable assumptions about risk aversion: People generally seem to prefer low deductibles even in policies that cover risks that are small relative to their wealth.

Indeed, when I show my students at Wharton a numerical example where the increase in the deductible is actually *smaller* than the reduction in premium (such that their guaranteed premium saving is more than the worst that could happen to them under the higher deductible), some still say they prefer the low-deductible policy.

How to explain this? One strategy is to posit a different (or at least an enriched) utility function in which "peace of mind" and "freedom from regret" have positive values (rather than only gain or loss, as predicted by the expected utility [EU] model), and that "peace of mind" extends on down to losses that are actually inconsequential relative to the person's income or wealth (but presumably large enough to be upsetting). A related view is this: Especially if your wealth is ample, why worry yourself to death to save a few dollars on insurance?

One modification of the EU model that would predict low deductibles has been proposed by Schlesinger and Doherty (1985): It may be that there are "losses" associated with the uncertain event that are not directly insurable. In a second-best sense, it may then be preferable to overinsure the insurable event (e.g., monetary damage or cost) to compensate for the inability to insure the other event. The substitution cannot be perfect, of course, but paying for coverage in this indirect way may be better than no coverage at all.

These two different explanations imply two potentially different roles for public policy. If the EU model were accepted, the discovery of a rational explanation for deductible aversion would obviate the need for government to take corrective action regarding overinsuring. In contrast, if the explanation were one based on behavioral motivations, a literal interpretation is that government should hinder, or at least nudge people away from, low-deductible policies that would not be good for them.

My own personal opinion is that practical public policy will tend to ignore this kind of welfare economics–based argument. If people have preferences differing from those of the benchmark model, the most "democratic" reaction is to say "So be it" and to let them waste their money in the way they choose.

However, it is not always possible to take such a hands-off attitude; it's one thing for preferences to be merely eccentric, quite another for them to be impoverishing. But on top of this, in a society where government caters to what voters want rather than to what welfare economists want, politicians interested in maximizing their tenures or political fortunes may well find it desirable to go along with these mistaken preferences, whether in pursuit of first dollar coverage, dread disease insurance, or even poor investment vehicles disguised as whole life insurance.

Usually it is the extended EU model, rather than the behavioral (peace of mind) explanation, that yields refutable hypotheses. Indeed, the circumstantial evidence supporting the behavioral explanation often amounts to a rejection of the EU hypothesis, and then one turns to the behavioral explanation as the only argument left standing. For example, in principle one could see whether deductible aversion is in fact stronger in cases involving uninsurable (but not unmeasurable) additional loss. Do people who choose low deductibles experience larger uninsured changes in their wealth (in multiple ways) than people who choose high deductibles? The answer to this is not yet known, but could be. If it turns out to be "no," the behavioral explanation would gain support.

CONSUMER WARRANTIES

Another example of a phenomenon that seems better explained by a behavioral theory rather than by EU theory is the purchase of warranties on consumer durables. Here again, the cost often exceeds the expected value of the benefit by a substantial amount, and yet many people still buy. To be sure, the warranty's cost is usually small relative to the price of the product (or even relative to the price of a visit from the repairman), but the rational consumer looks at the price relative to the *expected* benefit, taking into account the probability of the loss as well as the amount of the loss. The proportion of people engaging in this behavior is a minority (in contrast to the majority who choose low deductibles), but a substantial minority, about a third of buyers. One other important factoid: The demand for warranties, even if its existence is irrational, is (rationally) responsive to their prices. (I suppose the same might have been said about the demand for pet rocks.)

Buy why does this behavior occur? The obvious explanation is that buyers of warranties overestimate the probability of needing repairs (especially when experiencing the hard sell after an already costly purchase). Another possible explanation is that, having made the effort to shop for and choose an item, at least some people may attach special value or affection to it—an argument that has been made in a more general framing (Kunreuther and Hsee, 2000), but usually with respect to "old favorite" and difficult-to-replace items, not brand-new merchandise still in the box. Warranties also protect buyers against higher prices for replacements, and may be priced favorably by a manufacturer whose marginal cost of replacement is much below the selling price—a real possibility for many relatively low-priced consumer electronics. Then, too, warranties give buyers peace of mind and freedom from regret.

An interesting question is whether the willingness of some buyers to buy warranties that would not be a good deal even if they were not overpriced results in a lower price for the product itself; could the product be a loss leader (as are razors), with the money to be made on warranties and/or repairs? Perhaps, but this seems like a stretch.

There is reason to go slow on a behavioral explanation here. In addition to the fact that most people do *not* buy warranties, competitively sold warranties are available for large purchases like automobiles (after the "free" manufacturer's warranty expires). It may also be that warranties are a form of price discrimination. A buyer who considers himself lucky for having gotten a good deal on a good product may be more willing to pay for a warranty than a buyer who thinks his particular purchase and purchase price are run of the mill and par for the course. The first buyer, having discovered "treasure," may be more willing to invest in protecting it. Finally, the price responsiveness of demand for warranties implies that, even if the preferences are not so rational, consumer behavior in fulfilling those preferences does repeat the standard model.

Regulation of warranty pricing or terms is a possible public policy solution, although at present it is uncommon (but not unknown). An alternative policy intervention would be the provision of information on frequency of repairs, so that buyers could make a better calculation of the expected value of a warranty. Indeed, such information would be useful across a whole range of insurance products, from warranties to long-term care insurance, where information on probabilities tends to be either absent or grossly distorted.

THE NONPOOR HEALTH UNINSURED

The two examples above are cases of overpurchase of insurance. What about behavioral versus rational explanations for under- or nonpurchase? The most familiar example from my perspective is the nonpurchase of health insurance. Some of the uninsured people in the United States have such low incomes that the explanation for nonpurchase is obvious: They can afford neither to pay for care nor to pay for insurance. But a fraction known to be "sizeable" could afford health insurance, in the sense that, had they bought it (even in the expensive individual market), they would have had enough left over for decent levels of other consumption. Many other people facing the same circumstances do have and pay for insurance, so how can that fraction say they cannot afford insurance? (Bundorf and Pauly, 2006; Gruber, 2008). Bear in mind, too, that while they may get some free care if their bill is enormous, they risk having to pay the bill themselves up to that point.

So why are some of the nonpoor uninsured? The all-purpose explanation is that their tastes for insurance are weaker than those of otherwise similar people, but a "tastes" explanation is distinctly unsatisfying. For this population, the consequence of not paying an insurance premium is not a guarantee that they will have that much more income available for other types of consumption; there is still the real prospect of expected out-of-pocket expenses. In short, the alternative to insurance they think they cannot afford is not *no expense* but, rather, a risky prospect of high expenses that they can even less afford. (That the uninsured are charged much higher retail or undiscounted prices for hospital inpatient and outpatient care is another reason why insurance is a better buy than noninsurance.) Even with the likelihood of nonpayment for catastrophically large expenses, the real chance of severe financial distress should motivate purchase by everyone with income or wealth above some relatively low level. Why doesn't it?

There are plausible explanations from the behavioral side. To begin with, it appears that some people are just not risk averse enough to be willing to pay the administrative loading for health insurance. This loading can be high—just look at the individual insurance policies that people were initially offered on the Internet—but, in principle, the great bulk of the uninsured population has access to lower prices and tax-subsidized employment-based group insurance (the insurance negotiated by a company for all its employees is likely to be cheaper). A substantial fraction (perhaps a fifth) of the uninsured have turned down group insurance for which they are eligible. Even more could find jobs that carry coverage if they really wanted to get coverage and were willing to put up with less than their "dream job."

A more plausible explanation from a behavioral perspective is that they do not have enough information to see the value of insurance. A study of the nonpoor uninsured in California provides some confirming, if circumstantial, evidence: Nonpoor people without health insurance are also likely to lack other kinds of insurance (life, homeowners, collision), to be maxed out on their credit cards, and to believe that individual insurance is much more expensive than it really is. These are people who are just not into risk protection of any sort. But there is an economic explanation as well. Group insurance tends to charge explicit premiums that are independent of risk (though with much lower than expected benefits) and thus seems to discriminate against lower risks, sometimes creating a situation where lower-risk employed people are less likely to take coverage than the higher-risk employed. (It probably helps the risk pool that a person must at least be able to work to get group insurance, such that the possibility of severe adverse selection is reduced.) A low-risk person will face the same explicit premium as a high-risk person working in the same firm, but the options available in firms employing mostly lower-risk people and the existence of a lower wage offset for coverage cause premiums to be somewhat reflective of risk.

Here, the best outcome is probably a compromise. Insurance prices facing the uninsured are not especially attractive, and the uninsured tend to underestimate the value of insurance. Behavioral factors and rational factors reinforce each other.

The role of public policy in this context has recently been much debated. Public subsidies for moderate-income uninsured people, which exceed the subsidies they get for group insurance, are a part of every health reform plan. And most plans purport to be able to offer coverage at lower administrative cost through exchanges or pools of some kind. Intererestingly, behavioral issues—motivation, salience, and framing—have not been a major part of the debate.

One approach that sidesteps these issues in practice but makes them more important in theory is the use of mandates for coverage (for children or adults). The strongest argument for mandates has to do with the spillover costs that the uninsured impose on others—costs that recent research shows are much larger than those related to hospital-level charity care, but that extend to lower quality for insured people in the community, because larger fractions of the uninsured make high quality less profitable (whether they use such care or not) (Pagán and Pauly, 2006).

INSURANCE AND A TRANQUIL LIFE

A theme common to the cases discussed in the preceding three sections is that people have other objectives than getting their insurance purchases just right. Howard Kunreuther and I formalized this idea in a study that postulated a decision-making cost to investigating insurance purchasing—collecting information on the best premiums, the best coverage, and the true loss probabilities (Kunreuther and Pauly, 2000). We found that where a risk really matters—fire insurance for the home, collision insurance, an extended warranty for a new car, insurance for dependents against a parent's premature death—insurance does commonly exist. That is, where expected utility might really be impacted by a loss, people usually care enough to start looking for insurance and eventually buying some coverage, though perhaps not the literally ideal amount. How long they persist in searching for coverage depends on how much a good price matters to them; for example, we found that low-risk young people paid premiums that were less than optimally reflective of their expected expenses for health insurance—a phenomenon consistent with the cost-of-search hypothesis but also with others.

One important consideration that has both rational and behavioral implications is how people think about insurance pricing. If they believe that insurance premiums generally reflect relatively modest profits for insurers across the board, they can greatly simplify their lives. Given such an assumption, the premium an insurer charges you to insure a given asset against a particular peril tells you what the insurer thinks the loss probability is.

Suppose you are considering buying insurance coverage that you know to be priced close to cost against the possibility of an event that imposes a loss of $L, where L = dollar amount of loss. You do not have to worry about how likely the event is or try to collect some data or ask others about it. Instead, you need only plug in your estimate of how much of the premium goes for loading, interpret the rest as a measure of expected loss (and expected benefit from insurance), and decide whether or not your risk premium (which you can calculate when you know the loss and its probability) is or is not greater than the loading. This information will also tell you how large a deductible to choose.

This means that the first question a rational person should ask when confronted with an offer of insurance coverage in an unfamiliar setting (say, long-term care insurance) is not how much the loss (or loss probability) might amount to but, rather, what the loading (including profit) on the offered coverage is. Unless you have some inside information that your loss probability is much different from what the insurer would think is average, knowing the loading and knowing the premium will give you almost all the information you need—if not for a perfect choice, then for one that is pretty good.

Unless there is a conscious attempt at secrecy, finding out the loading embodied in an insurance offer is usually easier than trying to find the data on losses and their frequencies. If the insurance market has multiple sellers, if there are past data on premiums paid in and benefits paid out, and if you expect the future to be much like the past, the needed information is in principle available from the insurer's own accounting data. Often these data must be submitted to a state insurance regulator; alternatively, a prospective buyer may ask the insurer for this information. If the insurer refuses to furnish it, that alone speaks volumes about the likely low value of the insurance relative to its cost.

The key point here is that rational insurance purchasing can be based on a small amount of fairly objective data (or assumptions about data) and need not depend on the feelings and facts currently known by insurance purchasers.

CONCLUSION: WHEN RATIONAL AND BEHAVIORAL DECISION MAKING COMPLEMENT EACH OTHER

My conclusion from these applications is that the rational and the behavioral need not be in serious conflict if there is reason to believe that insurance markets are working reasonably well. Given that entry into insurance is relatively unrestricted, "working reasonably well" should be the rule rather than the exception, although spirited discussion about how well is "reasonably well" will be commonplace. There are some exceptions to rational behavior for relatively small and linked risks, such as warranties and rental car insurance. But for those risks that might (if uninsured) make a big difference to a person's expected utility, we can expect markets to work reasonably well, and usually they do. Of course, a large number of little risks can mount up to a big risk, but insurance firms seem adept at bundling risks to a given asset in a given use (as in the form of all-perils coverage). Things are not going to work that well for new, large, unknown losses—but you have probably guessed that. This is precisely the focus in the next part of the book.

RECOMMENDED READING

Arrow, K. J. (1963). "Uncertainty and the Welfare Economics of Medical Care." *American Economic Review* 53, no. 5: 941–973.

Bundorf, M. K., and M. V. Pauly (2006). "Is Health Insurance Affordable for the Uninsured?" *Journal of Health Economics* 25, no. 4: 650–673.

Gruber, J. (2008). "Massachusetts Health Care Reform: The View from One Year Out." *Risk Management and Insurance Review* 11, no. 1: 51–63.

Kunreuther, H., and C. K. Hsee (2000). "The Affection Effect in Insurance Decisions." *Journal of Risk and Uncertainty* 20, no. 2: 149–159.

Kunreuther, H., and M. V. Pauly (2000). *NBER Reporter*, March 22.

Pagán, J. A., and M. V. Pauly (2006). "Community-Level Uninsurance and Unmet Medical Needs of Insured and Uninsured Adults." *Health Services Research* 41, no. 3: 788–803.

Schlesinger, H., and N. Doherty (1985). "Incomplete Markets for Insurance: An Overview." *Journal of Risk and Insurance* 52: 402–423.

17 The Hold-Up Problem
Why It Is Urgent to Rethink the Economics of Disaster Insurance Protection

W. KIP VISCUSI

As other contributors to this book have suggested, how people make decisions involving risk and uncertainty and how economists think people should make these decisions are often quite different matters.

For many decisions that we make the stakes are modest, so whether we stray a bit from economic efficiency norms may be of professional interest to economists but of little societal import. When the stakes are large, however, the soundness of decisions truly matters. In situations involving risks posed by disasters and catastrophic events, mistaken choices may impose considerable costs both on the individual and on society.

For example, although for decades economists have devoted substantial attention to the economic evaluation of the merits of flood control projects and other public works designed to offer protection from natural disasters, comparatively little attention has been given to individual decisions that affect the losses these disasters impose. Some economists, armed with expected utility theory and the economic analysis of insurance (both of which are discussed in previous chapters of this book), seem to rest assured that people perceive the risks accurately and make sound decisions regarding insurance and self-protection.

THE CASE OF FLOOD INSURANCE DECISIONS

It was in this context that Howard Kunreuther and his colleagues produced a landmark empirical investigation in the 1970s that documented the failures of individual insurance decisions.[1] I would like to use this study as an illustrative example and source of information here. The original study focused on risks posed by earthquakes and floods. These hazards pose potentially large losses for which rational people should find actuarially fair insurance policies attractive. Because disaster insurance is heavily subsidized by the government, purchasing such insurance should be especially attractive. However, even under these favorable cost conditions, people often chose not to purchase the insurance. And indeed, they usually didn't even know the basic parameters of the available insurance opportunities. In the case of flood insurance, a 1976 study found that for those who were insured, 17 percent of consumers did not know the cost of their flood insurance and 44 percent didn't know the size of their deductible. Among those who were not insured, 68 percent didn't know the cost of the insurance and 82 percent didn't know the possible choices of the deductible. The failure of people to purchase insurance, coupled with this failure of knowledge that is counter to the usual economic assumption of perfect information, led to this strong conclusion: "The expected utility model, as traditionally used by economists, provides relatively little insight into the individual choice process regarding the purchase of insurance."[2]

Economists' expected utility theory predicts that the subsidized insurance should be more attractive for people who expect greater financial damage from a severe flood. Among those who believed their damage claims would be zero, 24 percent purchased insurance.[3] Overall, 46 percent of those expecting finite damage claims not exceeding $10,000 purchased insurance, with the percentages rising to 61 percent for those expecting a loss of between $10,001 and $30,000 and to 67 percent for those expecting a loss above $30,000. Likewise, the purchase of insurance was positively correlated with the expected probability of a flood, which is what we would expect if people behave in a sensible manner.

What is to be concluded here? Certainly these data do not imply that all is well with rational economic theories of behavior. Rather, they suggest that, as indicated by Mark Pauly in the previous chapter, even for smaller potential losses the report card for insurance decisions for natural disasters is mixed. Some aspects of the choices are broadly consistent with rational choice, but there is also evidence that the standard economic paradigm fails to reflect the substantial failures in individual risk beliefs and decision making. One can, of course, mount other defenses of expected utility theory in this context, but they tend to be somewhat ad hoc. The fixes represent possible amendments to the basic economic model rather than features already incorporated into it.

BEHAVIORAL CONSIDERATIONS

As discussed in previous chapters, how individuals treat low-probability events has continued to be a recurring concern in the economics and psychology literatures. People tend to both overestimate low-probability events and underestimate the very large risks that they face. Disasters often carry a low probability, so one would expect these risks to be easily overestimated. Moreover, highly publicized, dramatic events are prone to overestimation; natural disasters such as floods and earthquakes garner substantial press attention, which should lead the public to believe the risks are more common than they actually are. Given these biases, highly publicized risks would theoretically lead people to be excessively insured with respect to such hazards. However, insurance decision purchases seem to reflect biases in the opposite direction.

Another characteristic of disaster risks other than the level of risk probability is the precision of our knowledge of the risk. People may not know the actual probability of possible disasters, making the risks highly ambiguous. To the extent that people exhibit aversion to poorly understood risks (a widely documented phenomenon), one might expect them to err on the side of excessive insurance and self-protection. Yet, the apparent inadequacy of insurance purchases suggests that on balance this effect of risk ambiguity is not dominant.

Another possible explanation as to why individuals fail to purchase adequate coverage against disasters is that there are real personal costs to becoming fully informed. The percentage of people who have read their insurance contract in its entirety is likely to be very low. Learning about the terms of available insurance contracts involves transactions costs (e.g., making calls to different insurers to compare what they would offer, or carefully reading the entire car or home insurance contract; many consumers just don't), so people may not know all of the conditions under which they are covered or not.

However, given the opportunity to purchase subsidized insurance, people may need to know little about the insurance terms as long as they know that it is heavily subsidized by the government. Similarly, if purchase of insurance is a requirement of obtaining a mortgage, then no element of choice is involved. Those who expect the government to bail them out completely after a major disaster may not see a need for insurance either, so here, too, the incentive to learn about insurance and to buy appropriate coverage is diminished.

The main implication of these and other findings is that decisions concerning low-probability events appear to be fraught with error. The low probabilities involved are hard for people to think about, and making reliable probability judgments requires substantial personal experience. Some people overestimate the risks, and others may underestimate the risk. The losses they suffer from the errors that lead to underinsurance and inadequate protection are likely to be greater than the losses from excessive insurance. Regardless of the direction of the errors people make, however, it is clear that many of their decisions fall short of the prescriptions of rational choice based on models of rational economic choice.

WHY WAS NEW ORLEANS, STILL HIGHLY EXPOSED TO FUTURE HURRICANES, REBUILT IN THE SAME PLACE?

A salient societal issue raised by these decision errors and the resulting market failure is determination of the appropriate role for government. After Hurricane Katrina in August 2005, the government initially fell short in its response but subsequently has spent billions to compensate the victims and increase the protections against future flood risks. Many economists debated the wisdom of rebuilding New Orleans and strengthening the protections against future flooding given the inherent riskiness of the Gulf Coast region. Such musings may have academic interest but are of little practical consequence: The city is being rebuilt. A well-established finding in behavioral economics is the "endowment effect," whereby people place an inordinately large value on assets in their possession. New Orleans itself might be viewed as one such asset that we collectively possess, as it ranks among the most important cities in the United States in terms of historical and architectural interest. Individual property values there certainly understate the worth of New Orleans to the country. So, politically, any plan of action that does not ensure the survival of New Orleans is simply a nonstarter.

THE HOLD-UP PROBLEM

There are additional difficult policy issues pertaining to disaster assistance. What, for example, is the appropriate future compensation policy given that the presence of hurricane risks to New Orleans is well known? If residents return to New Orleans and suffer from a future hurricane, should the government again provide substantial compensation for the losses incurred? A national survey undertaken in April 2006—eight months after Hurricane Katrina—found that a representative national sample expressed little support for additional aid. Specifically, whereas 82 percent of the American public supported compensation of disaster victims generally, only 36 percent supported compensation of victims in New Orleans after the next hurricane.[4] Saying that one will not support assistance after a future hurricane may, of course, be a form of hypothetical trash talk. It is a very different matter to actually deny assistance once there are identified victims and their stories are featured on the evening news. In health-risk contexts, the sentiments people express about saving the identified lives of people who will otherwise die if there is no intervention are quite different from the valuations involved in reducing small probabilities of death within a large population, where the persons who will be saved are not known in advance. In much the same way, aiding those actually in need will be a more pressing concern than aiding those who may prospectively be in need.

As a society, then, we are faced with a *hold-up problem*. People may underinsure despite the offer of subsidized insurance and then seek and obtain post-disaster assistance, which is difficult to deny. The analytic phenomenon is not unlike that posed by aid to the elderly in the United States. If people did not save for retirement, there would be millions of destitute elderly who would be prime candidates for government assistance. Denying such aid would be difficult. To avoid these enormous aid costs, the government requires savings for retirement through Social Security. For those who do not have sufficient earnings to reap these retirement benefits, the Supplemental Security Income program provides assistance.

POLICIES TO FOSTER ADEQUATE SELF-PROTECTION AND INSURANCE

Cognizant of the failure of people to buy adequate disaster insurance coupled with the U.S. government's inability to deny post-disaster aid, Howard Kunreuther and Mark Pauly have proposed a comprehensive approach for disaster risks to deal with the possible consequences of disasters in a more anticipatory manner.[5] Under their proposal, the government would impose zoning restrictions to prevent people from putting valuable property at unnecessary risk and require insurance for people in disaster-prone areas so that they would be forced to have some coverage for the financial risks. Special accommodations would be made for those with low income, similar to those provided to the elderly poor by current programs of income assistance. The Kunreuther-Pauly strategy recognizes the failures of private decisions; it also recognizes the likely societal willingness to provide assistance to victims of disasters, even though the severity of the consequences is due to their own inadequate self-protection and underinsurance. If this policy strategy is adopted, it might compel people to internalize the disaster costs imposed by their choices—thereby influencing, in a socially efficient manner, longer-term decisions regarding the location of businesses and homes.

Risk-rated insurance and regulation proposals such as these work best in situations where we have substantial historical data, making it possible to distinguish the risk levels and differences in risk by locale. For other disasters, however, this is not feasible. The risks from mega-terrorism posed by events such as the 9/11 attacks are low-probability events that pose even greater challenges for rational choice than that posed by natural disaster risks. The single concentrated cluster of events associated with the 9/11 attack provides little basis for assessing the likely frequency of such attacks in the future or where they might occur. The risks themselves are dimly understood, involving considerable uncertainty and highly diffuse probability judgments. Research indicates an extremely wide range of assessed risks following the 9/11 attack. In a survey Richard Zeckhauser and I undertook after 9/11, the mean value of respondents' percentiles for the expected number of deaths due to terrorism in the next year was 33 at the 5th percentile, 404 at the median, and 35,200 at the 95th percentile—a very wide range indeed.[6] The actual number of terrorism deaths in 2002 from attacks in the United States was zero, though 27 U.S. citizens were killed in anti-U.S. terrorist attacks in other countries.[7] Although the analytical issues pertaining to terrorism risk insurance share many commonalities with natural disasters, they pose considerably greater obstacles for individuals and insurance firms.

Moreover, post-disaster compensation may become a potentially recurring policy issue for terrorist attacks just as it is for natural disasters. After 9/11, the government-funded compensation effort provided income support for the families of the deceased and limited the liability claims and costs imposed on the affected airlines and other businesses. In some respects, such post-disaster relief parallels the assistance efforts that are undertaken for victims of natural disasters. However, perhaps because of the novel circumstances of the 9/11 attacks, the government-provided aid was even more generous than that provided to victims of Hurricane Katrina and other natural disasters. Whether very generous post-disaster assistance will be forthcoming for future terrorist attacks will depend on the frequency of terrorist attacks, whether the victims engaged in behavior that put them at risk, the cost of compensation, and the public's general concern with the welfare of those who have suffered the losses.

These less well anticipated disasters will pose problems that neither individual decisions nor insurance markets can address in a fully reliable manner. Even government policies may fall short. Understanding the sources of the failures and the likely departures from full economic rationality will continue to be a pivotal prerequisite for addressing the consequences of such disasters. The lessons learned from the literature on protection from natural disasters provide substantial guidance and cautionary warnings with respect to the ability of people to make the even more difficult decisions involving terrorism risks. There is no reason to believe that people will better understand these risks or make more rational insurance decisions, especially given that terrorism risks depend on many factors that evolve over time (protection in place, foreign policy, etc.). In addition, the societal response to those harmed by such hazards is likely to be fraught with errors. As with natural disasters, it is important to establish mechanisms that foster self-protection and insurance so as to bolster what is likely to be the inadequate role of individual decisions.

RECOMMENDED READING

Kunreuther, Howard (1976). "Limited Knowledge and Insurance Protection." *Public Policy* 24, no. 2: 227–261.

Kunreuther, Howard, et al. (1978). *Disaster Insurance Protection: Public Policy Lessons.* New York: Wiley.

Kunreuther, Howard, and Mark Pauly (2005). "Insurance Decision-Making and Market Behavior." *Foundations and Trends in Microeconomics* 1, no. 2.

National Safety Council (2004). *Injury Facts.* Itasca, IL: National Safety Council.

Viscusi, W. Kip, and Richard J. Zeckhauser (2003). "Sacrificing Civil Liberties to Reduce Terrorism Risk." *Journal of Risk and Uncertainty* 26, nos. 2–3: 99–120.

Viscusi, W. Kip, and Richard J. Zeckhauser (2006). "National Survey Evidence on Disasters and Relief: Risk Beliefs, Self-Interest, and Compassion." *Journal of Risk and Uncertainty* 33, nos. 1–2: 13–36.

PART FOUR

MANAGING AND FINANCING EXTREME EVENTS

P ART FOUR BUILDS ON the first three sections of the book and on what we now know about human behavior in a catastrophic environment. Here, the focus is on how *individual* behavior translates into *collective* actions (or the lack of such actions). In other words, how do we deal with catastrophic risks as a society? And how can decision sciences and economics show us how this could be radically improved?

The first two chapters (18 and 19) look at how the U.S. government prepares for, manages, and ensures financial recovery after natural disasters and terrorist attacks, and what that means in the aftermath of the global financial crisis. The authors disclose how the federal government has, over the years, played an increasing role in providing financial coverage and relief to many more people and for a larger range of risks. However, federal disaster expenditures nowadays are rarely aligned with good economic rules and sound insurance principles. Relief is mainly dictated by political and media pressure in the aftermath of a disaster, rather than being based on clear attribution rules defined and known to all beforehand.

The next two chapters (20 and 21), more technical, focus specifically on the 2008–2009 financial meltdown to analyze how the combination of individual behavioral biases and misaligned incentive systems led to this historic crisis. A lot has been written on this matter already, but the authors show in a very novel way how economic theory and lessons from other major crises (e.g., with respect to post-catastrophe insurance markets) can shed some new light.

The next four chapters (22 to 25) look at environmental risks and climate change—an issue that includes the irrational politics of environmentalism and the question of how some conservatives in the United States abandoned the responsibility to conserve. Today, the citizen, the politician, the entrepreneur, and the judge are concerned about environmental problems and about how to efficiently allocate limited resources given the great uncertainty surrounding the future climate, yet they don't necessarily have a strong scientific basis for decision making. But this can change. In a more technical discussion (Chapter 24), we will also look at an innovative proposal for long-term insurance contracts (as opposed to the traditional one-year contracts we currently know). Such contracts, if adequately designed and marketed, could address a host of concerns ranging from climate change to land use. But will insurers agree?

Part Four ends with a discussion of one critical policy question. Climate change is predicted to severely affect the poorest countries on the planet, which will likely be devastated more often by droughts, intense floods, and other extreme weather-related catastrophes. What is the responsibility of rich countries—countries that, for decades, have been emitting a large portion of the greenhouse gases currently in the atmosphere? More specifically, can the international community create an innovative financial safety net for the poor? In a more dangerous and interdependent world, this should matter to all of us.

18 The Peculiar Politics of American Disaster Policy

How Television Has Changed Federal Relief

DAVID MOSS

Particularly since the 1960s, the federal government has played a significant role in financing disaster losses in the United States.[1] The federal government may thus be thought of as providing an implicit form of public disaster insurance. However, unlike many long-standing public insurance programs, which collect premiums to cover expected losses, federal disaster "insurance" collects no premiums other than for flood risk.[2] And even here, in the case of the National Flood Insurance Program, premiums have traditionally been subsidized.

Why doesn't the federal government administer its disaster expenditures in line with conventional insurance principles, instead of funding them mainly *ex post* out of general revenues (and borrowing) and typically on the basis of emergency supplemental appropriations? More concretely, why is public disaster relief financed differently from other forms of public insurance, such as unemployment insurance and deposit insurance?

Although there are many possible explanations for this puzzle, one that deserves particular attention relates to the peculiar politics of disaster policy at the federal level and the special role that the news media appear to play in driving policy outcomes. As is well known, media coverage surges upward in the immediate aftermath of a disaster, throwing a bright spotlight on the victims, and then quickly dissipates. As a result, although the accumulated costs of disaster relief are quite high, the politics are typically played out one disaster at a time, in line with the media coverage. This dynamic appears to focus public attention more on the immediate benefits of emergency disaster assistance than on the long-term costs. Unless and until the public discussion can be reframed to look across disasters, rather than focusing on one disaster at a time, insurance-based policy reform may remain exceedingly difficult to achieve.

A BRIEF HISTORY OF FEDERAL DISASTER RELIEF

Although Americans have always faced the scourge of natural disasters, attitudes about the proper role of government in addressing disaster losses have changed dramatically over time. The change has been particularly striking with regard to the federal government.

Congress provided assistance to the victims of a major fire in New Hampshire as early as 1803, and historians have counted 128 specific acts of Congress providing *ad hoc* relief for the victims of various disasters over the years 1803 to 1947. Nevertheless, disaster relief was not generally viewed as an ongoing federal responsibility in the United States until well into the twentieth century.[3] In 1887, for example, President Grover Cleveland vetoed a bill that would have provided $10,000 in assistance to the victims of a drought in Texas. "I can find no warrant for such an appropriation in the Constitution," Cleveland declared, "and I do not believe that the power and duty of the General Government ought to be extended to the relief of individual suffering. . . . [T]hough the people support the Government, the Government should not support the people. . . . Federal aid in [cases of misfortune] encourages the expectation of paternal care on the part of the Government and weakens the sturdiness of our national character."[4]

Forty years later, in 1927, a massive flood on the Mississippi prompted a new level of engagement from the federal government—and especially from President Calvin Coolidge's activist secretary of commerce, Herbert Hoover. Hoover took charge of the federal relief and rescue efforts and helped to distribute roughly $10 million in federal funds. Although the effort was seen as Herculean at the time, it was minuscule by modern-day standards. Federal expenditures in 1927 covered only about 3.3 percent of total damages and were considerably smaller than the $17.5 million in cash contributions (and $6 million of in-kind contributions) collected by the Red Cross that year for the relief of flood victims. Hoover himself recalled some years later that "those were

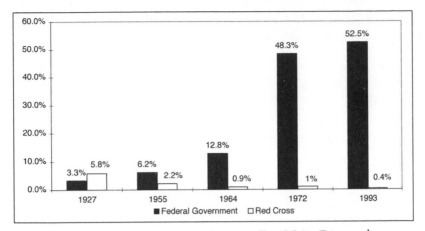

FIGURE 18.1 Approximate Coverage Rates[a] on Five Major Disasters[b]
(Federal Government and the Red Cross)

[a]Ratio of disaster spending to total estimated damages (in percent).

[b]The five disasters are the Mississippi Floods of 1927, Hurricane and Flood Diane
(1955), the Pacific Northwest Floods (1964), Tropical Storm Agnes (1972), and the
Mississippi Floods of 1993.

Source: David A. Moss, "Courting Disaster? The Transformation of Federal Disaster
Policy since 1803," in Kenneth A. Froot, ed., *The Financing of Catastrophe Risk*
(Chicago: University of Chicago Press, 1999), figure 8.2 (p. 328).

the days when citizens expected to take care of one another in time of disaster
and it had not occurred to them that the Federal Government should do it."[5]

Federal involvement in disaster relief continued to expand over the ensu-
ing decades. Congress passed the first general disaster relief act in 1947 and
created the first permanent relief fund as part of the Federal Disaster Act of
1950. Even so, federal spending remained modest by current standards. In the
wake of Hurricane and Flood Diane in 1955, for example, federal relief spending covered only about 6.2 percent of total damages—although this was now
higher than Red Cross spending, which covered just 2.2 percent of damages
in 1955. Federal coverage rates (i.e., federal spending as a percentage of total
disaster losses) rose rapidly over the next twenty years, reaching 48.3 percent
in response to Tropical Storm Agnes in 1972 (see Figure 18.1).

Howard Kunreuther has characterized the great Alaskan earthquake of
1964, which struck on Good Friday that year, as a "turning point in the federal government's role in disaster relief."[6] Certainly, federal officials mounted
a significant effort in response to the terrible Alaskan quake, and from that

point forward the federal role in disaster relief grew by leaps and bounds. Over the remainder of the 1960s, federal disaster policy was "expanded to include funding for the repair of damaged higher education facilities, debris removal from private property, and unemployment compensation and food coupons for hard-pressed disaster victims. The federal government had also increased the availability of SBA [Small Business Administration] and FmHA [Farmers Home Administration] disaster loans."

The Disaster Relief Act of 1970 codified these developments while also "[s]trongly emphasizing relief for individual victims"; and this followed the National Flood Insurance Act of 1968, which provided federally subsidized insurance for flood risk. Subsequent federal actions established the Federal Emergency Management Agency (FEMA) in 1978, dramatically expanded crop insurance in 1980, and consolidated (and expanded) federal disaster policy as part of the Stafford Act of 1988.[7]

Recent estimates suggest that from 1989 to 2006, federal disaster spending totaled $212.9 billion on disaster losses of $483.1 billion. This implies an average federal coverage rate of almost 45 percent. Moreover, since nearly 40 percent of total disaster losses were covered by explicit (contractual) insurance, federal aid as a percent of total uninsured losses ran considerably higher (approximately 75 percent) over these years. It is also worth noting that almost four-fifths of federal disaster spending across this period came through emergency supplemental appropriations, suggesting that relief spending was for the most part highly reactive.[8]

Clearly, the federal role in disaster relief has changed dramatically over the nation's history. In 1985, Howard Kunreuther and Louis Miller observed:

The role of the federal government with respect to hazards has been changing over the past 30 years. Although Congressmen and federal agencies have become more concerned with finding ways to help communities struck by severe disasters, there has also been a realization that government has been viewed as the protector of risks in ways that would have been unthinkable 50 years ago. Even 30 years ago there was a reluctance by local communities to rely on federal relief for recovery purposes.[9]

Substantial federal assistance in the aftermath of major disasters had emerged as an accepted feature of American life. Indeed, not even a century after it was first articulated, President Cleveland's dictum that "the Government should not support the people" would represent near political suicide for a modern American president, particularly if declared against the backdrop of a large-scale disaster.

RELIEF OVER INSURANCE: A PROBLEM OF CONCENTRATED BENEFITS AND DIFFUSE COSTS?

Today, there can be little doubt that federal disaster policy represents an implicit form of insurance. Although the victims of natural disasters typically have no contractual claim on federal assistance (outside of federal flood and crop insurance), past experience suggests that substantial federal aid will almost certainly be forthcoming in the wake of a major disaster. It is widely recognized that at least some federal role is necessary in addressing disaster losses, given numerous weaknesses in the private management of catastrophe risk, including long-standing—and apparently growing—gaps in private insurance coverage.[10] The question, though, is why implicit federal insurance against disaster losses has never been converted into explicit insurance, along the lines of workers' compensation, public unemployment insurance, or federal deposit insurance.

As compared to open-ended relief (i.e., *implicit* insurance), explicit federal disaster insurance or reinsurance could foster appropriate incentives for loss prevention through the assessment of risk-based premiums. The collection of premiums would also provide an important source of funds for compensating victims in the aftermath of disasters, and truly risk-based and actuarially appropriate premiums would reduce or eliminate existing cross-subsidies. President Franklin Roosevelt introduced federal crop insurance in the late 1930s, and federal lawmakers enacted the National Flood Insurance Program in 1968. For a long time, however, both of these programs remained limited in scope and highly subsidized. Even today, as subsidies for federal flood insurance have been reduced, both programs continue to be dwarfed in magnitude by general disaster relief. The fact is that despite repeated calls for comprehensive disaster insurance, Congress never moved to convert *implicit* disaster insurance (relief) into *explicit* disaster insurance or reinsurance.[11] What accounts for this seemingly suboptimal outcome?

One plausible answer is that the preference for relief over insurance is simply the political product of concentrated benefits and diffuse costs, a la Mancur

Olson.[12] To be sure, those living in hazard-prone areas have much to gain from an open-ended system of federal disaster payments, funded out of general revenues, whereas everyone else has relatively little to lose, since the per capita cost of such relief is relatively small, at least for any given disaster. As a result, those living in hazard-prone areas may have a strong incentive to organize politically (in support of federal relief), whereas average taxpayers may have little incentive to expend resources to lobby in the opposite direction.

Although this explanation carries strong intuitive appeal, it nonetheless suffers from a number of possible problems. First, one has to wonder why federal disaster expenditures grew so dramatically beginning in the 1960s if the political dynamic of concentrated benefits and diffuse costs had always favored large federal relief spending. Second, although concentrated interests are normally expected to achieve their political objectives through organization and lobbying, there exists no visible political organization representing the interests of hazard-prone areas—that is, there is no "Disaster Relief Promotion Association" or comparable organization. Third, if concentrated interests were driving the politics of disaster relief, it is not clear why they would favor funding most of it through emergency supplemental appropriations, which require many separate congressional votes (each of which is presumably costly to organize).

Finally, and most important, numerous public opinion polls indicate that in the immediate aftermath of a major disaster, public support for generous federal relief has been remarkably strong, suggesting that aggressive lobbying by potential recipients might not have been necessary. In September 2005, for example, when asked in a CBS News/*New York Times* poll "Which is more important to you right now—cutting taxes or rebuilding New Orleans," 73 percent said "Rebuilding New Orleans" and 20 percent said "Cutting taxes." When asked in the same poll "Would you be willing or not willing to pay more in taxes to help with the recovery from Hurricane Katrina," 56 percent answered "Willing," 37 percent "Not Willing," and 7 percent "Don't Know." Similarly, when informed as part of an Associated Press/Ipsos poll that "the U.S. Congress is expected to appropriate up to 200 billion dollars to help the affected areas recover from Hurricane Katrina," 52 percent thought that this was the "right amount" and 15 percent thought that Congress should "spend more," while only 24 percent thought it was "too much" and 7 percent were "unsure."[13] Apparently, Americans generally—and not just disaster victims— favor generous federal relief in times of disaster.[14]

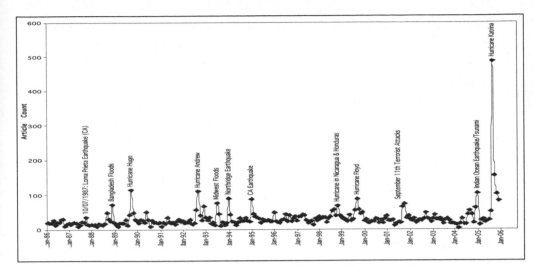

FIGURE 18.2 Natural Disaster Coverage in the *New York Times*, 1986–2005
Note: This figure was prepared by Stephanie Lo, using the Proquest Historical Database. Search terms were defined as ("disaster" or "catastrophe") and ("storm" or "earthquake" or "flood" or "hurricane").

AN ALTERNATIVE EXPLANATION: THE POWER OF THE PRESS IN SHAPING DISASTER POLITICS

Another possible explanation for continued federal reliance on disaster relief, rather than explicit disaster insurance, stems from the extraordinary media coverage that catastrophes typically generate. It is well known that major disasters are often heavily covered in both local and national media. As shown in Figure 18.2, the number of articles about natural disasters in the *New York Times* predictably spikes in the face of major disasters. (Not surprisingly, a very similar pattern emerges when the same search is conducted on all newspapers in the Lexis-Nexis database.)

Presumably, heavy media coverage of disaster victims inspires sympathy in their fellow citizens (i.e., outside of the disaster area) and, in turn, stimulates broad public demand for disaster relief. With regard to international disasters, Thomas Eisensee and David Strömberg have found that U.S. relief for the victims of disasters abroad is greater when news coverage of the disasters on the major television networks is higher. Significantly, they have also found that such relief is smaller when network coverage of large foreign disasters is crowded out by other major news events. Based on this evidence, Eisensee and Strömberg conclude that "relief decisions are driven by news coverage of disasters."[15]

Given the power of news coverage—and particularly television news coverage—to influence disaster policy, it is possible that the rapid growth of federal spending on disaster relief that commenced in the 1960s (again, see Figure 18.1) derived at least in part from the dramatic rise of television news during the same decade.[16]

Following major advances in television technology in the 1950s, FCC Chairman Newton Minow's 1961 characterization of television as a "vast wasteland" prompted a "renewed emphasis on news by the networks, and enhanced news coverage by local television stations. That same year, President John F. Kennedy allowed the networks to broadcast a presidential news conference—live."[17] Two years later, in 1963, stunning coverage of Kennedy's assassination in Dallas catapulted network news to a new level. "'Live' became a defining word," explains Phillip Kierstead, "indicating the powerful advantage television news was developing over print media."[18] In fact, a Roper poll in November 1963 found for the first time that more Americans relied on television, rather than on newspapers, as their main news source.[19]

It may have been more than coincidence, therefore, that the Alaskan earthquake of 1964, which marked a "turning point in the federal government's role in disaster relief," was itself prominently and poignantly covered on the evening news at the time, with dramatic on-scene reporting and graphic video of the devastation.[20] By bringing the tragedy of natural disasters into America's living rooms, television likely increased public pressure for federal relief of the victims. This dynamic may also help to explain why Congress has relied so heavily on emergency supplemental appropriations in funding disaster expenditures, since public demands for action, probably driven in part by intense bursts of media coverage at times of disaster, are themselves episodic.

What remains less clear is why public attention to disasters—fostered perhaps by media coverage—has translated into large disaster expenditures but *not* into fundamental reform of the way those expenditures are financed. In many other contexts, intense media coverage of major tragedies or scandals has helped to provoke significant policy reform, even over the objections of powerful concentrated interests. The media's exposure of the Love Canal toxic-waste tragedy in upstate New York in 1978, for example, led directly to the enactment of Superfund, despite strenuous (and well-financed) opposition from the chemical industry, which was expected to bear much of the cost. Similarly, the extraordinary civil rights protests and violence in Selma, Alabama, in 1965 attracted nationwide media coverage and led directly to passage of the Voting Rights Act that same year.[21] Why hasn't comparable coverage of major natural disasters pushed Congress to reform federal disaster policy, bringing it more in line with traditional insurance principles?

One possible answer to this question relates to the nature of the media coverage that natural disasters elicit. News reports about natural disasters, which surge when disasters strike and then quickly dissipate, tend to focus on loss of life, physical damage, and harrowing stories of those who survived the onslaught. There is generally much less attention to what preventive measures could have been taken, and even less to the intricacies of how federal relief could (or should) be financed. In the case of Love Canal and Selma, leading news stories focused not only on the victims but also on the alleged perpetrators, thus virtually ensuring that demands for punishment and appropriate policy reform would loom large on the national agenda. In the case of natural disasters, by contrast, the most obvious culprit, Mother Nature, cannot be punished or easily reformed. Accordingly, the stories generally focus on victims rather than on perpetrators, sparking sympathy rather than outrage—that is, unless, as in the cases of Hurricane Andrew in 1992 (during the presidency of George H.W. Bush) and Hurricane Katrina in 2005 (during that of George W. Bush), seemingly inept relief and recovery efforts themselves invite public outrage.[22] The point is that, by its very nature, news coverage in cases of natural disaster generally directs public attention toward the need for immediate relief of the victims, and federal lawmakers appear (for the most part) to respond accordingly.

CONCLUSION: REFRAMING THE DISCUSSION AS A PREREQUISITE FOR REFORM

It is no secret that the current (and long-standing) federal approach to financing disaster losses is far from perfect. Since disaster risk is spread unevenly across the country, financing federal relief out of general revenues involves large cross-subsidies, from low-risk to high-risk areas. Many critics claim, moreover, that generous federal relief creates a large "moral hazard" problem, ensuring greater losses over the long term by encouraging building in hazard-prone areas and generally reducing incentives for investment in preventive measures.

Nor is there any lack of good policy alternatives. One reasonable option would be to make private disaster insurance mandatory and to create a federal reinsurance program, allowing private insurers to transfer some portion of the risk to the government reinsurance agency, in return for an appropriate premium. Howard Kunreuther suggested a solution along these lines as early as 1968, and I proposed my own variant on the idea three decades later.[23]

The most difficult challenge, however, is not designing the program but finding a way to give the relevant ideas political salience. So long as public discussion of disaster policy is set within the context of a specific disaster, it is hard to imagine lawmakers not focusing on the disaster's victims and their immediate needs. Only by looking across multiple disasters will lawmakers—and the American public—begin to see advantages in reforming the way the federal government finances disaster losses. As a result, constructive reform of federal disaster policy may, ironically, become more likely against the backdrop of a fiscal disaster than of a natural disaster. Whereas a natural disaster focuses our attention, appropriately, on how best to assist the victims, a fiscal emergency could focus our attention on the enormous long-term costs of disaster relief, across many disasters. Thus, as we now move into a period of unprecedented fiscal challenge, it may be a particularly good time to take up disaster policy anew.

19 Catastrophe Insurance and Regulatory Reform After the Subprime Mortgage Crisis

DWIGHT M. JAFFEE

INTRODUCTION

The U.S. federal government and individual states now actively participate in providing catastrophe insurance for all major natural disasters (earthquakes, hurricanes, and floods) as well as terrorism. At this time, the subprime mortgage crisis is also creating catastrophic effects in U.S. loan markets and associated goods markets that clearly require governmental intervention. The experience with catastrophe insurance markets is useful for re-regulating loan markets facing severe distress because originating risky loans with highly correlated loss patterns is tantamount to writing catastrophe insurance.

LESSONS LEARNED FROM CATASTROPHES AND GOVERNMENT CATASTROPHE INSURANCE

Although the focus of this section is on the lessons learned from governmental provision of catastrophe insurance, it is useful to start with those learned regarding the behavior of economic agents—individuals, firms, and government—in anticipating past catastrophes and providing emergency aid in the immediate aftermath of the events. Subsequently, I will address the lessons learned regarding catastrophe insurance and how this may help inform the regulatory reform of the U.S. financial system.

Lesson 1: Limited Preparation and Mitigation in Anticipation of Catastrophic Events

It is remarkable the degree to which individuals, firms, and governments fail to take precautions to avoid catastrophic natural disasters or to mitigate their effects, even when historical precedents indicate that future events are likely. For one thing, homes and commercial structures continue to be built on earthquake fault lines and flood plains and within hurricane belts. In addition, the available insurance is often not purchased and cost-effective mitigation investments are often ignored.[1] As an example of a specific failure, recall that the World Trade Center was the focus of a serious terrorist attack eight years before the fateful attacks of September 11, 2001, and yet few precautions were instituted to stop a new attack or to mitigate its effects.

In the same fashion, few precautions were taken to avoid or mitigate the effects of the subprime mortgage crisis. A clear warning sign was the bubble in U.S. housing prices, with home prices far exceeding any normal criterion of affordability for many of the borrowing households. Anticipation of further house price increases maintained the bubble for a while, but a crash was inevitable. Nevertheless, borrowers, lenders, investors, rating agencies, and government agencies either participated actively or watched with benign neglect as the bubble expanded. Of course, once the crash began, the government was immediately called to the rescue.

A continuing behavioral question is why economic agents with huge stakes ignore the warning signs of forthcoming catastrophes and then suffer the consequences. In some instances, perhaps individuals believe "it will not happen to me" or they consider the events to be of too-low probability and then act as if the probability is actually zero. In others, government bailouts may be anticipated, leading some to take risks they would not otherwise take. And in still others, maybe economic agents underestimate the magnitude of the consequences, possibly because they have failed to recognize the externalities and systemic reactions the event will create, or otherwise have used an improper model to generate the loss distribution. This last factor seems particularly relevant to the subprime crisis, since the systemic effects have far exceeded the direct losses on subprime mortgages.[2]

Lesson 2: Government Intervention is Essential in the Aftermath of a Catastrophe

Following a catastrophe, "Who you gonna call?" The government, of course. The reality is that private markets regularly fail in the face of a catastrophe, and government or associated nonprofit entities are often the only available responders. This clearly applies to the emergency aid needed in the very short run, although the government response is not always effective, as was evident in New Orleans following Hurricane Katrina in 2005. In the medium run, government aid to reconstruct structures and infrastructure is often very limited, even if the conventional wisdom is to the contrary. By contrast, reconstruction aid following the 9/11 terrorist attacks and Katrina has been more substantial. Total federal assistance following 9/11 was approximately $30 billion, only slightly below the insured losses of about $35 billion. And government assistance following Katrina may well have exceeded the insured losses relating to that event. The subprime mortgage crisis has elicited strong calls for government aid, and it is fair to say that the government response so far has been disorganized, ineffective, and remarkably opaque in terms of its goals and strategies. This is all the more disturbing given the dollar costs of the subprime crisis, which far exceed those of past natural disasters or the terrorist attacks of 9/11. Due to regulatory "forbearance," the response to the savings-and-loan crisis of the 1980s was also inefficient. One implication is that a greater role could be assigned to well-designed government insurance programs as "automatic stabilizers" to counter future financial crises.

Lesson 3: Government Catastrophe Insurance Responds to Private Market Failures

Over the last forty years, private insurance firms have withdrawn from providing primary coverage over the entire range of natural disaster and terrorism risks in the United States.[3] The federal government started providing primary coverage against floods in 1968, following a decade of extremely heavy flooding. The state of Florida has provided primary reinsurance against hurricanes since Hurricane Andrew in 1992, and the state of California has sponsored the state's primary earthquake coverage through a quasi-public entity since the Northridge quake of 1994. Most recently, the private market for terrorism insurance stopped functioning immediately after the 9/11 attacks, leading to the current system backed by free federal government reinsurance up to $100 billion.

To be sure, a fringe of private insurers remains in most of these markets, either by cherry-picking risks where the government's premiums are too high or by providing special coverage. In addition, in all of the government programs, private insurance agents and firms still write, administer, and settle the insurance policies, for which they earn fees. Nevertheless, the government itself or a government entity always bears a significant component of the risk, if not all of it.

The calls for government catastrophe insurance always emphasize the negative ripple effects that would arise in the absence of an insurance market to provide financial protection. For example when terrorism insurance became unavailable after the 9/11 attacks, there was widespread concern that construction and mortgage lending would stop at least in the urban areas. The 9/11 experience, however, also provides a caution. The Terrorism Risk Insurance Act (TRIA), which established the arrangement between private insurers and federal government to cover commercial firms in the United States against terrorism, was not signed until November 2002—more than fourteen months after 9/11. Contrary to the industry's alarmist threats, real estate and mortgage activity continued at what could be considered the normal rate conditional on the slower economic growth that occurred in the overall economy.

While all the government catastrophe insurance programs have served their primary goal of providing insurance in the absence of private market alternatives, two key problems remain evident:

- *Limited Risk-Based Pricing and Subsidized Insurance.* Governments generally fail to impose meaningful risk-based insurance premiums, even when the programs technically require an actuarial basis. Since the higher risks are underpriced, this failure to use risk-based pricing creates a subsidy. It also removes the economic incentive for those who are exposed to properly invest in risk reduction measures. In the worst cases, the government is actively encouraging people to put their homes and commercial structures in harm's way, since the cost of government insurance makes little or no distinction among locations or risk mitigating activities.

- *Crowding Out of Private Markets.* None of the private insurance markets have recovered in any substantial way once the government insurance plan was created, which is not surprising in view of the subsidies that are provided.

Lesson 4: Public-Private Insurance Partnerships Can Be Attractive

This lesson can be illustrated by reference to the TRIA legislation, first passed in November 2002 to provide federal reinsurance for qualifying losses from a terrorist attack. Since TRIA provides a useful starting point for developing government reinsurance plans to cover financial catastrophes, I provide a summary of its key and relevant features below.[4]

- *Industry Loss Trigger.* The government's terrorism reinsurance is triggered only when the industry's aggregate losses for a qualifying terrorist attack exceed a specific amount (currently $100 million).
- *Government Excess of Loss Coverage.* Each insurer has a deductible amount as a percentage of its premiums written for commercial property and casualty insurance. The insurer must pay all losses up to this deductible, and must also pay co-insurance (15 percent) for the losses above this deductible (to an event limit of $100 billion).[5] The deductible and co-insurance have the effect that private insurers will receive little or no government reimbursement except for the largest terrorist attacks. This leaves insurers with a strong incentive to use risk-based pricing and to induce property owners to take action to mitigate the risks where possible. The government's reinsurance, however, is provided without charge and thus the overall program does retain an element of subsidy; the subsidy offsets the incentive for property owners to mitigate their risks.
- *The "Make Available" Requirement.* This legislation requires that all property and casualty insurers continue to "make available" terrorism coverage on the same conditions (but not at the same prices) they offered prior to 9/11.[6] Perhaps surprisingly, the result has been a well-functioning and reasonably priced market for terrorism insurance. Indeed, the industry has enthusiastically supported the program through two renewals. It is possible that the "make available" clause helped to coordinate a new

diversified equilibrium in which all firms desire to participate knowing that all other firms must also participate.

- *Crowding Out.* Since the government reinsures the top tier of risk at no charge, it clearly crowds out any private reinsurance market for these risks. However, it is unclear whether any reinsurance firms would offer such coverage even in the absence of the government program. The experience of European countries is telling: Reinsurers have reentered this market but their participation is always extremely limited and embodied in public-private programs (e.g., Gareat in France, Extremus in Germany). Moreover, under TRIA, private insurers bear the major risks below that threshold, and it could be said that the government is "crowding in" the private markets, since private terrorism insurance might not exist in the absence of TRIA.

RE-REGULATING LOAN MARKETS IN THE AFTERMATH OF THE SUBPRIME CRISIS

I now apply the lessons learned from the long U.S. experience with catastrophes and governmental catastrophe insurance to the issue of regulatory reform in the aftermath of the subprime mortgage crisis. It is important to recognize in this context that making or investing in risky loans with possibly highly correlated losses is tantamount to providing catastrophe insurance. Indeed, the subprime mortgage crisis has created a set of conditions that strongly echoes this country's experience following the occurrence of major natural disasters and the 9/11 terrorist attacks:[7]

- Private insurance/loan markets have systematically failed.
- Private markets and institutions are calling for government help, basing their claims largely on negative externalities that otherwise would affect the real economy.
- Government appears to be the only currently available and dependable remedy.

The experience with the government's catastrophe insurance programs suggests that governmental loan guarantees/insurance may provide an efficient mechanism to revive the failing loan markets. Loan guarantees would allow private market participants to continue originating risky loans and transferring them to final investors, given that the upper tail of catastrophic losses is covered by government insurance.[8] Loan guarantee programs may also be, and should be, designed to maintain private-sector expertise in evaluating the default risks and setting the proper risk-based interest rates. In this fashion, the worst negative externalities of the subprime crisis on loan markets and associated goods markets may be eliminated, while using the available private-sector expertise for loan analysis and underwriting. In addition, if the government program is designed to protect only against the largest systemic failures, it could then be maintained on a continuing basis as a low-cost automatic stabilizer against future financial catastrophes.

The details of applying governmental loan guarantees and insurance to revive loan markets can best be illustrated by reference to an application to municipal bonds and municipal bond insurance, which I discuss in the next section. (In the Summary and Conclusions, I suggest additional applications.)

GOVERNMENT REINSURANCE FOR MUNICIPAL BOND INSURANCE

For more than twenty years, there has been an active U.S. market to provide insurance against municipal bond default risk. This insurance expedites the purchase of state and local government bonds by delegating the analysis of the underlying default risk to the insurers. Municipal bond insurers are chartered under state laws requiring that they be "monoline," meaning that their capital is available only to pay claims against municipal bond losses. The goal is to make the municipal bond insurer bankruptcy remote from losses that might occur on other insurance lines covered by the same holding company (i.e., with no possible contagion). In addition, the chartering laws have imposed relatively high capital requirements on the firms.

Quite irrationally, in recent years, insurance regulators have also allowed municipal bond insurers to provide coverage against default risks on subprime mortgage securitizations and related collateralized debt obligations (CDOs) and credit default swaps (CDSs). It is unclear why the insurance regulators allowed the insurers to mix the relatively limited credit risks on municipal bonds with the high risks on subprime mortgages and their derivatives, since this clearly violated the monoline principle on which the insurers were chartered.

Worse yet, losses on the subprime mortgage derivatives now threaten the solvency of the municipal bond insurers.[9] The failure of these firms would have significant negative externalities in two regards. First, it would become difficult for many state and local government to issue new bonds in the absence of credible insurance. Second, many municipal bonds are held by depository institutions, motivated in part by the relatively low capital requirements allowed on bonds backed by highly rated insurers; if these insurers lost their high ratings, or even failed, the depository institutions could face significantly higher capital requirements. Moreover, if both the bonds and insurers defaulted, the investors would face the losses directly.

In this setting, the government faces the question of how to maintain a functioning market for municipal bonds, dependent as it is on a functioning market for municipal bond insurance. An immediate issue is how to separate the losses that are already present on the existing books of subprime and municipal bond insurance from the task of insuring newly issued municipal bonds.

For this purpose, I propose a good insurer/bad insurer model, and I first consider how to insure newly issued municipal bonds (the good insurer). The basic plan is to create a new government excess of loss reinsurance program that would backstop the risk on newly insured municipal bonds.

The TRIA program already in place for terrorism risks provides a useful template. The basic feature is an excess of loss insurance contract, with a deductible high enough to place all of an insurer's contributed capital in the first loss position. The monoline bond insurers already face significant capital requirements, and these should be continued, possibly even expanded, for the newly restructured insurers.[10] A further refinement, and one that differs from TRIA, would make the reinsurance payouts a minimum of the insurer's actual losses (above its deductible) and a prorated share of the industry losses based on the principal amount of insured bonds. This would provide insurers an incentive to hold diversified—"market portfolio"—books of business, for otherwise a firm would face a "basis risk" whereby its actual losses might significantly exceed its reinsurance payout.

Dealing with the losses that are embedded in an insurer's existing book of business represents a more complex problem. This has not been a difficulty for the existing government programs that insure natural disaster and terrorism risks because, by and large, all the extant claims had been settled by the time the government program started. But for the current municipal bond insurers the problem is particularly complicated by the fact that their existing books combine moderate losses on municipal bonds with vast losses on CDO and CDS subprime mortgage derivatives. If the two lines could be separated, then it might be sensible to bail out the existing municipal bond policies while allowing the insurer to default on its CDO and CDS policies. Indeed, had the regulators properly enforced the monoline principle, this would be an available option. In the actual case at hand, the government must either bail out the entire firm or allow it to default on all of its policies. In the latter instance, the government could still bail out the municipal bond investors.[11]

SUMMARY AND CONCLUSIONS

In this chapter I have proposed that an economist's view be applied to the United States' long-standing experience with government-backed catastrophe insurance (covering natural disasters and terrorism) to regulatory reform in the aftermath of the subprime mortgage crisis. Specifically, I discuss a proposal to apply the concepts of government catastrophe insurance to help maintain a functioning market for new municipal bond default insurance. The same principle could be applied, if necessary, to other loan markets—such as credit card and auto loans—if these markets were to fail. The motivation in all these cases is to forestall a negative externality through which a failure in a loan market brings down associated markets for real goods, thus enlarging the systemic crisis.

Mortgage loan markets represent an even greater concern, both because they are particularly stressed as a result of the subprime mortgage losses and because they are simply much larger in size (given approximately $11 trillion in outstanding single-family home mortgages). As with the example of municipal bonds, there is the dual problem of how to deal with the existing losses, including mortgage foreclosures, and how to reform the market to carry on new business. Dealing with the existing losses is particularly complex, and again there is no relevant past experience with governmental catastrophe insurance plans to fall back on. Regarding new mortgages, there may well be a role for excess-of-loss government catastrophe insurance, in parallel with the plan offered here for municipal bonds and with the existing Federal Housing Administration mortgage insurance for low-income borrowers. I have also proposed elsewhere a plan to replace Fannie Mae and Freddie Mac with a direct government program by applying the same basic concept of government-backed excess-of-loss catastrophe insurance.[12]

RECOMMENDED READING

Jaffee, Dwight (2009). "The U.S. Subprime Mortgage Crisis: Issues Raised and Lessons Learned." In Michael Spence, Patricia Clarke Annex, and Robert M. Buckley, eds., *Urbanization and Growth*, World Bank (http://www.growthcommission.org/storage/cgdev/documents/ebookurbanization.pdf).

Jaffee, Dwight, Howard Kunreuther, and Erwann Michel-Kerjan (2008). "Long Term Insurance for Addressing Catastrophe Risk." NBER Working Paper No. 14210, National Bureau of Economic Research, Cambridge, MA.

Jaffee, Dwight, and Thomas Russell (1997). "Catastrophe Insurance, Capital Markets, and Uninsurable Risks." *Journal of Risk and Insurance* 64, no. 2: 205–230.

Kunreuther, Howard, Daniel Kahneman, and Nathan Novemsky (2001). "Making Low Probabilities Useful." *Journal of Risk and Uncertainty* 23:103–120.

Kunreuther, Howard, and Erwann Michel-Kerjan (2009). *At War with the Weather*. Cambridge, MA: MIT Press.

Kunreuther, Howard, and Mark Pauly (2006). "Rules Rather Than Discretion: Lessons from Hurricane Katrina." *Journal of Risk and Uncertainty* 33: 101–116.

20 Toward Financial Stability

Lessons from Catastrophe Reinsurance

KENNETH A. FROOT

UNDERSTAND WHY THIS HAPPENED: TWO DIVERGENT VIEWS

As this chapter is being written, the United States and world economies are experiencing probably the most intense contractions witnessed since the Great Depression. There is much debate about the downturn's underlying drivers and their respective primacy, but the discussion can be categorized under two main views.

One view is the "bubble-has-burst" hypothesis. It holds that excessive consumer demand fueled by lax borrowing standards, principally in the United States, drove asset prices to high levels generally, and real estate in particular, to levels not previously seen. These bubbles then popped. And, before they popped, upward price movements first stalled in mid-2007. The timing was driven by concerns that newly incurred and poorly qualified subprime and alt-A mortgage debt would be unserviceable by borrowers without continued price appreciation or interest rate decline. As borrowers began to feel pinched and housing values began to decline, consumption naturally fell. Households needed to pay their debts, without the benefits of continuing home-price appreciation. This recession is necessarily deep, this view holds, because asset prices have to fall a long way before reaching a more normal multiple of cash flow. And current and expected future consumption needs to adjust downward to reach sustainable levels with more realistic assumptions about future growth. The bubble-has-burst hypothesis emphasizes what I refer to as a "demand shock": It revolves around a boom-and-bust cycle of the demand for credit at its core.

The second view focuses on levered financial institutions and their role in morphing what was otherwise a garden-variety macroeconomic adjustment into an all-out crisis. This view holds that a relatively small perturbation—the excessive real estate borrowing of a small group of homeowners—negatively affected financial intermediaries' balance sheets. These intermediaries—banks and "shadow" banks that jointly fulfilled the function of credit extension to a wide universe of companies and investors—essentially cut back on lending to investors and to their market-making desks. Investors who depended on credit to hold securities had to sell them. And the lack of dealer market-making funding made the situation worse, substantially undermining the liquidity of many dealer-centric markets.[1] So the de-leveraging process, which by itself is the mechanical result of an initial reduction in asset values, had to take place in the context of increasingly illiquid and nonfunctioning dealer-centric markets. With liquidity low and falling, additional selling brought falling prices down even more dramatically than would otherwise have been the case. As a result, prices fell further than the current fundamentals might have justified and credit became expensive and scarce. Unfortunately, the fear and concern around these declining markets led to runs—not only on markets and institutions, such as money market funds, but also on consumption. This resulted in dramatic and precipitous declines in economic activity that ultimately, though unnecessarily, validated the low levels of asset prices. This financial-intermediaries view emphasizes what I refer to as a "supply shock"—a collapse of internal capital in financial intermediaries that greatly magnifies a small price change and turns it into a crisis in the macroeconomy.

These two versions of the current financial crisis are clearly illustrated in Figure 20.1. It shows an equilibrium in the pricing and availability of intermediary-provided capital. This capital is used by households to gain access to mortgages and other forms of credit (such as automobile-purchase credits or credit-card receivables), by corporations for borrowing from financial institutions, and by investors and traders who rely on dealers to help provide liquidity and who obtain financing in order to buy securities or other investments.

The bubble-has-burst hypothesis describes a leftward shock to the demand curve. A reduction in customers' demand for credit is equivalent to a leftward shift in the demand curve. As expected, the quantity of intermediary-provided credit falls. So, too, does the cost of credit. At the original rates charged by in-

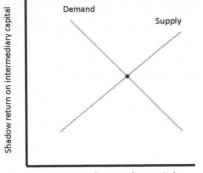

FIGURE 20.1 **Equilibrium in the Market for Intermediary-Supplied Capital**
Source: Copyright © Ken Froot.

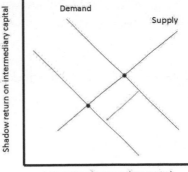

FIGURE 20.2 **A Negative Shock to the Demand for Intermediary Capital**
Source: Copyright © Ken Froot.

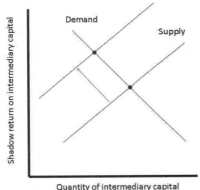

FIGURE 20.3 **A Negative Shock to the Supply of Intermediary Capital**
Source: Copyright © Ken Froot.

termediaries, there is excess supply of credit, so the shadow return on intermediary capital must decline.

The levered-intermediary view describes a supply shock—the leftward move in the supply curve shown in Figure 20.3. Here, too, the amount of credit supplied in equilibrium falls. However, because the cause is a reduction in the capacity of intermediaries to lend, the shadow cost of intermediary capital rises.

There seems to be little controversy about what has happened in this financial crisis to the quantity of credit extended by intermediaries: It has fallen considerably. The critical, and decisive, question regarding the distinction between these two hypotheses is whether the shadow cost of intermediary capital has gone down or up.

SOME PARALLELS WITH THE CATASTROPHE RISK MARKET

Before I turn to some direct evidence on this, I want to draw some parallels with the catastrophe risk market. This market has in the past witnessed dislocations that are similar to that of the 2008–2009 credit crisis. Yet it is in many ways a far less complicated and more easily interpreted marketplace.

In fact, the "cat" marketplace lends itself to a readily understood analogy, and there are several reasons for this. First, natural disasters are exogenous. In the case of the credit crisis, we know that the housing and commodity price bubbles have burst. But rather than reflecting concern over what exactly caused it, the cat risk example suggests we can and should move on, and look at the effects on capital provided to financial intermediaries. Second, cat risks and the damages they cause are physical phenomena that can be scientifically modeled. The likelihood of a given dollar amount of hurricane damage is much more objective and transparent than the likelihood of a deep recession, or, more accurately, of AAA securities trading at only pennies on the dollar. We can objectively simulate storm frequency, severity, and trajectory based on our knowledge of physical systems. We cannot objectively simulate the "madness of crowds"—by which I mean shifts in sentiment, so-called animal spirits, or runs on banks, runs on markets, or runs on consumption. Finally, cat risk is not systematic—it is not correlated with the risks of major financial markets. This means that we have a good idea of what the "fair market" price of cat risk should be. Specifically, because cat risk is diversifiable, the fair-value premium for a reinsurance contract that incurs no losses 99 percent of the time and incurs losses up to a given limit 1 percent of the time is 1 percent. That is, fair-value premiums are just equal to expected losses (probability × consequences). And since expected cat losses can be reasonably accurately and scientifically modeled, fair-value premiums can consequently be readily observed. This valuation process is far simpler than its counterpart in the financial world; while the market may try, no one has any real knowledge of what most underlying financial securities are worth. The same applies to real estate: Who can say convincingly that houses were too cheap or too expensive (or fairly priced) this year? Indeed, it is the lack of reliable markers of fair valuation that allow for enormous swings in the values of financial securities. During the most extreme bubbles we've witnessed (and there have been many over the past decade alone), pundits have argued compellingly that both the bubble and the bubble-has-burst prices are fair.

So what happens in the catastrophe markets in the aftermath of an event? As with the current crisis, some observers have contended that immediately following a hurricane is the best time to sell insurance (and reinsurance) because it's then that the demand for protection is high. Those who bought plenty of insurance see its value, and those who didn't feel once-burned, and, going forward, twice shy. With demand high, prices should be high. This is just the demand-shock view. And there are those who argue that, after an event, capital is depleted in the relevant financial intermediaries—reinsurers, in the case of cat risk—so that supply is low. Both arguments suggest that prices should be high after the event. And indeed they are. However, the high prices in each argument have opposite implications for what happens to quantities of intermediary risk sharing supplied.

The behavior of cat reinsurance prices in the aftermath of events is shown in Figure 20.4 with respect to Hurricane Andrew in 1992 and in Table 20.1 with respect to the three large hurricanes of 2005. These data make several points. First, they demonstrate that, in the aftermath of such events, the price of reinsurance rose substantially relative to actuarial, or fair, values. Prices on hurricane insurance jumped to more than six times actuarial value in 1994 and to five times or so in 2006. There is little question that the reinsurance was expensive and that writing cat reinsurance was an attractive proposition after these events. This brings us to the second point—namely, that while the cat risk was badly mispriced, and despite the fact that the cat risk market is fairly transparent and simple, it nevertheless took *years* after Hurricane Andrew for prices to return to normal (again, see Figure 20.4). Capital did flow into this sector to take advantage of the attractive opportunities available, and it eventually brought rates down. However, a long time was required. Competition among capital providers exists, but it is far from instantaneous. Capital arrives slowly when such opportunities arise and the early arrivers earn excess returns for a while before they are essentially competed away.

Figure 20.5 then makes the point that this cycle is predominantly a supply-shock story: The depleted capital of reinsurance intermediaries requires prices to rise *and* quantities of reinsurance transacted to fall. This result cannot be

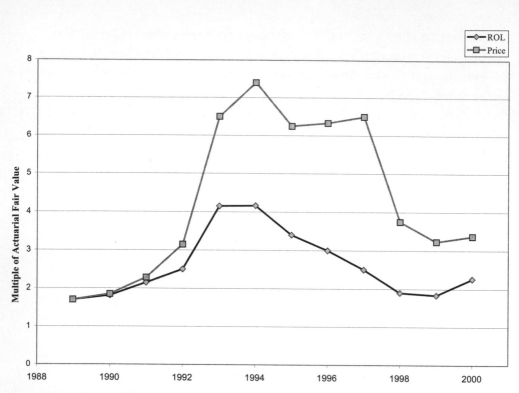

FIGURE 20.4 Prices of U.S. Property Reinsurance Relative to Actuarial Value Following Hurricane Andrew in 1992 (1988–2000)
Source: Ken Froot 2001.

TABLE 20.1 Prices of U.S. Property Reinsurance Relative to Actuarial Value Following the Hurricanes of 2005 (Katrina, Rita, and Wilma)
Source: Nephila Capital, Ltd. © Ken Froot.

Region	Strike	Expected Loss	2005	2006
US hurricane	$50B	2.5%	1.4x	6x
US hurricane	$30B	4.9%	1x	5.1x
US hurricane	$20B	8.1%	1.4x	4x
US earthquake	$15B	4.3%	1.7x	3.5x
US earthquake	$20B	3.2%	1.8x	3.6x
US 2nd event	$10B	5.2%	1.4x	4.8x
US 2nd event	$20B	1.2%	n/a	10.4x

Pricing shown as a spread to risk-free (typically 3m UST)

Expected losses shown as market standard model output (not NCL estimates)

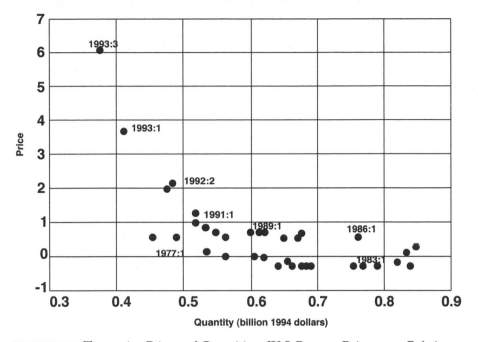

FIGURE 20.5 Transaction Prices and Quantities of U.S. Property Reinsurance Relative to Actuarial Value (industry price-quantity pairs, 1975:1–1993:4)
Source: Ken Froot 2001.

driven by a demand shock, because higher demand after an event generally results in both high prices and high quantities of reinsurance provided. In fact, the amount of reinsurance falls considerably in the aftermath of an event, tracing out the negative correlation between price and quantity. This is the pattern suggested by supply—not demand—shocks.

UNDERSTANDING THE 2008–2009 FINANCIAL CRISIS

This correlation between price and quantity is very similar to what we have seen on a broad scale in the 2008–2009 crisis. Much has been made of the fact that credit extension by financial intermediaries has fallen considerably as the crisis has worsened. See, for example, the evidence on overall bank lending during the second half of 2008 and early 2009 highlighted by Ivanisha and Scharfstein (2009). There is also evidence of this behavior in the securities markets.

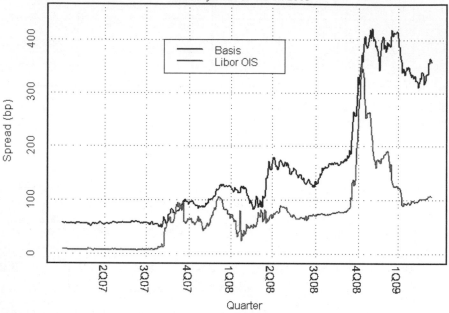

FIGURE 20.6 Difficulties in Bank Financing Were Coincident with Underpricing in Corporate Bonds Relative to CDS, but Dissipated Faster
Source: Ken Froot 2001.

At the point when Lehman Brothers collapsed, many financial intermediaries faced real difficulties financing themselves: Balance sheets were over-leveraged and there was substantial risk that counterparties would not get paid in time. These circumstances virtually destroyed lending to major banks. Overnight rates spiked to extraordinary levels, high not only in absolute terms but also relative to longer-term borrowing to the same institutions. In other words, the market seemed to sense that either banks would fail then and there or, if they survived, they would go on to operate more normally in the future. Intermediaries had difficulty tapping external markets for capital and so the initial reaction was a decline in the quantity of intermediary capital.

Figure 20.6 makes this point by showing the LIBOR OIS spread (which compares overnight to three-month LIBOR rates)[2] and its behavior beginning in 2007 and through the end of first quarter of 2009. While the onset of the problems in mortgage markets in the summer of 2007 shows up in this figure, it is dwarfed by the shock that occurred around the time the

Lehman Brothers failed. In September, intermediary capital was clearly constrained: No one was going to put funds into additional intermediation at that time.

But this is only the first part of the story. The authorities at the major central banks, especially the Federal Reserve, understood that the shortage of intermediary capital was a potentially catastrophic threat to the financial system. Through a series of programs and facilities they quickly moved to help provide capital to intermediaries, both directly and through indirect federal guarantees. This brought the chaotic situation of bank capital under control relatively quickly. While the long-term health of these intermediaries remained in question, they were receiving sufficient funding over the short and medium terms so as to allow them to access capital at more normal prices. LIBOR OIS declined precipitously.

However, the shortage of capital in banks also resulted in very high shadow rates (usually not reported to the general public) for use of intermediary capital. This outcome is represented in Figure 20.6 by the black line, which delineates the bond-CDS basis—that is, the difference between the spreads on corporate bonds and the derivative contracts that insure them (i.e., credit default swaps, or CDS).[3] Why the bond-CDS spread, and what does it tell us? CDS contracts are relatively liquidly traded contracts that measure the credit risk on bonds. In theory, this basis, the difference between bond and CDS yields, should be near zero, since the cost of insurance against a bond's default should be about the same as the additional yield demanded by bondholders to compensate them against this same default. Thus, in terms of credit risk, bonds and CDS are approximately the same. However, in terms of liquidity, they are dramatically different. Intermediaries allow customers to write CDS insurance by putting up only a small amount of collateral relative to what they must put up to buy a bond. Moreover, bonds are generally traded far less frequently (this was true even before the current financial crisis), and with considerably higher bid-ask spreads, than CDS. All of this makes bonds riskier in terms of liquidity, though no different in terms of credit risk.

In September 2009, the bond-CDS basis exploded to levels never previously seen. Intermediaries, who faced real capital shortages, called in capital everywhere they could. The bond-CDS liquidity difference was an indication that their clients' bond positions were far more collateral-intensive than were their CDS positions. So effectively, as intermediaries called in their capital, it became impossible (or inordinately expensive) to finance bond positions. Many investors were forced to sell their bonds—to de-lever because leverage was no longer available to many. Others who retained access to leverage sold voluntarily for fear that the last one out of the bond market would be left to shut off the lights. Some were also forced to liquidate CDS positions. Yet bond liquidation predominated: It released more collateral than CDS liqua-tion, and, in any case, liquidation of CDS positions acted only to *reduce* the bond-CDS basis. By both cause and effect, liquidity disappeared from bond markets: The uncertainty around what bonds would actually fetch became further magnified. Bonds therefore rapidly became much cheaper than their associated CDS. The magnitude is stunning: The 400 basis point bond-CDS spread represents an undervaluation of bonds relative to CDS of between 20 percent and 25 percent.[4]

The behavior of LIBOR OIS suggests that intermediaries quickly re-gained access to capital after the seizure of markets in September 2008. In-termediaries could then fund themselves in debt markets. But they were willing to do the same for their clients because of the scarcity of equity cap-ital. In essence, the shadow required return on intermediary risk capital rose to very high levels, so high that intermediaries would not lend capital out at anything like the normal lending rates. This is the analog of the relative in-crease in bond rates—and the relative decline in bond prices. The cycle of intermediary capital shortages, so pronounced in this recent financial crisis, is the same pattern we saw above in the catastrophe risk market—a decline in the supply of intermediary capital along with an increase in the price at which intermediary capital is available. This is powerful evidence that a sup-ply shock—not a demand shock—was the predominant operative factor in both cases.

THREE LESSONS ON MARKET BEHAVIORS

What lessons can we draw regarding the current crisis from our experience with natural catastrophe reinsurance? First, when the intermediary sector's capital is damaged, replacement capital does not arrive quickly. Instead, it is as though the intermediaries essentially try to self-heal: They charge a lot for access to their capital. Over time this helps them repair their balance sheets, along with capital inflows. But no cavalry bringing additional capital arrives to ensure that there is sufficient liquidity or capital to keep prices fair. Prices may be distorted for a period of time while intermediaries remain broken or weak. The system is sensitive—systemically sensitive—to shocks to the supply of intermediary capital.

The second lesson we can draw during the healing process is that this return toward fair pricing is going to be even more painful and slow in banking than it has been, repeatedly, in reinsurance. Why? Remember that the shocks to reinsurance capital are essentially flips of a coin: They are chance outcomes whose *ex ante* probabilities are unaffected by the *ex post* occurrence. In the financial crisis, the risk of lending was endogenous to the system. (In any crisis, lending is obviously going to be more risky.) Indeed, the worse the breakage of bond markets and the more bond underpricing we experience, the more stressed intermediary capital levels become. Markets that break therefore worsen the crisis and make the prospect of ongoing lending even more risky. So the sensitivity of intermediary capital to supply shocks affects, in turn, both the severity and the duration of the downturn.

The final lesson is that the concentrated risks of intermediary capital are both systemically dangerous and preventable. In reinsurance, traditional reinsurers are slowly being replaced by a diffuse set of agents who manage dedicated but reinsurance exposures for many investors—hedge funds, mutual funds, and so forth. Reinsurance can be, and increasingly is being, written in small pieces by many portfolio managers acting as agents for their beneficial investors. This allows for far wider sharing of reinsurance risk and less concern with "too big to fail." The financial crisis has been made worse by the mistake of allowing intermediaries to accumulate large portfolios of securities whose markets the dealers were supposed to support. When those security values fell, intermediaries' stressed capital levels made it impossible for them to support these markets. And when the intermediaries' support of these markets waned, the public-good of liquidity declined, allowing for even less funding and even lower security vales.

This vicious cycle was an important but unnecessary magnifier of the current crisis. We have begun to make reinsurance markets more competitive by reducing intermediary concentration and by encouraging intermediaries to compete with investors directly. We need to do the same for bond markets— making them less reliant on exposed intermediary dealers, both by increasing the markets' competitiveness and by using regulation to prohibit substantial dealer warehousing of risk. The cost and protracted nature of this crisis is a direct result of preventable problems that we allowed to emerge in the regulation and organization of bond markets.

RECOMMENDED READING

Ivashina, Victoria, and David S. Scharfstein. "Bank Lending During the Financial Crisis of 2008." Harvard Business School Working Paper, July 2009.

21 Economic Theory and the Financial Crisis
How Inefficient Incentives Can Lead to Catastrophes

KENNETH J. ARROW

One does not have to study deeply to find that the failure of markets for various kinds of derivative securities to perform properly is an essential element of the current financial crisis.[1] Actually, financial crises are not a new phenomenon. The history of capitalism has been marked by repeated collapses of the financial system, situations in which the "markets" for loans disappear for extensive periods of time. The eighteenth century saw some bubbles, but these might not be quite modern. But from 1819 on, there have been a succession of failures of banks and other financial institutions. These have typically been unpredicted and did not correspond in time to any particular exogenous event (e.g., wars). Economists did recognize the phenomenon; for example, John Stuart Mill's survey of economic theory (1848) has a chapter on commercial crises (Book 3, Chapter 12) in terms that resonate with the latest news today. But the discussion on crises is not at all integrated with the general exposition of classical economics that unifies the rest of his fairly long book. This disjunction has remained in modern economics. No one could be a more vigorous advocate of unrestrained markets than economist Milton Friedman; yet, to my reading, the account that he and Anna Schwartz gave of monetary developments in the United States and particularly with regard to the Great Depression, emphasizes not prices, not even interest rates, but the supply of money and, by inference, of liquidity (Friedman and Schwartz, 1963).

I start with the neoclassical general equilibrium framework, to which I have given a good deal of attention and effort. I seek to identify a possible point at which it fails to supply a coherent theory of securities markets and so might possibly lead to some understanding of the repeated crises of the financial system underlying the development of capitalism. As my analysis will mainly build on economic theory, which might not be familiar to some of the readers, I will aim at presenting it through a natural progression.

GENERAL EQUILIBRIUM AND CREDIT INSTRUMENTS

The concept of general equilibrium was always implicit in any serious use of standard economic analysis, but it became explicit in the work of French economist Léon Walras (1874, 1877). The elements of the analysis are competitive markets in the individual commodities, each characterized by a large number of participants on both sides, all facing the same price, and by market clearing (buyers purchase the commodity from the sellers at this market price). Under these assumptions, there is no question of liquidity; any individual, taken to be small compared with the total market, can buy or sell at the unique market price. Money plays no essential role, except as a useful tool of accounting.

The markets are linked because the same individuals appear in all or at least many markets, and make choices as consumers or producers based on all prices. Hence, the price of one commodity affects market behavior on all other markets. Under these and other conditions, some remarkable theoretical results have been obtained. There will be a set of prices (possibly not unique) such that equilibrium (market clearing) can be achieved on all markets (with a suitable meaning for clearing when there is excess supply at zero price). Further, assume that individual behavior is rational, in the sense that individuals in these markets are maximizing the utility they derive from the goods they acquire. Then the allocation achieved at a competitive equilibrium is efficient in the sense that there is no other allocation in which some other individual is better off and no individual is worse off.

The bulk of the above analysis, however, was static in nature, dealing with a single time period (i.e., only today matters and tomorrow does not count). But a capitalist system is intrinsically forward-looking. Many economic decisions have implications for the future as well as the present and concern the tradeoff between the two. For instance, saving is a tradeoff between your present and future consumption. Investment is an expenditure today with a view to output in the future.

Value and Capital, which was published by British economist John Richard Hicks in 1939, brought a simple integration of general equilibrium theory with the theory of supply and demand of capital to the attention of economists. He recognized that goods to be supplied in the future were different from those supplied now, even if physically equivalent. If a market were created for each dated good, then, for example, a steel firm would buy a blast furnace today and simultaneously sell steel for delivery in many subsequent years. It would thus know today its stream of future profits and choose today its inputs and outputs in the present and future so as to maximize total profits. (The price today of a future delivery is what would ordinarily be interpreted as a *discounted* price.)

Of course, if all these markets existed, all the previous analysis of the static market would be applicable. Prices that would clear all markets would exist, and the resulting allocations would be optimal.

Unfortunately, this conceptual description of the economy fails to conform with everyday observation. Markets for future delivery ("futures markets") exist only to a very limited extent, and only for a specialized range of commodities. We do have futures markets in agricultural commodities (wheat, cotton, and a few others) and in some minerals, but not in manufactured goods. We also, and more importantly, have markets that trade not ordinary goods but various forms of money at different points in time—that is, the whole panoply of credit instruments.

Hicks was perfectly aware of this failure. He suggested that individuals form *expectations* of future prices and then prepare plans today based on current prices and expected future prices.[2] Only the current markets are active and equilibrate (so-called *temporary equilibrium*). Provision for the future can take the forms of durable goods and of credit instruments (loans and bonds).

It is important to note here that there is no intrinsic reason so far addressed that ensures that different economic agents have the same expectations of the future prices. But the efficiency characteristics of markets depend on the assumption that all individuals face the same tradeoffs (i.e., the same relative prices). Hence, there is no guarantee of efficiency in this broader approach to general equilibrium over time.

There is one assumption, mentioned by Hicks and given much greater emphasis in the work Gérard Debreu and I published in 1954, under which expectations do yield efficiency. This is the assumption of *perfect foresight*;

individuals predict future prices correctly. In this case, of course, all individuals' expectations are the same. This assumption is consistent, as was demonstrated, but it ascribes an econometric ability to economic agents much beyond that of academics. In principle, it requires that all agents know the utility functions and production possibility sets of all other agents. This condition is not only empirically false; it is also inconsistent with one of the chief claims of economists, that efficiency can be achieved by trading among individuals who know only about their own tastes and productive capabilities.[3] I return to this point in the third section below.

Once it is recognized that a great deal of allocation takes place on the basis not of markets but of expectations about future markets, two questions emerge: Why don't the missing markets come into being, and what are the implications of expectations-driven allocations? I here intend only to broach these questions and make a few preliminary remarks towards an analysis.

GENERAL EQUILIBRIUM UNDER UNCERTAINTY

One obvious explanation for the nonexistence of futures markets is the uncertainty about the future. There are many causes for uncertainty, but one of great importance is surely uncertainty about technological developments. To make a contract now for future delivery at a given price bears a risk because technological change in the coming years may make the cost different from that expected. Another risk may be the future emergence of new products whose qualities are random variables from today's viewpoint.

That the uncertainty about the future is a significant factor in affecting the outcomes of current markets was long understood in a general way, but there was no systematic way to incorporate uncertainty into the framework of general equilibrium theory. In the 1950s and 1960s I introduced one approach, derived from the usual formulations of probability theory and statistical decision theory (Arrow 1953, 1963–1964); it was subsequently extended by Debreu (1959, Chapter 7).

In this approach I assumed that the parameters of the economic system, the preferences and production possibilities of the economic agents, were themselves random variables, in general changing over time according to known probability laws. A specification of the values of all these random variables is called a *state of nature*. I suggested that a market was defined not just by the physical characteristics of the commodity and the time of delivery (as in Hicks) but also by the state of nature prevailing at that time. The unit of transaction was the *contingent contract*, that is, contingent on the state of nature prevailing.

With this reinterpretation, the standard apparatus of general equilibrium theory could be used to demonstrate the existence and efficiency of equilibrium. I also suggested a role for securities (payable in money, at least in the sense of a unit of account). If individuals had what has been referred to as *contingent perfect foresight*—that is, the ability to predict the prices that would prevail if a given state of nature occurred—then it would be sufficient to have securities paid in money contingent on states of nature. These securities would be very much like the insurance policies we are well acquainted with, which reimburse you if you suffer a loss that is covered in the insurance contract; the insurance payment is *contingent* on the loss occurring.

There are indeed a large number of securities with payment conditional on some events. Apart from standard insurance policies, there are common stocks, clearly very numerous. In addition, corporate bonds and bank loans have payments that are nominally fixed in time and amount, but it is fully understood that there is a risk of default from the borrower, an event that is contingent on some events. What is noteworthy, however, is that these securities are contingent not on exogenous states of nature but on occurrences determined at least in part by economic variables within the system, especially prices but also quantities. A firm will fail to repay a bond or will pay a dividend when the input prices are high relative to the output prices. That the contingent contracts in the real world depend in major part on variables endogenous to the economic system has been especially emphasized by Mordecai Kurz (1974 and 1996, among other papers).

LIMITED INFORMATION OF ECONOMIC AGENTS

Probably the most important innovation in economic theory in the last fifty years has been the emphasis on what has been called *asymmetric information*. The term *information* is properly and appropriately used in the sense given by mathematical statistics or communication theory: an observation on one random variable that changes the probability distribution of some random variables relevant to decision making. It is clear and reasonable that different individuals have access to different information; they have varying life experiences and varying opportunities to make observations. A number of economists came to stress this concept from varying points of view; I myself came to it by considering the economics of medical care (Arrow, 1963).[4] Insurance companies had long understood the consequences of asymmetry of information under such headings as *moral hazard* and *adverse selection*.

It is not always recognized that the most neoclassical approaches in economics also assume asymmetry of information. It is a standard claim for the usefulness of a system of markets that it requires an individual to know only his or her own utility function and production possibilities. The only information about the rest of the world is contained in the prices.

This has an implication for the relation between contingent contracts in general and the limited set of contingent claims on exogenous events that Debreu and I had postulated in our treatment of general equilibrium under uncertainty. After all, general equilibrium prices are going to be functions of the state of nature. Hence, if there are enough markets for contingent contracts depending on economic events (standard securities or those derived from them, such as options), one could infer what the value of insurance policies on states of nature would be. But this inference would depend on knowing the entire system of general equilibrium relations, and this knowledge is not available to individual agents.

The more standard problems raised by asymmetric information are also relevant here. A contingent market can exist only if the contingency can be verified by all parties, and this condition will frequently not hold. This is probably the most basic reason why the full set of markets called for in the theory of general equilibrium under uncertainty does not exist.

INFORMATION AS A COMMODITY

The last set of remarks has put increasing importance on the role of information in modulating the organization of the economy and, in particular, the types of securities (contingent contracts) that are possible and the terms on which they are exchanged. Now the distribution of information cannot simply be taken as given. On the contrary, information can be acquired but it usually comes at some cost. For example, the physician acquires information by attending medical school, by his subsequent residencies, and from his own practice. He or she illustrates the special properties of information as a commodity. The same information is used over and over again; *unlike other inputs, it is not consumed by being used.* This property implies that it is efficient to specialize. It does not pay that everyone in a society acquires this information, but only a number needed to supply the necessary services.

Bankers have traditionally supplied this function in the financial world. Here, the basic information is training and experience, permitting the evaluation of specific information about potential borrowers. However, the relation ceases to be easily described by a market, because each extension of credit not only involves knowledge about specific borrowers but also requires money.

There is therefore a tendency toward small numbers of suppliers—that is, toward the absence of "perfectly competitive" markets (in which there is such a large number of buyers and sellers that none of them alone can influence the price at the equilibrium). Consequently, there is a set of assets whose tradability is limited, and so is of limited liquidity. This in turn means that holding money begins to have a value, since other assets are not easily used to purchase other goods.

The advantages of marketization remain real, so that there are recurrent attempts to revive it, as with mortgage-backed securities. But the additional complications mean that there is a degradation of information. For example, the bank initially extending a mortgage has information that will not be transmitted to buyers of mortgage-based securities. Further, the fact that the initial mortgagee is planning to resell the mortgage means that it has less incentive to gather information and to monitor the mortgagor. The same principle applies to any securitization that increases the number of steps between the original source of the risk and the ultimate risk-bearer. These remarks point to some of the tensions marking financial markets recurrently in the history of capitalism.

INEFFICIENT INCENTIVES: AN ENDEMIC PROPERTY OF CAPITALISM?

In a discussion of the current financial crisis, Alan Greenspan, who was chairman of the Federal Reserve of the United States from 1987 to 2006, raised a very pertinent question: Why did the financial concerns make such risky loans? They had obvious incentives not to put themselves at risk; they would be the losers, as indeed turned out to be the case. Also, they had as much information as anyone could have about the risks; this was not a case of ill-informed speculators.

One possibility, of course, is that suggested by behavioral economics: The financiers were subject to cognitive biases. Because of the specialization induced by the nature of information as discussed in the last section, the transactions were large on the scale of the market and so had important consequences for the system as a whole.

However, there is an alternative view, suggested by many in the media and in academic circles, that, given the incentives, the agents were actually behaving rationally. The root of the matter is that liabilities are limited from below. A firm can go bankrupt, but that is the worst that can happen to it. Similarly, an executive of a company can at worst be dismissed (at least if he has not committed any fraudulent activity). The extra bonuses compensating him or her for performance in the event that things went well are not paid back in bad times. As a result, a risky investment that is socially unprofitable (a negative expected value or a positive expected value insufficient to compensate for the market-determined risk level) may be privately rational for the decision maker, because the latter will not bear all the negative consequences he or she imposed on others.[5]

This incentive problem is intrinsic to the nature of modern capitalism. It is built into the concept of limited liability. Obviously, one aim of this policy is to increase the ability to take risks. The only question is whether, in a world of imperfect and asymmetric information, it does not lead to excessive risk-bearing. These are problems that need to be addressed.

RECOMMENDED READING

Arrow, K. J. (1953). "Le role des valeurs boursières pour la repartition la meilleure des risques." In *Économetrie*, Colloques Internationaux du Centre National de la Recherche Scientifique, Vol. 11, pp. 41–47.

Arrow, K. J. (1963). "Uncertainty and the Welfare Economics of Medical Care." *American Economic Review* 53: 941–973.

Arrow, K. J. (1963–1964). "The Role of Securities in the Optimal Allocation of Risk Bearing." *Review of Economic Studies* 31: 91–96. (English translation of Arrow [1953].)

Arrow, K. J., and G. Debreu (1954). "Existence of Equilibrium for a Competitive Economy." *Econometrica* 22: 265–290.

Debreu, G. (1959). *Theory of Value*. New York: Wiley.

Friedman, M., and A. J. Schwartz. (1963). *A Monetary History of the United States, 1867–1960*. Princeton, NJ: Princeton University Press.

Hicks, J. R. (1939). *Value and Capital*. Oxford: Clarendon Press.

Kane, E. J. (1989). "The High Cost of Incompletely Funding the FSLIC Shortage of Explicit Capital." *Journal of Economic Perspectives* 3: 31–47.

Kurz, M. (1974). "The Kesten-Stigum Model and the Treatment of Uncertainty in Equilibrium Theory." In M. Balch, D. McFadden, and S. Wu, eds. *Essays on Behavior Under Uncertainty*. Amsterdam: North Holland Publishing.

Kurz, M. (1996). "Rational Beliefs and Endogenous Uncertainty: An Introduction." *Economic Theory* 8: 383–397.

Laffont, J.-J., and D. Martimort (2002). *The Theory of Incentives*. Princeton, NJ: Princeton University Press.

Mill, J. S. (1848). *Principles of Political Economy*, 7th ed. (1909). William J. Ashley, ed. London: Longmans, Green and Co.

Morgenstern, O. (1935). Vollkommene voraussicht und wirtschaftliches gleichgewicht. *Zeitschrift für Nationalökonomie* 6: 337–357.

Walras, L. (1874, 1877). *Éléments d'économie politique pure*. English translation by W. Jaffé (1954). *Elements of Pure Economics*. Homewood, IL: Irwin.

22 Environmental Politics
Are You a Conservative?

GEOFFREY HEAL

Environmental conservation need not, and indeed should not, be a partisan political issue. Conservatives, after all, are in principle interested in conserving, and that is what conservation is about.[1] Two of the best presidents from an environmental perspective were both Republicans—Teddy Roosevelt and Richard Nixon. The third of the top three environmental presidents was Lyndon Johnson. Yet environmental conservation in the last several decades has nevertheless become primarily a Democratic concern.

Roosevelt is widely seen as one of the founders of the American environmental movement. "The conservation of our natural resources and their proper use constitute the fundamental problem which underlies almost every other problem of our national life," he told Congress in 1907. In the same year he also said that "[t]he nation behaves well if it treats the natural resources as assets which it must turn over to the next generation increased and not impaired in value." These remarks presage two important contemporary ideas: that conservation can be central to good economic performance, and that we should see the environment as an asset, as natural capital on which we can earn a return if it is well managed. Roosevelt seems to have understood this a century ago, long before it was clear to the environmental community.

On its website the environmental group Environmental Defense Fund (EDF) lists Roosevelt as an Environmental Hero. Roosevelt proclaimed that " [a] nation that destroys its soils destroys itself. . . . Forests are the lungs of our land, purifying the air and giving fresh strength to our people" and backed up these words by protecting 150 national forests. In all, according to EDF, Roosevelt protected some 230 million acres of national land. He also founded the National Park system, creating five National Parks and the National Park Service to manage them.[2]

Roosevelt's role in environmental conservation is widely known; Lyndon Johnson's and Richard Nixon's roles are not, and so deserve to be set out in more detail. Johnson commented that

> [t]he air we breathe, our water, our soil and wildlife, are being blighted by poisons and chemicals which are the by-products of technology and industry. The society that receives the rewards of technology must, as a cooperating whole, take responsibility for [their] control. To deal with these new problems will require a new conservation. We must not only protect the countryside and save it from destruction, we must restore what has been destroyed and salvage the beauty and charm of our cities. Our conservation must be not just the classic conservation of protection and development, but a creative conservation of restoration and innovation.

Johnson's administration was responsible for the following items of legislation:

- Clear Air, Water Quality and Clean Water Restoration Acts and Amendments
- Wilderness Act of 1964
- Endangered Species Preservation Act of 1966
- National Trails System Act of 1968
- Wild and Scenic Rivers Act of 1968
- Land and Water Conservation Act of 1965
- Solid Waste Disposal Act of 1965
- Motor Vehicle Air Pollution Control Act of 1965
- National Historic Preservation Act of 1966
- Aircraft Noise Abatement Act of 1968
- National Environmental Policy Act of 1969

Many of these were the predecessors of legislation that today still forms the backbone of America's environmental policy: The Endangered Species Preservation Act is the forerunner of the Endangered Species Act, and the Clear

Air, Water Quality and Clean Water Restoration Acts and Amendments set the framework for the air and water quality legislation that we have today. At times, Johnson was passionate on environmental issues: He commented that "[t]here is no excuse for a river running red with blood from slaughterhouses. There is no excuse for paper mills pouring sulfuric acid into the lakes and streams of the people of this country. There is no excuse—and we should call a spade a spade—for chemical companies and oil refineries using our major rivers as pipelines for toxic waste. There is no excuse for communities to use other people's rivers as a dump for their raw sewage."[3]

Nixon continued this torrent of environmental legislation and, on occasion, was almost as passionate in his comments. I quote here at length from his 1973 State of the Union Address, because to a generation that thinks of Nixon largely in terms of Watergate, it is so surprising. Here are some parts of that address:

President Abraham Lincoln, whose memory we are honoring this week, observed in his State of the Union message in 1862 that " [a] nation may be said to consist of its territory, its people, and its laws." "The territory," he said, "is the only part which is of certain durability."

In recent years, however, we have come to realize that what Lincoln called our "territory"—that is, our land, air, water, minerals, and the like—is not of "certain durability" after all. Instead, we have learned that these natural resources are fragile and finite, and that many have been seriously damaged or despoiled.

To put it another way, we realized that self-destructive tendencies were endangering the American earth during the 1960s in much the same way as conflicting political forces had endangered the body politic during the 1860s.

When we came to office in 1969, we tackled this challenge with all the power at our command. Now, in 1973, I can report that America is well on the way to winning the war against environmental degradation—well on the way to making our peace with nature.

Day by day, our air is getting cleaner. In virtually every one of our major cities, the levels of air pollution are declining.

Month by month, our water pollution problems are also being conquered, our noise and pesticide problems are yielding to new initiatives, our parklands and protected wilderness areas are increasing. . . .

We can be proud of our record in this field over the past 4 years. But a record is not something to stand on, it is something to build on. Nineteen important natural resources and environmental bills which I submitted to the last Congress were not enacted. In the coming weeks, I shall once again send these urgently needed proposals to the Congress so that the unfinished environmental business of the 92nd Congress can become the first environmental achievements of the 93rd Congress. . . .

The energy crisis was dramatized by fuel shortages this winter. We must face up to a stark fact. We are now consuming more energy than we produce in America. A year and a half ago I sent to the Congress the first Presidential message ever devoted to the energy question. I shall soon submit a new and far more comprehensive energy message containing wide-ranging initiatives to insure necessary supplies of energy at acceptable economic and environmental costs. In the meantime, to help meet immediate needs, I have temporarily suspended import quotas on home heating oil east of the Rocky Mountains. . . .

Second, because there are no local or State boundaries to the problems of our environment, the Federal Government must play an active, positive role. We can and will set standards. We can and will exercise leadership. We are providing necessary funding support. And we will provide encouragement and incentive for others to help with the job. But Washington must not displace State and local initiatives. We shall expect the State and local governments—along with the private sector—to play the central role in this field.

Third, the costs of pollution should be more fully met in the free marketplace, not in the Federal budget. For example, the price of pollution control devices for automobiles should be borne by the owner and the user, not by the general taxpayer. People should not have to pay for pollution they do not cause.

I include Nixon's comments about energy policy because they are still so relevant today and because they show how little has actually been done since the need for action was first recognized in 1973, over thirty years ago. Both Johnson and Nixon were riding an environmental wave, generated by recognition of the impact that industrial growth was having on air, water, and the countryside, and by concerns about the impact of this pollution on human health. Strangely, this was an issue that had not been a part of the public policy debate earlier. One of the main forces driving this wave was Rachel Carson's 1962 book *Silent Spring*, which spoke out about the impact of pesticides on the health of human and nonhuman creatures. Her work led to the eventual banning of DDT, one of the main pesticides of that era, and more generally to an awareness that many applications of science and technology have unintended consequences for people and for other animals. The title *Silent Spring* is a reference to the impact of pesticides on bird populations, many of which were threatened by the bioaccumulation of pesticides used on crops. Pesticides remain long after their application on both crops and insects: Birds eat crops and insects, and as a result the pesticides accumulate in their bodies. And when birds of prey eat the smaller insect-eaters or crop-eaters, they receive a concentrated dose of pesticides. DDT accumulated in the bodies of predators, leading to the thinning of eggshells, and populations of hawks feeding on smaller birds experienced a sharp drop in reproductive rates. *Silent Spring* had a huge impact, becoming the subject of a movie and a TV documentary and staying at the top of the *New York Times* best-seller list for several weeks.

This was the background that allowed Johnson and Nixon to pass environmental legislation unprecedented in scope and extent. In 1970 Nixon commented to the leaders of the Sierra Club that "[a]ll politics is a fad. Your fad is going right now. Get what you can, and here's what I can get for you."[4] And he proceeded to get a remarkable amount for them. His legislative achievements include the National Environmental Policy Act, the establishment of the Environmental Protection Agency, the Clean Air Act, the banning of DDT, the Clean Water Act, and the Endangered Species Act. All of this legislation has continued to form the basis of our environmental policy for the last three decades, and no subsequent president has come close to this level of environmental activism.

Perhaps surprisingly, there is no evidence that the state of the environment actually mattered personally and emotionally to Richard Nixon, as it clearly did to Teddy Roosevelt. But as indicated by the above-cited remark he made to the Sierra Club, Nixon saw that the times required environmental action and provided the voting public with what it wanted.

On the one hand, the times we're in today are rather like the 1960s and early 1970s: There is again a widespread intuition that we are doing something potentially disastrous to the environment. There is nobody as eloquent as Rachel Carson in *Silent Spring*, but Al Gore's documentary *An Inconvenient Truth* and his Nobel Prize have had an impact, as have the reports of the Intergovernmental Panel on Climate Change, the Stern Review, other official bodies emphasizing the changes we are forcing in our most basic environmental systems, and the stream of television documentaries about the threats to forests and marine life.

On the other hand, there is a major difference between the environmental issues we face today and those that precipitated the flurry of legislation under Johnson and Nixon. The difference is local versus global, pollution that damages the area in which it is created versus environmental damage that affects the world as a whole. Ozone depletion, climate change, and deforestation affect the entire globe. Their consequences are truly global—and may paradoxically often be invisible to the people who are causing the damage. We humans are impinging on the operation of global systems on which all creatures depend: That is different from the more localized pollution that was recognized in the 1960s and addressed, quite successfully, by Presidents Johnson and Nixon and in equivalent legislation in other advanced countries in the 1960s and 1970s. Another difference is that the population of the earth has roughly doubled over the intervening forty years, and living standards have risen by a factor of between two and three so that the impact of economic activity is now vastly greater than when Rachel Carson was writing. The potential for damage has risen massively.

Why are conservatives in the United States currently so hostile to environmental issues, when there is a great tradition of environmentalism from the conservative side—and an obvious need for action? Why do conservatives make an exception for environmental conservation?

I think there are two answers to these questions. One is that there has been a change in conservative ideology, and the other concerns the rise of climate change and its threat to powerful corporations in the United States.

When I say there has been a change in conservative ideology, I am speaking loosely: Conservatism was for many years without an overarching ideology, and has recently developed one: belief in the power of free markets. Reagan was referring to this when he stated that the government is the problem, not the solution. From about the 1980s on, a strong component of American conservatism was a belief that unaided and unfettered markets represented an ideal state. In this respect, conservatives were following the preaching of their demi-god Milton Friedman. From an economic perspective this faith is unfounded, and Friedman in his role as a scholar was aware of this fact and even alluded to it in footnotes. But his followers were not aware of it, and are still not. From the perspective of an ardent free-marketer, environmental problems are a threat: They require government intervention in the economy. It's hard to believe both that we need to solve environmental problems and that the government is the problem and not the solution! Believing both leads to cognitive dissonance. Many conservatives ignore environmental problems, pretending that they don't exist. Roosevelt and Nixon did not have this conflict: In their day, conservatism was consistent with a role for the government.

Compounding this ideological change is an empirical one: the rise of climate change as an issue. Climate change threatens the fossil fuel industry, the oil, coal, and gas industries. They are the sources of most greenhouse gases and stand to be affected most by restrictions on their emissions. The United States, more than any other industrial country, is a major producer of fossil fuels. In fact, though relatively few know this, it is the world's third-largest oil producer. First is Saudi Arabia at 10 million barrels per day, then Russia at about 8 million, and then the United States at about 7 million. No other country consistently produces more than 4 million. So America is a petro-state, and the oil industry is a powerful political force. The United States is also a major coal producer, and the coal industry, too, has been active in lobbying against the reality of climate change: When the reality was accepted, it moved to lobbying against the need for action.

Worth mentioning is one other possible contributor to the conservatives' lack of interest in conserving the environment: the growing hostility to science in some parts of the conservative movement. This originates, at least in part, in the conflict between those who take the Bible literally and the scientific consensus that life on earth evolved by natural selection. Skepticism toward science bred of religious disagreement spills over to the belief that one can pick and choose which parts of science one wishes to accept. As climate change and the ozone layer are invisible and we need sophisticated science to measure and understand them, someone who can reject natural selection simply because it conflicts with his prior beliefs can surely do likewise with any other science-based argument.

The rise of free-market conservatism and the power of the coal and oil lobbies, coupled perhaps with a willingness to reject science when its conclusions are inconvenient, explain why American conservatives no longer wish to conserve the environment, notwithstanding the fact that their predecessors played a noble and very decisive role in this endeavor. There is a chance that this may change: As I write, in the midst of the financial crisis of 2008–2009, the belief in the power of unadulterated markets is visibly waning. It will be interesting to see in the coming years if conservatives redevelop a taste for conservation in the environmental realm. This would be a rational choice for them.

RECOMMENDED READING

Carson, Rachel (1962). *Silent Spring*. Boston: Houghton Mifflin.

23 Act Now, Later, or Never?
The Challenges of Managing Long-Term Risks

CHRISTIAN GOLLIER

The publication in 1972 of "The Limits to Growth" by the Club of Rome marked the emergence of a public awareness about collective perils associated with the sustainability of our development. Since then, citizens and politicians have been confronted by a never-ending list of environmental problems: nuclear wastes, genetically modified organisms, climate change, biodiversity. . . .

This debate has recently culminated with the publication of three reports. On one side, the Copenhagen Consensus in 2004 put top priority on public programs yielding immediate benefits (fighting malaria and AIDS, improving water supplies, etc.) and rejected the idea of investing much in the prevention of global warming. On the other side, the Stern Review in 2006 and the fourth report of the Intergovernmental Panel on Climate Change in 2008 put a tremendous pressure on acting quickly and strongly against global warming. The absence of consensus among the experts on this question has translated into public debate and public action, notably with respect to the current limitations of the Kyoto Protocol to encourage all countries to seriously reduce their greenhouse gas emissions.

A striking aspect of the recent debate on climate change is the transfer of the most pressing scientific challenges from the so-called hard sciences (e.g., climatology, oceanography, chemistry) to the social sciences, and more specifically to economics. Yet the economic community remains divided on the way to approach long-term environmental risks. The absence of consensus about efficient public policy for the environment may be explained by several factors.

First, there is still no consensus within the scientific community about the intensity and future impact of many underlying long-term environmental risks. Second, scientists disagree about whether we should wait to get better information before implementing strong actions. Third, they disagree as well about how much effort should be expended to improve the environment for future generations. The bottom line is that there is no agreed-upon rule about how to evaluate long-term environmental risks and therefore no consensus yet about how to shape environmental policy.

But this does not have to be the case. Recent advances have been made toward providing a unified scientific framework to evaluate and make policy recommendations regarding collective long-term risks. This progress puts a new light on concepts such as "sustainable development" and "precautionary principle," increasing their suitability as efficient guidelines for collective decision making.

The state-of-the-art methodology for evaluating an environmental project is based on a benefit-cost analysis in which the net present value of the future monetarized benefits is compared to the cost of the project. This methodology has been applied to the reduction of emissions of carbon dioxide, which are bad for the environment: Specifically, the cost of reducing CO_2 by one ton (e.g., through the substitution of nuclear or solar technologies in place of fossil fuel for example) is compared to the discounted value of the flow of future marginal damages generated by one more ton of CO_2 in the atmosphere—the so-called carbon value. Two crucial elements explain the very diverse estimations of this carbon value: selection of the discount rate (one dollar today will not be equal to one dollar in thirty years) and uncertainty about the damages. Similar attempts to evaluate environmental policy in favor of biodiversity versus a moratorium on genetically modified organisms, for example, led to similarly ambiguous conclusions.

The consequence of the absence of consensus is an inefficient allocation of our resources invested for the future. Its cause—namely, the lack of a consensual methodology—originates from a unified theory to evaluate long-term risks. Economists disagree about the rate at which one should discount far-distant environmental benefits, about how to take uncertainties into account, and about how to optimize the distribution of preventive costs over time. In short, the judge, the citizen, the politician, and the entrepreneur are concerned with current and future environmental problems, but they don't have a strong scientific basis for decision making.

THE PROBLEM OF DISCOUNTING THE DISTANT FUTURE

Consider the Stern Review on climate change, written under the direction of British economist Sir Nicolas Stern, former chief economist of the World Bank. Most criticisms of the Stern Review are related to the discount rate, which was fixed at 1.4 percent per year in the Review. It asserts that most of the consequences of global warming will not appear before the year 2100. Thus, it isn't the current generation but future ones who will bear the costs stemming from global warming. A crucial issue, then, is to determine how much the current generation should be ready to pay to reduce these future costs. We all agree that one dollar obtained immediately is better than one dollar obtained next year, given the positive return we can get by investing this dollar. This argument implies that costs and benefits occurring in the future should be discounted at a rate equal to the rate of return of capital over the corresponding period.

Because it is hard to predict the rate of return of capital for several centuries, one should instead select the discount rate, which, in turn, entails careful evaluation of the welfare effect of the environmental policy under consideration for each future generation. Because one compares consumption paths in which costs are redistributed across generations, it is important to make explicit the ethical and economic assumptions underlying these comparisons. Most environmental policies will generate winners and losers, but economists evaluate the welfare gain by defining an intergenerational welfare function that is a (discounted) sum of the welfare of each generation.

The welfare approach to discounting is based on the additional assumption that future generations will be wealthier than us. Suppose that the real growth rate of the world GDP per capita will be 2 percent per year over the next 200 years (as was the case over the last two centuries in the Western world), which implies that people will enjoy a real GDP per capita 50 times larger in 2200 than it is today. Suppose also that, as in the Stern Review in which the representative agent has a logarithmic utility function, doubling the GDP per capita halves the marginal utility of wealth. Combining these two assumptions implies that one more unit of consumption now has a marginal impact on social welfare that is 50 times larger than the same increment of consumption in 2200. This wealth effect corresponds to a discount rate of 2 percent per year.[1] But is the future a simple mirror of the past?

In my view, it is absolute nonsense to justify discounting the future based on this argument without taking into account the enormous uncertainty affecting the long-term growth of the world economy. Estimating the growth rate for the coming year is already a difficult task. No doubt, any estimation of growth for the next century/millennium is subject to potentially enormous errors. The history of the Western world before the industrial revolution is rife with important economic slumps (as a consequence of the invasion of the Roman Empire, of the Black Death, of worldwide wars, etc.). Some experts argue that the effects of the improvements in information technology have yet to be realized, and that the world faces a period of more rapid growth. But others insist that natural resource scarcities will result in lower growth rates in the future. Still others posit a negative growth of GNP per capita in the future, due to deterioration of the environment, population growth, and decreasing productivity. These disparate views cast doubt on the relevance of the wealth effect as justification of the use of a large discount rate.

We see here that the choice of the discount rate is one of the key elements in the definition of the notion of sustainable development, just as the interest rate is the key economic variable for economic growth. If we are very uncertain about the sustainability of our development, it would be advisable to reduce the discount rate—and especially the rate at which distant cash flows are discounted—in order to induce more investment for the (distant) future.

Growth uncertainty thus needs to be analyzed as well. This is required for the sake of realism, and it is essential if one wants to provide a credible economic approach to the notion of sustainable development. Instrumental to the standard analysis is the concept of prudence, which refers to consumers' willingness to save more in the face of an increase in their future income risk. Indeed, people are generally willing to sacrifice current consumption when their future becomes uncertain. Macroeconomists who have been measuring the precautionary saving motive can tell us much about how cautiously people spend when their own future becomes uncertain. This well-documented observation justifies selecting a smaller social discount rate, implying more investments for the future. In *The Economics of Risk and Time*, which I wrote in 2002, I explain how the benefits of these investments should be targeted for the time horizons with the largest uncertainty, *ceteris paribus*. This provides an argument for implementing a decreasing term structure of the discount rate, if the precautionary effect dominates the wealth effect for longer time horizons.

The existing literature is based on a completely standard expected utility modelling, whereby the welfare of each future generation is evaluated by computing its expected utility based on a probability distribution for the GDP per capita that it will enjoy. A major difficulty, however, is that these probability distributions are ambiguous, in the sense that they are not based on scientific arguments, or on a database large enough to make them completely objective. Indeed, more than one stochastic process is compatible with existing methods for describing economic growth. The Ellsberg paradox tells us that most human beings are averse to ambiguity, which means that they tend to overestimate the probability of the worst-case scenario when computing their subjective expected utility. This suggests that agents systematically violate Savage's "Sure Thing Principle" (Savage, 1954). More precisely, it seems that the way we evaluate uncertain prospects depends on how precise our information about the underlying probabilities is. Hence, a natural question to ask is, Given ambiguity aversion, does a standard subjective utility model systematically underestimate (or overestimate) the socially efficient discount rate?

As explained in Hogarth and Kunreuther (1989), Kunreuther, Hogarth, and Meszaros (1993), and Kunreuther et al. (1995), introducing ambiguity aversion into a discussion of the discount rate is crucial if one wants to have evaluation tools that are compatible with social welfare. It is also appealing as a normative concept to transform the precautionary principle into an operational rule that distorts collective beliefs in a pessimistic way. The degree of ambiguity aversion will determine the intensity of the pessimistic bias in the socially efficient collective evaluation of uncertain prospects compared to their objective equivalent risky prospect. The problem is that we don't have any clear indication of the degree of ambiguity to be applied in the calibration of our evolution models.

THE PROBLEM OF DYNAMIC RISK MANAGEMENT

Most environmental projects have uncertain future benefits. For example, according to the Stern Review, the best estimate for losses in the year 2200 is 13.8 percent of GDP, with a 90 percent interval of confidence that the true loss will be between 2.9 percent and 35.2 percent of GDP. Because future generations are risk averse, the certainty-equivalent loss is larger than 13.8 percent. In practice, with the notable exception of the Stern Review, most evaluations of environmental policies are made by assuming risk neutrality, which tends to underestimate the value of risk prevention.

The state-of-the-art methodology is to use either (1) an expected utility approach with an appropriate degree of risk aversion to compute certainty-equivalent benefits of preventive actions or (2) an asset pricing model from the theory of finance. The latter should be combined with the use of option values attached to more flexible dynamic strategies. However, this general methodology fails to take into account important aspects of certain economic problems, as I explain now.

Ambiguous Benefits, Small Probability Events, and the Precautionary Principle

It is difficult to assess the precise probability distribution to describe the uncertainty faced by decision makers who are dealing with environmental policies such as those associated with global warming or genetically modified organisms. The problem of imprecise probability is particularly crucial with respect to very unlikely events, whereby the speed with which one can learn from the empirical frequency is low. We must recognize that, because people are ambiguity averse, the ambiguity on the distribution of impacts has an adverse effect on social welfare. What are the consequences of ambiguity aversion on the optimal investment in prevention? The general idea is that ambiguity aversion reinforces risk aversion, rendering people more reluctant to undergo ambiguous risky acts. The same idea can be found in the debate about the precautionary principle. This principle has been discussed in various international forums, including the Conference of Rio on Environment and Development and the Maastricht Treaty. It states that "*lack of full scientific certainty shall not be used as a reason for postponing cost-effective measures to prevent environmental degradation.*" Indeed, the precautionary principle has widely been interpreted as a recommendation for reducing collective risk exposure in the presence of ambiguous probabilities. In short, ambiguity aversion should make us behave in a more precautionary way.

The Value of Flexibility, the Debate Between Mitigation and Adaptation, and the Energy Problem

In a risky environment, new information usually generates new decisions. Furthermore, what can or cannot be done *ex post* affects the optimal action *ex ante*. In the context of climate change, there is an important debate emerging on the interaction between mitigation of global changes (limiting the emissions of greenhouse gases) and adaptation to them (preparing to deal with the effects of global warming). The optimal mitigation strategy depends on our beliefs about society's ability to adapt to changes in its environment. Moreover, new information about the intensity of the impacts of climate change, and about the availability of cheap technologies to limit emissions, affects the optimal mitigation strategy—and this flexibility should be taken into account as we determine our optimal effort today.

The emergence of the energy question in the public debate and the reduction of the stock of nonrenewable resources raise similar policy questions. How fast can/should we extract this resource, if we don't know the total amount of resource available? The same question applies when the evolution of the cost of renewable energy sources is stochastic (Dasgupta and Stiglitz, 1971).

What is the effect of flexibility on the optimal risk attitude? One needs to compare the choices under risk in two different contexts. In the flexible context, the decision maker first selects a risk position in a choice set and then, after observing the risk outcome, takes an action. In the rigid context, the agent must commit to an action before observing the state of nature. Intuition suggests that the agent should be more risk-prone in the flexible context than in the rigid one. This point is related to the irreversibility effect and real option values first developed by French economist Claude Henry in 1974.

The value of flexibility and its effects on collective risk attitude are often overlooked in environmental economics. For example, in the Stern Review, it is implicitly assumed that all decisions about the mitigation of climate change should be made immediately. I suggest that one should instead approach the climate change problem and the energy problem by solving them via stochastic dynamic calculus, as in continuous-time finance with predictable assets returns. (This approach was developed in 1969 by American economists and Nobel Laureates Robert Merton and Paul Samuelson.) There are indeed clear links to the literature of dynamic finance: (1) Preserving a nonrenewable resource, or reducing emission of CO_2 under a constraint of maximum concentration, is equivalent to an increase in saving; (2) the uncertainty about the stock of the resource, or the uncertainty about the desirable maximum concentration of CO_2, is parallel to income uncertainty in the standard consumption-portfolio problem; (3) emitting greenhouse gases when the environmental impact is uncertain is equivalent to investing in a risky asset. However, an important difference is due to the absence of an objective probability distribution for the impacts of climate change, or for the speed of technological progress.

Economics and the Psychology of the Precautionary Principle

The normative theory of the efficiency of long-term environmental risks is based on standard assumptions: expected utility (possibly generalized to smooth ambiguity aversion), rational expectation, and exponential discounting of future felicity. This theory has a strong normative basis (e.g., the independence axiom) but a relatively weak positive power to predict real behaviors. Recent developments at the frontier between psychology and economics have revealed that people often evaluate, behave, and judge other agents' decisions under uncertainty in a different way than predicted by the standard theory.

An important aspect of the political economy of the precautionary principle is related to the way people evaluate and judge *ex ante* collective decisions after new information is obtained about the risk. From a normative point of view, information not available at the time of the decision should be irrelevant to evaluation of the optimality of the initial decision in the face of uncertainty. In reality, people have difficulty behaving in that way. For example, they usually feel regret. Regret is a psychological reaction to making a wrong decision, where the quality of decision is predicated on the basis of actual outcomes rather than on the information available at the time of the decision. How does the aversion to regret affect the optimal level of prevention of a future risk? How do people weight the two types of regret/error? In other words, do they (1) invest a lot in the reduction of CO_2 emissions before learning that the economy can easily adapt to climate changes, or (2) avoid doing anything in terms of mitigation before learning that the economy is badly hit by the increased temperature? And how do public decision makers react to the expectation that they will be judged by regret-sensitive agents?

Another promising direction of research is related to the formation of beliefs about long-term risks. If people have anticipatory feelings about the future, they may distort their beliefs in order to fight their anxiety. This willingness to bias beliefs is limited by the knowledge that too much optimism or wishful thinking yields bad risk management for the future. Economists want to explore an alternative explanation based on the fact that too much optimism *ex ante* increases the chance of disappointment *ex post*. We will characterize the optimal distortion of individual and collective beliefs, and the equilibrium collective level of prevention of the risk (as a function of the duration between the decision and the realization of the risk).

IN CLOSING

As more economists are asked to think about, and advise on, global long-term risks, these theoretical questions will come closer to the heart of the debate on the evaluation and management of climate change. Up to now, most economists who specialized in climate change focused their attention on the production of Integrated Assessment Models that combine a climate module and an impact module, with a relatively crude approach to risk evaluation. The extraordinarily vivid debate that followed the publication of the Stern Review in the fall of 2006 was mostly concentrated on the treatment of risk and time. The prospect that much progress will be achieved in the next few years is considerable. As evidenced by the path-breaking career of Howard Kunreuther, an economist who is not so irrational himself, this will take place at the boundary of various disciplines: psychology, sociology, political science, neuroscience, and economics.

RECOMMENDED READING

Dasgupta, P., and J. E. Stiglitz (1971). "Differential Taxation, Public Goods and Economic Efficiency," *Review of Economic Studies* 38: 151–174.

Gollier, C. (2001). *The Economics of Risk and Time*. Cambridge, MA: MIT Press.

Hogarth, R.M., and H. Kunreuther (1989). "Risk, Ambiguity, and Insurance." *Journal of Risk and Uncertainty* 2: 5–35.

Kunreuther, H., R. M. Hogarth, and J. Meszaros (1993). "Insurer Ambiguity and Market Failure." *Journal of Risk and Insurance* 7: 71–87.

Kunreuther, H., J. Meszaros, R. M. Hogarth, and M. Spranca (1995). "Ambiguity and Underwriter Decision Processes." *Journal of Economic Behaviour and Organization* 26: 337–352.

Savage, L. J. (1954). *The Foundations of Statistics*. New York: Wiley. Revised and enlarged edition, New York: Dover (1972).

24 Climate Change
Insuring Risk and Changes in Risk

NEIL DOHERTY

INTRODUCTION

The defining feature of climate change seems to be uncertainty, and uncertainty, it seems, deters the functioning of insurance.[1] There is an emerging scientific consensus that anthropomorphic factors are changing the atmosphere. However, projections of the resulting climatic impact vary. Most scientists agree that temperatures and sea levels will rise if we continue to pump out greenhouse gases, but the extent and timing of anticipated changes are surrounded by a large margin of error. When it comes to extrapolating from broad indicators of climate change (mean global temperature and sea level) to changes in natural hazard risk (storms, droughts, etc.), the belt of uncertainty expands. If we drill down to the impact of climate change on regional hazard risk, our knowledge of future risk levels is scant. Thus, we summarize the potential impact of climate change on the hazards we typically insure by the phrases *increasing risk* and *enormous uncertainty*. We simply do not know with any precision how the risk that we seek to insure will change over time.

How will insurance function under such conditions? If climate change follows a slow evolution, the problem might take care of itself. Insurance contracts typically are for short periods, typically one year, and each year insurers and policyholders will update with the latest information and write new contracts. True, risk levels may change a little, but premiums will be fine-tuned, and the impact will be gradual.

But what if climate change is more rapid and sudden? In this case, actuaries cannot rely on a long historical data record to estimate future loss distributions. Old data degrade, thus compromising the sample size. This implies that statistical updating on the basis of very recent loss experience can be quite dramatic. Rate increases following single events such as Hurricane Andrew in 1992 or the cluster of storms that occurred in 2005 (including Katrina) were large.[2] In an unstable climate, much of the risk that people face is the *risk that risk itself may change*. Thus, even if insured over the long haul, people face the risk that future premiums may change dramatically, and quite fast. Accompanying these changes in the level of risk will be changes in the market values of assets that are exposed to risk. We may expect climate change to affect home prices according to changes in local hazard.

Thus, an unstable climate not only generates uncertainty about future risks, it generates new risks. These new risks include uncertain premiums and uncertain asset prices. What are the challenges to insurance markets introduced by climate change? Will the normal conditions for insurability be present? Do insurance contracts need to be redesigned? Can insurance cover the new risks of volatile premiums and an uncertain real estate market? It is helpful, in addressing these questions, to examine the nature of the risk that faces people and businesses in an unstable climate.

I will argue that climate changes can be represented in a simple way as a "compound lottery" with risk present in both the first and second stages. The *stage 1* risks are the instability of insurance premiums and asset price volatility, whereas the *stage 2* risks are those we normally associate with insurance (i.e., whether a loss occurs or not). However, the first and second stages exhibit very different characteristics that, in turn, carry different implications for insurance. I will then use this characterization to address long-term insurance for hazard risk.

CLIMATE CHANGE AS A COMPOUND LOTTERY

The evolution of risk under conditions of climate change is depicted in Figure 24.1 as a sequence of risks, or "multi-stage lottery." Currently, the risk for a particular insurance portfolio is to some degree known, and this can be shown as a probability distribution. How will this risk change over time? Consider the risk in some future year t, let's say in fifteen years. We cannot

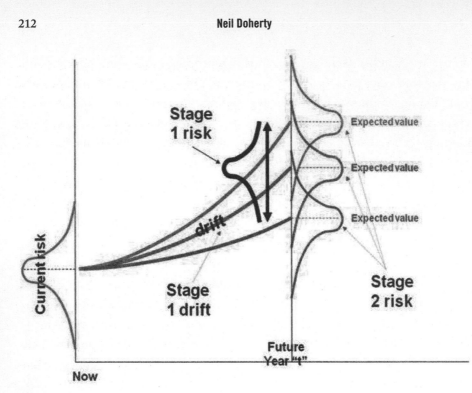

FIGURE 24.1 Risk as a Multi-Stage Lottery

specify now what the risk might be in that year. Indeed, there are many probability distributions that could occur, each with their own expected value and
level of risk.[3] Between now and time t, climate risk will change. I have shown
three possible change, or "drift," paths; each depicts a potential evolution of
the expected value of loss at time t. As future year t approaches, we will learn
more about how climate is changing and, therefore, about how uncertainty
will be resolved, but only to some extent. We will still not have the luxury of
a long and stable climate historical record with which to estimate the year t
risk, and we will rely on other methods (e.g., meteorological models) to estimate the distribution.

Stage 2 Risk

We can see different types of risk. When future time t arrives we will have
conventional contemporaneous risk: There will be a more-or-less known distribution of loss, and actual losses will represent draws on that distribution. We
will call this *stage 2* risk. If climate change is sudden and rapid leading up to

time t, we may not place much confidence in our best estimate of the distribution, and I will refer to *stage 2* ambiguity. Thus, *stage 2* risk is the conventional insurance risk that future underwriters will face in the future, though future actuaries and modelers may be unusually challenged when it comes to estimating this distribution. Some adjustments might be expected:

- Exposures for which risk has increased (decreased) will face higher (lower) premiums.
- If the correlation among risks increases (e.g., if there are more expansive weather systems that can cause multiple storms, or if sea-level rises make more locations vulnerable to even modest storms), insurance supply may be more constrained or capital will need to be increased or contracts will need to be rewritten to limit aggregation of risk. Such contracts will essentially mutualize risk and I will address this later. If, in addition to correlation, there is also considerable ambiguity, insurers may require more capital to cover the possibility that risk will be underestimated and therefore that premiums will be too low.
- Insurers will rebalance their exposures as the geographical exposures shifts.

Stage 1 Risk

Let me be clear about what *stage 1* risk is *not*. If there is a foreseeable upward drift in climate hazard, then people are expected to face an increasing hazard cost, which will be manifest in increasing insurance premiums and declining property values in exposed regions. These are anticipated real costs but they are not risk; they are predictable. Rather, the *stage 1* risk relates to the *uncertainty in the path* assumed by the *stage 2* risk. More specifically, it refers to the uncertainty in evolving *knowledge* as to how future risk is changing. However, that evolving knowledge will affect real decisions and will coalesce into real changes in wealth. The main *stage 1* risks will be the risk of volatile premiums, volatile asset prices, and volatile tax liabilities.

- If we assume that the market for insurance continues to be one with short-term insurance contracts, then *stage 1* risk implies that future insurance premiums will be random.

- The second major form of *stage 1* risk lies in asset price risk. Assets that are exposed to a changing risk will be re-priced. For example, coastal homes will tend to devalue as the risk is perceived to increase.
- There are other forms that the *stage 1* risk could assume. For example, if future governments bail out uninsured property owners, then climate change implies a random tax liability to fund these bailouts.

There may be a demand to insure these risks. I will focus on only two of the *stage 1* risks: the insurance of risky premiums (i.e., premiums may be volatile going forward) and risky asset prices. However, to explore the potential for insuring these risks, I need to be more specific about the generic properties of the *stage 1* (and *stage 2*) risks, and what these properties imply for the feasibility and design of insurance contracts.

While relatively little is known about the properties of *stage 1* risk, some conservative conjectures can be offered. First, there seems to be a general (perhaps a better word is "vague") consensus that the trend is upward. It is difficult to predict the impact of climate change on future tropical storm risk in a specific area for a given year. Nevertheless, the general view is that global warming will lead to more intense (though not necessarily more frequent) tropical storms in some regions.[4] Note that, insofar as an upward trend is expected, wealth transfers associated with this trend are not amenable to normal risk transfer mechanisms. Rationally, the expected increase in risk should already be impounded in house prices. Moreover, the expected increase in hazard risk in a given region translates into an expected increase in insurance premiums.

A safer conclusion one can draw is that while the mean predictions of future regional storm activity are unclear, the uncertainty surrounding those predictions is likely to increase. This uncertainty or ambiguity could be transferred under a hedge or insurance contract; clearly recognizing that the risk to be hedged is the unexpected change in the level of hazard, one might contemplate an insurance against *unanticipated* premium increases. However, the availability and pricing of such insurance might depend on whether the ambiguity is independent in different places (e.g., we could underestimate risk in one place and overestimate it in another) and whether the ambiguity relates not just to the year-by-year estimates of loss but also to the long-term trend.

Trending or momentum in the hazard path implies uncertainty about the long-term hazard and diminishes the possibility of inter-temporal diversification.[5] With such momentum, we could find that, if we underestimated the hazard risk for year *2020*, then we would likely also have underestimated for *2021, 2022*, and so on. In addition, there might be contemporaneous correlation. Suppose that nature chooses a general path for climate change (e.g., a 2° increase in mean global temperature over a fifty-year horizon). With such a path, how correlated will the impacts on different hazards in different regions be? If storms will be more severe/frequent in some regions and less severe/frequent in others, then the uncertainty about which regions will have more or fewer storms is diversifiable. However, if there is more correlation across regions, then insurers will find it increasingly difficult to diversify risk and therefore will be constrained in offering insurance. Similarly, will the chosen path simultaneously increase most risk types (storm, flood, drought, etc.)? Again, a high degree of correlation will degrade the effectiveness of risk transfer mechanisms.

ALTERNATIVE DISPOSITIONS OF STAGE 1 RISK

Stage 1 risk is uninsured, and stage 2 risk is insured through short-term insurance contracts.   This is "business as usual"; insurers continue to offer year-by-year contracts with premiums based on updated estimates of the risk level. But even if contracts continue to look as they do at present, climate change presents enormous challenges to insurers. Increasing risk will require more capital, and climate instability will lead to problems in estimating contemporaneous loss distributions and therefore difficulties in setting premiums. Re-estimating loss distributions based on rapidly evolving hazard levels could lead to violent premium changes, and this premium volatility is a risk that policyholders face. Compounded difficulties would arise if policyholders and insurers differed in their assessment of the likelihood of the risk, which, in turn, could lead to excess supply or demand of insurance. As mentioned earlier, additional challenges will arise if climate change leads to changes in the correlation structure of the world insurance portfolio. (For example, El Nino/La Nina currently present correlated weather patterns across widely separate parts of the world, but we know little about how these would change with global warming.)

Stage 1 risk is insured in constant premium long-term insurance contracts. Can insurance cover both the *stage 1* and *stage 2* risks? A paper by Howard Kunreuther, Erwann Michel-Kerjan (at Wharton), and Dwight Jaffee (at UC Berkeley) advocates long-term insurance in which much of the premium risk is absorbed by the insurer.[6] The appeal of this proposal lies with the demand side of the market—risk-averse homeowners who would clearly benefit from offloading the joint risks of actual losses, volatile premiums, and the future availability of insurance.

The problems lie on the supply side. This long-term insurance proposal cleverly links insurance to preexisting long-term contracts that are rooted in value (i.e., mortgages). In doing so, they acknowledge that lenders already accept a long-term risk position insofar as the revealed risk (either decline in house prices or uninsured losses) will affect their collateral. Could one go further and formally establish a market for long-term insurance contracts that offer some protection against premium volatility (whereby, for example, premiums and coverage remain constant over the whole period of the contract, or are guaranteed for sub-intervals such as three years, five years, etc.)?

There is a precedent. Life insurance is routinely sold on terms of twenty, thirty (etc.) years with uniform premiums. But comparing life insurance with long-term catastrophe insurance can be alarming. The three conditions that facilitate long-term life insurance—predictable risk, uncorrelated trends in risk, and a beneficial trend in risk (declining mortality)—are unlikely to be present in the context of climate hazards. If, as one fears, an upward trend in catastrophe risk is associated with (serially and contemporaneously) correlated ambiguity, then the *stage 1* risk would not be amenable to diversification. In this event, the amount of insurer capital required to secure that risk at an acceptable credit rating could be enormous. On the other hand, if the pool was not adequately prefunded with capital, then credit quality would deteriorate perhaps to the level of unacceptable counterparty risk.

I will mention another issue that is addressed by the long-term insurance proposal: Unless such contracts are binding on policyholders, then competing insurers offering short-term contracts can pick off those policyholders for whom risk might decrease. Such slippage will, of course, diminish the degree of risk pooling. This issue will bedevil most long-term solutions, including those noted below. (A different approach to long-term insurance contracts is to optimize separately on the *stage 1* and *stage 2* risks.)

Stage 1 risk is semi-mutualized in binding long-term contracts with separate treatment of stage 1 and stage 2 risk.   Let us assume that *stage 2* risk is reasonably well behaved in the sense that it is not highly contemporaneously correlated across regions and insurance markets can secure geographical diversification. These are strong assumptions, but they establish the minimal conditions under which ongoing short-term insurance would function. Now let us assume that *stage 1* risk is subject to serial and contemporaneous correlation. To the extent that it is, diversification does not help. However, we know much about insurance design under such circumstances. The mutual structure allows all idiosyncratic risk to be effectively insured. Yet the systematic risk is shared by all policyholders through equity participation in the overall risk pool.[7] This can be achieved through organizational structure (mutual or reciprocal insurance companies) or by contract design (participating policies issued by a joint stock insurance firm).

One might conjecture that an optimal long-term insurance contract would have the following structure. First, idiosyncratic and diversifiable *stage 1* premium risk would be mutualized. Each policyholder would have his or her premiums indexed to changes in the total risk in the pool. This would both ensure overall premium adequacy and provide some degree of risk protection for those in regions where risk increased more rapidly. *Stage 2* risk would then be insured under normal conditions. In short, the *stage 2* risk would be borne by short-term insurance contracts secured by insurer capital in the usual way, whereas the *stage 1* risk would be borne communally by means of indexed premiums. However, if it did transpire that *stage 2* risk exhibited higher correlation, then one could have a secondary level of mutualization under which all policyholders funded actual deficits (or shared surpluses) in the annual results by means of additional premiums or refunds.

Both types of contracts—the semi-mutualized insurance and the constant premium contract—raise concerns about the disincentives for homeowners to take measures to mitigate their own risk. In both cases, policyholders are protected from, at least, idiosyncratic changes in risk; but would this erode homeowners' incentive to mitigate? Certainly, either form would compromise incentives for short-term mitigation. For long-term mitigation, the issue is more complex. Perhaps the central issue is that incentives for mitigation rest largely on the prospect that home values do indeed reflect risk. If long-term insurance were bundled with home ownership (such that rights to the policy transferred with ownership of the house), then insurance would provide a hedge against falling house prices due to increased hazard. However, it is apparent that decoupling house prices from hazard risk would simply encourage people to continue to move to high-risk areas, as we have seen in the state of Florida. Under normal insurance practice, the policy attaches to the policyholder rather than to the home, so this may not be an issue.

Stage 1 risk is hedged through non-insurance mechanisms.   The benefits of a mutual approach to *stage 1* risk also could be achieved by non-insurance mechanisms. To hedge against local changes in insurance premiums caused by changes in local risk, one could take derivative positions in house prices. In fact, such derivatives are already traded in some metropolitan areas. A derivative trade can easily be constructed in which individuals are protected from the fall in their house price relative to the national average change in house prices. A market for such contracts would protect people from the idiosyncratic *stage 1* risk. Of course, the local changes in house prices would reflect not only changes in hazard risk but also changes in regional economic factors. Moreover, because some local prices would rise relative to the national average and other local prices would fall relative to the national average, then investors could enter this market without necessarily experiencing any systemic risk.

The same effect could, in principle, be achieved with weather derivatives. While these derivatives are usually designed to pay out on weather events, their prices would reflect local risk. A similar local-short/national-long strategy based on derivative prices should be able to isolate the deviation of the change in local risk relative to the overall change, thus mutualizing the risk. Doing this on weather derivatives provides more focus than with house price indices; it isolates the weather risk. However, the problem with both strategies lies in the term of the contracts. To be effective in hedging global climate change, the derivative strategy needs to cover the longer-term impact on insurance risk and futures contracts.

CONCLUDING THOUGHTS ON INSURER SOLVENCY

I have argued that, while long term contracts are, in principle, capable of covering the combination of *stage 1* and *stage 2* risks imposed by climate change, these contracts are problematic. Probably the most severe issue is whether insurers remain solvent over long time periods. In a period of capital scarcity, the additional capital needed by insurers for *stage 1*, solvency risk in a long-term contract, could severely diminish insurance capacity. Ironically, insuring *stage 1* risk, which does not score well against the normal criteria for insurability, could well crowd out the availability of the all-important *stage 2* risk.

A lesson from health insurance might well be heeded. As insurance has become more comprehensive (e.g., inclusion of mental health, more consumer choice over providers, the ability of consumers to conceal genetic information) insurance has become more expensive and less affordable and we now have an unprecedented number of Americans uninsured. Creating "Cadillac" catastrophe coverage courts the same risk. Thus, my lesson for insurers when "making decisions in a dangerous world" is "stick to what you are good at."

25 International Social Protection in the Face of Climate Change

Developing Insurance for the Poor

JOANNE LINNEROOTH-BAYER

"A TRULY INTERNATIONAL ENDEAVOUR"

In the previous chapter, Neil Doherty discussed how insurance companies might consider the insurability of climate risk in the future. While insurance is widely used in rich countries around the world, we know that radical changes in climate would have debilitating impacts on poor countries lacking an insurance system. Does the international community of wealthy nations—in light of their emissions of greenhouse gases—have responsibility for providing security to the developing world, and especially the poor within this world, as floods, typhoons, and other extremes in weather increasingly threaten their livelihoods and lives? This chapter examines the case for an international effort aimed at providing insurance as a form of social protection against weather extremes to vulnerable individuals and governments. Insurance is especially topical in the current climate negotiations, which are expected to create substantial funding for, among other activities, adapting to climate variability and extremes affecting the developing world.

The dire effects of such variability and extremes on the poor raise age-old issues of responsibility, equity, and efficiency in designing public policy. This is especially the case as poorly regulated financial markets threaten economic livelihoods across the world economy, as food insecurity leads to political discontent, and as climate change imposes the threat of greater local environmental damage and increasingly destructive natural disasters. As the threats become global, so too does responsibility for providing security to protect against them. According to UN Under Secretary-General for Economic and Social Affairs Shu Zukang:

> The responsibility for the choice and mix of policies required to guarantee prosperity, stability and justice, remains, of course, with national institutions and constituencies, but in an increasingly interdependent world and on a fragile planet, building a more secure home is a truly international endeavour.[1]

By calling for a "truly international endeavour," Shu Zukang set the stage for this discussion, which proposes a radical extension of national social protection systems in the direction of an international regime that would support insurance mechanisms as a way of providing financial protection against weather-related losses in vulnerable countries.

This topic is highly relevant to development organizations, humanitarian groups, and international financial institutions. Recognizing that disasters are a major impediment to local economic development and, hence, an important contributor to poverty, and that post-disaster aid has failed to sufficiently reduce this impact, many donor organizations are already switching from aid to social protection with insurance. Insurance for the most vulnerable is also a "hot topic" on the climate negotiation agenda, which, building on the Kyoto Protocol, is expected to include adaptation as an important response to climate change. Both the Framework Convention on Climate Change (UNFCCC) and the 2007 Bali Action Plan[2] specifically call for consideration of risk sharing and transfer mechanisms, such as insurance, as a means to adapt to weather-related loss and damage in developing countries.

My aim in this chapter is to make a case for including insurance in development assistance strategies as well as in the emerging climate adaptation architecture. I argue this case in full recognition that insurance is not appropriate in all contexts and that it must be designed to minimize inefficiencies through price-distorting subsidies. Donor-supported insurance programs, some of which introduce novel index-based pricing, are already serving the poor.

Below, after briefly discussing the implications of weather extremes on poverty, I review the costs, benefits, and challenges of these programs and then introduce a recent proposal for including insurance as part of the climate agreement expected, as of this writing, to emerge from the 2009 negotiations in Copenhagen. This proposal, known as the Munich Climate Insurance Initiative (MCII), offers a practical way of building an international regime for social protection.

WEATHER EXTREMES: WHY THE POOR SUFFER THE MOST

The impacts of natural hazards on economic well-being have escalated alarmingly in recent decades. Although increased population and wealth in vulnerable areas remain the main factors in explaining rising losses, the Intergovernmental Panel on Climate Change (IPCC) has predicted that extreme event impacts are "very likely" to change because of increasing weather variability.[3] There is even mounting evidence of a current "climate signal," with the IPCC (2007) reporting observations of widespread changes in temperature, wind patterns, and aspects of extreme weather, including droughts, heavy precipitation, heat waves, and the intensity of tropical cyclones.

With over 95 percent of disaster fatalities and far greater relative economic losses occurring in low- and middle-income countries, the poor suffer the most (see Figure 25.1). One reason is that developing countries employ many more people in the weather-sensitive agricultural sector. In sub-Saharan Africa, for example, 90 percent of the population relies on rain-fed agriculture for their basic food needs.[4] It is important to keep in mind that the losses from disasters in low-income countries are not only economic but often existential as well.

The data pictured in Figure 25.1 do not include the *long-term* consequences of disasters on economic development—consequences that can greatly amplify both economic and human losses. Due to limited tax bases, high indebtedness, and low uptake of insurance, many highly exposed developing countries cannot fully recover from disasters simply by relying on limited external donor aid. In turn, external investors are wary of the risk of catastrophic infrastructure losses, and small firms and farmers cannot receive the credit necessary for investing in higher-yield/higher-risk activities.

Climate disasters exacerbate poverty in two major ways. (1) They destroy human and physical assets, livelihoods, and public infrastructure, thus setting back gains from development. And (2) households, small and medium-sized enterprises, and farmers with high uninsured risk exposure often adopt

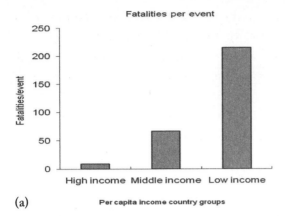

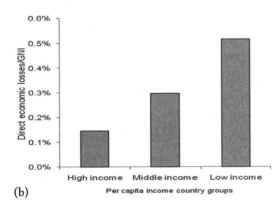

FIGURE 25.1
Differential Burden of
Natural Disasters:
(a) Fatalities Per Event and
(b) Economic Losses
According to Country
Income Groups
Source: Author's calculations
based on data from the
reinsurer Munich Re (2005).

low-risk, low-return strategies (e.g., placing relatives in low-paid but secure employment, planting low-yield drought-resistant seeds), thus reducing their ability to accumulate the assets needed to escape poverty through savings and investment.

INSURANCE FOR THE POOR AS SECURITY AGAINST WEATHER DISASTERS

Insurance and other financial instruments should be viewed within an overall risk management strategy. A cornerstone of risk management is investing in measures that limit exposure, increase preparedness, and reduce vulnerability. Estimates show that only about 2 percent of disaster management expenditures by bilateral and multilateral donors are spent on disaster risk reduction, whereas the benefits can be many times the expenditures. Reinhard Mechler from the International Institute for Applied Systems Analysis (IIASA) in Austria, for instance, has examined retrospective studies on disaster mitigation in developing countries and concluded that measures like building polder systems, planting mango trees, and relocating schools have demonstrated large benefits in relation to their costs. Risks, of course, will remain—and for this reason risk-sharing and risk-transfer mechanisms will increasingly be viewed as an essential component of risk management.

Insurance programs, which pool economic losses and smooth incomes, as well as transfer risks to the capital markets, are playing an increasingly visible role in developing countries. However, in countries where insurance penetration is low and the network of insurers on the ground is not that well developed, issuing a new policy and managing it over time can be quite costly. Moreover, there would be the high cost of handling claims that are spread over an entire region. To avoid these costs, new insurance programs have been developed in recent years that are index-based. By *index-based* I mean that the insurance claims issued by such programs are based not on the direct losses suffered by the insurance policyholders but, rather, on an external physical trigger, such as rainfall or wind intensity. If well defined, such a trigger is highly correlated with losses. An important advantage of index-based insurance is that it is simple to measure by anyone if good-quality weather stations are in place.

For example, herders in Mongolia can now purchase an index-based insurance policy to protect them against livestock loss due to extreme winter weather, or *dzuds*. Whereas the herders themselves absorb small losses that do not affect the viability of their business, larger losses are transferred to the private insurance industry and only the final layer of catastrophic losses is borne by the government with backing from the World Bank.[5]

Not only herders but also subsistence farmers are benefiting from index-based systems (e.g., in Malawi and India), and the potential for scaling up insurance programs to protect rural livelihoods is huge. For the most part, however, farmers and herders do not belong to the group referred to as the "poorest of the poor." Lacking assets, this group is probably best served by post-disaster government relief. Here, too, pre-disaster financial instruments can provide needed security by insuring the providers of relief. For instance, in

2006, the World Food Programme, which is the food-aid branch of the United Nations and the world's largest humanitarian organization, reduced its own risk of large aid outlays to drought victims by supporting—through a partnership with the French insurance giant AXA—an index-based risk-transfer instrument for the Ethiopian government. This insurance instrument holds large promise for supporting institutions that have traditionally provided humanitarian assistance.

Across the developing world, highly exposed governments face financial gaps in providing relief to the poor. In filling these gaps, post-disaster donor funds earmarked for relief and reconstruction consistently fall short of the desired level. Faced with this situation, a few innovative governments are transferring their risks to the international markets. This is the case in Mexico, where government officials recently issued a catastrophe bond to transfer the exposure to natural disasters of the government's catastrophe reserve fund directly to the financial markets and thus reduce the country's risk of a large fiscal deficit following hurricane and earthquake disasters. It is also the case in the Caribbean island states, which have formed the world's first multi-country catastrophe insurance pool to provide governments with immediate liquidity in the aftermath of hurricanes or earthquakes. International development organizations have committed funds to Haiti, for example, to ensure wide participation.

The possibilities for similar arrangements elsewhere in the world are significant, given the largely untapped potential for pooling uncorrelated risks of country governments ill prepared to respond to disasters with their own means.

BENEFITS, COSTS, AND CHALLENGES OF INSURANCE INSTRUMENTS

Insurance instruments provide security against the loss of assets, livelihoods, and even lives in the post-disaster period. They can also set incentives for reducing exposure and vulnerability, engage the private sector in vast markets, and, not least, spur economic development. For many in the developing world an insurance contract is viewed as more self-respecting than relying on humanitarian assistance. In the words of Oxfam expert Hari Krishna: "Communities value disaster insurance . . . because they see it as an instrument of dignity. Financial support to recover from a disaster becomes their right without sacrificing their self-respect. It is far more dignified to claim your right for recovery than to find yourself dependent on the *ad hoc* generosity of donors."[6]

Switching from post-disaster humanitarian assistance to supporting insurance contracts *ex ante* is attractive not only to disaster victims but also to international financial and donor organizations. If coupled with incentives for preventing disaster losses, insurance programs can ultimately reduce the human and economic toll that disasters take on the poor. Indeed, switching to pre-disaster assistance for insurance can be an efficient long-term strategy because of its potential ultimately to reduce the need for post-disaster humanitarian assistance.

While the benefits of insurance are largely uncontested, they are paid for in high associated costs. Premiums for catastrophe insurance are calculated on the basis of anticipated losses, and also include the costs of doing business (which can be substantial in the developing world) as well as a contingency load for holding capital and assuming very uncertain risks. Owing to the high capital requirements for insuring systemic risks (events that impact whole regions at once), the contingency load for catastrophe cover is far higher than the insurance cover for health, life, and other nonsystemic risks. Moreover, data on very infrequent events is scarce, meaning that insurers must guard themselves against vagaries in the statistical estimates.

The high costs of catastrophe insurance present challenges to the international community, but its benefits in terms of reducing poverty present very real opportunities. For example, donors can leverage their limited humanitarian budgets by replacing post-disaster aid with support for catastrophe insurance, and climate-change negotiators can use risk-pooling and risk-transfer instruments as an integral part of an adaptation strategy. The main challenge, of course, is to make these programs affordable to poor communities and governments without distorting markets and incentives.

Development organizations, international financial institutions, and NGOs are already providing support to make insurance affordable in the developing world. The aforementioned insurance programs in Mongolia, Ethiopia, Mexico, and the Caribbean have all received outside backing in the form of technical assistance, reinsurance facilitation, and, in some cases, direct subsidies. The efficiency and equity issues raised by this kind of assistance are discussed in the next section.

Another challenge is that badly designed insurance contracts can discourage investments in loss prevention or even encourage negligent behavior ("If I know I'm protected anyway, I can take more risk"), commonly referred to in economics as *moral hazard* or in the climate community as *maladaptation*. As a remedy, index-based contracts, by decoupling losses and claims, avoid moral hazard and can provide strong incentives for risk-reducing interventions and lifestyle changes. Two of my earlier examples illustrate this: In Mongolia, insured herders will face increasing premiums as climate change worsens weather conditions, giving them an added incentive to change their livelihood if animal husbandry becomes unproductive; and in Mexico, government officials will face higher interest on their catastrophe bonds by not taking measures to reduce risks to public infrastructure. This is the power of risk-based insurance premiums.

INTERNATIONAL SUPPORT FOR INSURANCE: EFFICIENCY AND EQUITY

A central challenge in economics is to find the "right" balance between a policy or a program that is not only efficient from an economic point of view but also equitable. This challenge applies especially to insuring the poor in developing countries.

Efficiency

Incentives provided by risk-based premiums, which price risk and thus couple prevention with price reduction, can be weakened by outside support, especially if such support takes the form of premium subsidies. If the premiums do not fully reflect risks, they may perpetuate vulnerability by discouraging investments in disaster prevention and making it possible for people to remain in high-risk livelihoods or locations. This concern is voiced in the present book by Wharton's economist Howard Kunreuther, who calls for risk-based pricing, although he is aware, especially given the devastation caused by Hurricane Katrina in 2005, that risk-based premiums may not be affordable to the poor in high-risk areas. In their new book *At War with the Weather*, Kunreuther and Erwann Michel-Kerjan suggest that vouchers (which are similar to food stamps) would enable the poor to purchase insurance.[7] Indeed, vouchers might serve as an alternative to subsidizing insurance systems in the developing world. Already direct cash transfers to the poor are replacing donor-financed projects in some countries; perhaps in those that also provide post-disaster assistance, these transfers could be made conditional on purchasing insurance. As a case in point, cash transfers to women in Mexico are conditional on their provision of child education and health care, and it would be a small step to make these transfers conditional on their uptake of insurance against disasters and other threats to their lives and livelihoods.

Even without insurance vouchers, subsidies and other forms of premium support may be justified by the failure of the market to provide the right price signals. In Mongolia, for example, government support for the syndicate pooling arrangement takes the form of absorbing losses from very infrequent extreme events (e.g., more than 30 percent animal mortality), and the government can call upon a World Bank contingent debt arrangement to back this commitment. The designers of this program argue that subsidizing the "upper layer" is less price distorting than subsidizing lower layers of risk because the market may fail to provide insurance.[8]

Equity

The authors of the "UN World Economic and Social Survey 2008" argue that security against disasters cannot be left solely to individual responsibility and market forces: "Transferring the responsibility for sufficient protection against disasters to individuals by merely ensuring that risk transfer and risk pooling, such as insurance, are available can therefore not be the primary pillar for addressing the insecurity challenge." The case for shifting a part of the responsibility from poor to wealthy nations is greatly strengthened by recent evidence that greenhouse gas emissions are likely contributing to increased weather variability and to the risk of extreme events, and disproportionately burdening vulnerable developing countries. According to the UNFCCC's principle of "common but differentiated responsibilities and respective capabilities," industrialized countries are arguably obligated to absorb a portion of this burden.

To help make this principle operational, IIASA scientists have assisted the Munich Climate Insurance Initiative in putting forward a proposal to include insurance instruments in the climate-change adaptation regime expected to be agreed upon in Copenhagen in December 2009. According to this proposal, a risk-management financing mechanism would include two pillars: *prevention* and *insurance*, which would act together to reduce the human and economic burdens on developing countries. The insurance pillar has two tiers.

The first is a Global Insurance Pool, which compensates part of the losses from high-level risks in vulnerable countries. IIASA estimates that if *all* losses to governments unable to cope with their financial burdens were compensated by an international fund, the annual costs would average about US$8 billion, a small fraction of average annual losses in the developed world. (After Hurricane Katrina in 2005, the U.S. government sought $105 billion for relief and reconstruction.) The second tier is an Insurance Assistance Facility, which provides technical and financial support to fledgling insurance systems (such as the ones in Malawi, Ethiopia, Mexico, and the Caribbean that I've mentioned above) to cover middle-layer risks. Both pillars would be fully financed by an adaptation fund expected to emerge from the Copenhagen Agreed Outcome, and thus by citizens of the developed world. A similar proposal has been put forth by the Alliance of Small Island States (AOSIS).

CONCLUSION: A ROLE FOR THE ECONOMIST

Shu Zukang's words remind us that "in an increasingly interdependent world and on a fragile planet, building a more secure home is a truly international endeavour." Accordingly, and in this spirit, the present discussion has examined the idea of an international social protection regime in the form of insurance against extreme weather that is affecting and worsening poverty in the developing world. Under the auspices of the UNFCCC, I strongly believe a rationale exists for such a regime. This rationale is based on three premises: (1) Insurance can have large benefits for low-income individuals and governments, not only enabling them to recover from catastrophic weather events but also providing the security necessary for productive investments and thus for escaping poverty. (2) The private market, alone, cannot provide this security to the most vulnerable because they are unable to afford catastrophe insurance premiums (the cost of which is far higher than anticipated losses) and because the market fails to offer protection for very rare and high-consequence events. (3) Climate change is likely already worsening weather disaster risks, and wealthy nations have committed themselves through the UNFCCC to respond according to the principle of "common but differentiated responsibilities and respective capabilities."

A practical way forward is to include a risk management mechanism in the adaptation architecture in the Copenhagen Agreed Outcome. The recent

MCII proposal for such a mechanism calls for two pillars, prevention and insurance, both of which would be fully financed by a climate-change adaptation fund expected to be part of this architecture.

Climate change will be on the social, business, and political agenda for decades to come. Economists, too, will have a growing influence in shaping this debate. As we do so, it is important for us to consider our responsibilities in helping develop innovative and actionable solutions to reduce vulnerability to disasters for the largest-possible number of people, both rich and poor. In an increasingly interdependent world, this is surely a wise posture to adopt in order to ensure an equitable balance between the North and the South.

RECOMMENDED READING

Cummins, J. D., and O. Mahul (2009). *Catastrophe Risk Financing in Developing Countries: Principles for Public Intervention*. World Bank Publications, Washington, DC.

Gurenko, E., ed. (2004). "Climate Change and Insurance: Disaster Risk Financing in Developing Countries." Special edition of *Climate Policy* 6: 599–684.

Linnerooth-Bayer, J., R. Mechler, and G. Pflug (2005). Refocusing Disaster Aid. *Science* 309: 1044–1046.

Thompson, M., and M. Verweij, eds. (2006). *Clumsy Solutions for a Complex World: Governance, Politics and Plural Perceptions*. Hampshire, U.K.: Palgrave Macmillan.

Mechler, R., J. Linnerooth-Bayer, and D. Peppiatt (2006). "Disaster Insurance for the Poor? A Review of Microinsurance for Natural Disaster Risks in Developing Countries." ProVention Consortium, IIASA.

PART FIVE

WHAT DIFFERENCE CAN WE MAKE?

*T*HE IRRATIONAL ECONOMIST ENDS with a somewhat unusual series of contributions regarding the role of economists and other social scientists in society. The first four parts of the book have provided us with in-depth analyses and evidence on how we make decisions in a dangerous world and how we can improve our decision processes to achieve better outcomes. But in order to truly modify our behavior, as individuals and as a society, this knowledge must be shared with many, from students to the very top decision makers, and integrated into new ways of making decisions.

How can we accomplish this? What are the roles and responsibilities of economists and other decision scientists here and abroad? What tangible initiatives can be launched to tackle the most pressing issues on both the national and the global agendas? Why does research funding matter so greatly? What concrete action principles can we recommend? In a nutshell, what difference can we make in the world?

26 Are We Making a Difference?

BARUCH FISCHHOFF

Howard Kunreuther's career has been dedicated to producing research and remedies, aimed at helping people to make better decisions. That commitment has led
him to an uncommon variety of methods and collaborations. He has conducted
field surveys, qualitative interviews, and laboratory experiments, in addition to
more conventional economic modeling and theorizing—in order to triangulate
on complex problems. He has spent time with insurance salespeople, regulators,
and executives—in order to understand problems more fully. He has written papers satisfying the editorial standards of economics, psychology, disaster research,
and risk analysis—in order to get the work to the most relevant academic audiences. He has convened unusual working groups. He has provided missing pieces
to similarly spirited work that others have undertaken, myself included.

How can we tell how well our joint experiment is working? We've had
a good time intellectually and made some great friends. Universities have
thought enough of the exercise to indulge us with positions and resources.
People attend our workshops, contribute to our journals, and study with us.
We get to opine, here and there—in the news media, before government, on
advisory panels, and in boardrooms. These experiences, in themselves, should
constitute satisfying careers. However, unlike Marx's philosophers, we want to
change the world, not just explain it.

Yet, we are not full-time consultants, entrepreneurs, or legislators, posi-
tioned to see our grand ideas through to practical realization. Accordingly,
unless we leave, neglect, or redefine our day jobs in order to close the deal,
others must apply our insights. Understanding what they are doing with our
work is essential to evaluating how we are doing.

UNREASONABLE FRIENDS AND ENEMIES

Being recognized is no guarantee of success. There are honest brokers in the world of deeds, eager for scientifically sound proposals that they can carry forward. But there are also practitioners with foregone conclusions, looking for experts whose work they can invoke, in order to justify positions that they have already adopted. They may care little about the quality of our work, as long as it points in their direction and can be cited as a "neutral" source of truth. If our fame advances their cause, then they may help us to find better speaking engagements, better luck with our op-eds, and better consulting opportunities. But we are just means to their predetermined ends.

How can we tell whether we are being "kept" by the powerful, rather than getting well-deserved audiences? One positive sign is finding that our supporters have followed a discovery process paralleling our own, independently discovering a behavioral regularity that we have documented and explained. A second positive sign is finding that our supporters care about the details of our work and the science underlying it—and not just about our convenient truths. A third positive sign is finding that our supporters are committed to empirical evaluation, meaning that they care about how well a program works and not just that it exists, bringing them wealth or power.

Just as acclaim can be embarrassing, if it means that we are being used, so can scorn be an honor, if it means that our ideas are so powerful that they must be attacked. Social scientists study basic human activities, which others are already addressing (e.g., politicians, pundits, public affairs offices). Unless we fashion roles for those incumbents, we threaten them. A community activist once told me that she knew that her views mattered, when her life was threatened. Without worthy enemies, perhaps we're not saying much.

OUR PROGRAM?

If we get the chance to implement our work, we then need to ask whether the programs that emerge are faithful to our ideas. Implementation always requires some adaptation. However interdisciplinary our research groups might be, they are unlikely to include all the relevant expertise. For example, Howard Kunreuther's early work on the National Flood Insurance Program (NFIP) found that, despite having many attractive features, the NFIP had not adequately addressed insurance agents' compensation. Without appropriate commissions, agents had less incentive to sell a policy, however attractive it might be for their clients. The federal government later adjusted those commissions—a result of the research project's commitment to empirical research, capable of producing surprising results.

As mentioned, evaluation research is essential, if one cares about a program's impacts (and not just its existence). Evaluation research begins by assessing how faithful a program's implementation is to its underlying concept. That assessment keeps programs from being judged unfairly, when flawed imitations bear their names. For example, the failure of poorly marketed flood insurance does not prove that insurance can never work, as a strategy for internalizing costs, reducing moral hazard, and sending price signals. Similarly, the failure of poorly executed risk communications does not prove that "information doesn't work." On the other hand, if a program cannot be implemented faithfully, then it may just be an ivory-tower idea.

As a risk management program becomes more complicated, its implementation requires more and more kinds of expertise—to the point where the big idea may be just a banner under which multiple specialties ply their crafts. If so, then we should be proud of having opened the door to those experts, even if the final product is less distinctively our own. Complex programs provide less clear tests for any contributing discipline or theory. If they don't succeed, then there are many places to assign the blame. Making such excuses can give us a second chance. If others make them, getting repeated chances for their own failures, then they can keep us from getting a first chance. If we don't get to try, it is hard to know whether our ideas lack merit or we lack the clout needed to get them a trial.

REINVENTING OUR PROGRAMS

Ensuring that our ideas are implemented faithfully requires collaboration with practitioners—observing and addressing the issues that arise, as they try to make our ideas work. The greater our insight, the more it may lose in the translation, as practitioners struggle to understand and implement our novel concepts (see Ralph Keeney's chapter in this book). Such a curse of insight can mean that the more we impress our colleagues, the harder it will be for practitioners to grasp our big ideas.

In addition to consuming our time and energies, such collaborations can cause discomfort, as practitioners assume ownership of our programs. Those practitioners may be enthusiasts, wanting to add their private stamp to our work, or they may be skeptics, stuck with our programs. Practitioners may need to make changes in our programs for change's sake, in order to demonstrate their value to their organization. They may misunderstand our concepts, and inadvertently distort them. They may add vital elements that never occurred to us. They may just let our programs die, convinced that their organization wasn't committed to them anyway. As these processes evolve, we will need to decide whether to assert or disclaim ownership, for programs that aren't quite what we had in mind.

REINVENTING OUR INSTITUTIONS

I once heard the president of a Pittsburgh foundation say, "When historians look back at our era, they will wonder why our universities were so little engaged with the problems surrounding them." Many contributors to this book have led in creating exceptions to that rule. For such exceptions to be sustainable, however, public service must be more than just an indulgence for tenured faculty.

Sustainable public service should be more likely when

1. We demonstrate that applications spawn interesting basic research, revealing new phenomena that complement ones that arise endogenously from normal disciplinary science. For that to happen, we must create research designs that domesticate these new phenomena, so that they can be studied by our colleagues who are more comfortable with normal science.
2. We change the currency of our disciplines, so that they accept the unconventional methods, collaborations, and products that applications require. For that to happen, we need to make the case that such work is unusually difficult—and not a refuge for those without the taste or talent for basic research.
3. We get our best students to pursue applications, for the intellectual challenge that they bring (and not for consulting fees or political influence). For that to happen, we need to get students with these tastes admitted to our programs, then effectively employed.

Sustainable change is likely to be maddeningly slow. People don't change their work patterns very quickly. Arguably, they shouldn't try, lest they lose the internal checks and balances that their disciplines have taught them. That is all the more reason for encouraging the kind of sustained, self-critical innovation that Howard Kunreuther has practiced throughout his career.

CHANGING THE TALK—AND PERHAPS THE WALK

Whereas changing how the world works might be our aspiration, our success depends on forces beyond our control, including organizational and electoral politics. Changing how the world talks, however, might be within our grasp, if we make our research accessible to people who might use its results. Communicating with nonspecialists requires listening, so that we provide relevant work in comprehensible terms. It may also require reining in our own natural enthusiasm. Outsiders have little way of knowing either the controversies within our disciplines or the assumptions that their members share. Unless we reveal our internal discourse, we may instill undue confidence in those who listen to us—or paralyze those who observe the confident, conflicting claims of different scientists.

Social scientists are often asked for sweeping generalizations about human behavior. Sometimes, they can provide them (e.g., "People rarely panic, unless in confined spaces with limited egress and strong time pressure"). Often, though, behavior depends on the interactions of multiple processes (e.g., "Whether people prepare for disasters depends on their resources, their access to relevant information, their trust in information providers, their ability to act, their dependence on others, their need to support others, their culture"). In such cases, simple answers, with universal application, are necessarily misleading ones, as are policies based on them.

As a result, our communications succeed when they encourage more thoughtful, respectful, informed discourse about the challenges to effective decision making. That means fostering a realization that people have both strengths and weaknesses; that intuitive choices are sometimes good enough, while informed ones are sometimes inadequate; that we need evidence, not just assertion; and that people differ in their intellectual and material resources.

THE SCIENCE AND PRACTICE OF DECISION MAKING

A distinctive feature of our science is that it considers both the decisions that people face and the resources that they bring to them. Our science also considers people and their decisions in terms that reveal how sensitive choices are to human frailties and to where help is most needed. Those comparisons embody the tension between economics, whose view of human performance can be unduly bright, and psychology, whose view can be unduly dour. Because disciplinary writing contains so many implicit assumptions, realizing the value of that tension requires more than just having economists and psychologists read one another's work. Rather, it requires communicating directly and working together.

Much of our joint success would not have happened without Howard Kunreuther's ability to convene people in ways that allowed them to learn from one another. One secret to his success has been his recognition that poor decisions are a sign that life is complicated, not that people are hopeless. Among the many meanings of irrational, his embodies a faith that people can make better decisions, given proper support, and a deep commitment to providing it. Expecting early, easy returns on this investment would be irrational.

RECOMMENDED READING

Fischhoff, B. (1992). "Giving Advice: Decision Theory Perspectives on Sexual Assault." *American Psychologist* 47: 577–588.

Fischhoff, B. (2005). "Cognitive Processes in Stated Preference Methods." In K.-G. Mäler and J. Vincent, eds. *Handbook of Environmental Economics*. Amsterdam: Elsevier.

Fischhoff, B. (2009). "Risk Perception and Communication." In R. Detels, R. Beaglehole, M. A. Lansang, and M. Gulliford, eds. *Oxford Textbook of Public Health*, 5th ed. Oxford: Oxford University Press.

Fischhoff, B. (2007). "Non-Persuasive Communication About Matters of Greatest Urgency: Climate Change." *Environmental Science & Technology* 41: 7204–7208.

Fischhoff, B. (2008). "Assessing Adolescent Decision-Making Competence." *Developmental Review* 28: 12–28.

27 Thinking Clearly About Policy Decisions

The Importance of Training Policy Makers in Decision Sciences

RALPH L. KEENEY

INTRODUCTION

I believe the following: Since a large majority of the individuals involved in the policy-making process have had no education or training in the decision sciences, they do not possess the fundamental knowledge necessary for clear thinking about policy decisions.

What fundamental knowledge and which individuals are being referred to in this claim? The simple answers are, respectively, the knowledge of decision sciences concepts and everyone involved in the policy-making process.

To answer the knowledge question thoroughly and to support my belief, it is essential to recognize why policy decisions are complex. The reasons are that in policy decisions the achievement of multiple objectives must be balanced, large uncertainties are relevant, multiple parties are involved, and often the scientific, economic, and political substance is sophisticated.

Thinking clearly about the substance of policy decisions requires a knowledge of how to specify the full set of objectives, ask the right questions, identify useful information, balance the pros and cons of the proposed alternatives, and communicate about all of this. To do this well, one needs a thorough understanding of numerous concepts that have been well developed in the decision sciences, which here include aspects of economics, behavioral decision theory, and decision analysis. These concepts concern the elements of decisions, such as objectives, alternatives, uncertainty, and value tradeoffs; the way people process information and knowledge, such as anchoring, satisficing, and ambiguity; and features relevant to many policy decisions, such as compounding, cause-effect relationships, sunk costs, and the amplification of risks.

In a democratic society, citizens must think clearly about policy decisions in order to provide useful input to the policy-making process. Also, numerous technical, professional, and managerial personnel in government agencies and legislative bodies have responsibilities for the clear thinking that is required for policy decisions. The results of their thinking are passed on to agency heads and legislators to frame the policy decisions, to define alternative choices, and to provide information about the pros and cons of those choices.

This chapter describes some simple experiments and experiences with well-educated individuals that reveal a lack of understanding of critical decision sciences concepts and the subsequent impacts on policy decision making. These individuals either influence policy or have an education representative of those who do so. The concepts discussed are illustrative of numerous other concepts that are likely not known or well understood. Since the book is about making better decisions in a complex world, I will use examples of policy decisions in a risky environment.

ARTICULATING AND UNDERSTANDING VALUE JUDGMENTS

Values are absolutely essential to policy decisions. If we do not have any values relevant to a decision, then we should not care about it and of course we should not spend any time thinking about it.

Over the last few decades while consulting on numerous policy decisions, such as siting a nuclear waste repository or setting a national ambient air quality standard, I have noticed that individuals responsible for recommending choices or making decisions cannot articulate all of their relevant objectives. In a series of recent experiments with colleagues at the Duke Business School designed to investigate whether people can identify objectives for problems of importance to themselves, my colleagues and I found that individuals typically can identify only about half of their objectives and the ones they miss are as important to them as those they identify.[1]

In one study we asked doctoral students the following question: "Suppose you have identified five potential dissertation topics and now have to choose one of them; list all objectives that are relevant for your selection." After they'd given their responses, we showed them a complete list from which they could check all the objectives that mattered to them. Comparing their original lists of objectives and those later checked, we found that a majority of the twenty-three participants missed many significant objectives. The missing objectives often included the following: "helps me build a coherent future research program," "helps me balance my career and personal life," and "addresses problems that are important." All of the students who recognized these objectives only after viewing the master list subsequently indicated that they were relatively very important.

In the early 1980s, I took part in programs intended to educate members of the media (e.g., television networks, newspapers) about various aspects of environmental and health and safety risks. To prepare participants prior to my talk, I developed a short questionnaire. One question asked: "In considering the clean-up of old hazardous waste sites, rank the following in order of importance: economic cost of the clean-up, potential human life lost or sickness due to the hazard, and potential damage to the natural environment." All of the approximately 100 respondents ranked economic costs as least important, and every respondent but one had potential human life lost or sickness as most important. In a subsequent discussion, very few of these individuals seemed to think that it would be worth a $2 billion increase in clean-up costs to avoid 20 people being sick for a week and then recovering completely. The point is that it is essentially meaningless to prioritize objectives without understanding how much of each of the objectives ($2 billion and 20 one-week illnesses) they are prioritizing.

One of the earlier questions in the same questionnaire asked: "In evaluating risks to lives of the public, judgments should or should not be made about the relative importance of the lives of different individuals?" The large majority of the respondents replied "should not." A later question asked: "Do you agree or not that in allocating government funds to reduce risks to citizens, the saving of the life of any individual should be counted equally?" In this case, almost all participants responded that they "agree." I pointed out that counting the lives of individuals equally was a value judgment and that the responses on these two questions conflicted. This caused some consternation. Then I asked about the relative evaluation of saving children versus the elderly. Most people preferred saving children, which also conflicted with their "agree" response to the question. Many participants became somewhat

disturbed, as they recognized that value judgments about the relative importance of saving the lives of different members of the public are essential to
health and safety policy decisions.

Another question asked: "If it were known for sure that an improvement in
the maintenance of air pollution control equipment on coal-fired power plants
would save two expected lives a year, what is the maximum dollar amount that
should be expended for this maintenance?" Possible responses were "$100k,"
"$1million," "$10 million," "$100 million," and "whatever it costs." The re-
sponses were rather evenly spread across these options. Many people, including
many involved in setting policy, do not understand that value tradeoffs between
economic costs and expected fatalities are an inherent part of numerous policy
decisions, nor do they seem to understand that spending $100 million to save
lives in one arena means that this money cannot be spent for other purposes including possibly avoiding many more potential fatalities elsewhere.

UNDERSTANDING THE STRUCTURE OF POLICY DECISIONS

In 1987, I gave a two-hour presentation on probabilities as part of a two-day
workshop for earth sciences professionals at the University of California. Preceding my presentation, I asked all eighty-one participants to fill out a questionnaire that asked the following: "Is it true or false that there is a reasonable
chance of a moderate to large earthquake in the San Francisco Bay area in the
near future?" Then I asked for separate definitions of reasonable chance, moderate to large earthquake, San Francisco Bay Area, and near future. I perused
the results and was able to begin my presentation as follows.

You are in complete agreement on the main question: Everyone indicated
that the statement was true. However, there were significant discrepancies
among the definitions. A reasonable chance ranged from 5 to 92 percent.
Does the term moderate to large earthquake include very large earthquakes? About half of you thought so and the other half didn't. Some defined this as a Richter magnitude in the range 5–6 and others had a
magnitude from 7.5 and above. The difference between the magnitudes of
these earthquakes is 100-fold. The San Francisco Bay Area was defined as
within 5 miles of downtown San Francisco at one extreme and over 140
miles in all directions on any of fourteen different fault zones at the other

extreme. And as everyone knows, the near future ranges from 3 weeks to 100,000 years.

A related situation occurred in the early 1990s, during a discussion of the potential risks associated with the Ghost Dance Fault that crosses through the designated nuclear repository site at Yucca Mountain in Nevada. I was working with a select group of seven seismologists who were the world's experts on that fault; they were also familiar with probability assessment. A key issue was whether the fault was active. I said to them, "Without communication with each other, write down your judgment of the probability that the fault is active." Then, before any discussion, I asked each to write down the definition of active, which is one of the most basic words in earthquake science. Everyone was surprised when we got six different definitions. Some of these referred to what happened on the fault in the past, others concerned what might possibly happen in the future, and still others concerned what would definitely happen in the future.

One of the seismologists then suggested that it would be interesting if they each wrote down their definition of the Ghost Dance Fault. Upon reviewing the definitions, we were astounded to find that we had two Ghost Dance Faults. The problem stemmed from the fact that a north-south fault segment ran from north of the repository southward through the repository to where it was covered up by a large landslide several thousand years old. There was also a smaller fault segment that ran under that landslide from the southwest. It turned out that some of the seismologists thought both segments were part of the same fault, which they referred to as the Ghost Dance Fault. Others felt that the Ghost Dance Fault was only the larger north-south segment. Clarifying that there were different definitions of the Ghost Dance Fault greatly facilitated our communication about the possible likelihood and magnitude of any earthquake on the fault.

The point of all these examples is that characterizing a policy decision using only general terminology is ineffective and can even be misleading. Yet the exclusive use of such general terms is often how policy issues are discussed. The decision sciences fields have long known that carefully defining terms and quantifying likelihoods clarify the meanings of qualitative terms and reduce ambiguity in many situations. This knowledge would be useful in the policy arena as well.

ASSESSING, UNDERSTANDING, AND COMMUNICATING ABOUT UNCERTAINTY

The problem of interpreting and manipulating probabilistic information is complex and likely the source of important misinterpretations on major policy problems. The following two examples give support for this assertion.

In 1988, I was a member of a working group sponsored by the U.S. Geological Service to specify probabilities of major earthquakes occurring on segments of various California faults. The other eleven members of the committee had substantial experience with and knowledge about California earthquakes. My role was to help them come up with internally consistent sets of probabilistic estimates. A major earthquake was defined as a Richter magnitude 6.5 or greater. Five segments were defined on the two major faults in the San Francisco area, namely the San Andreas Fault and the Hayward Fault. A 45-kilometer length of the San Andreas Fault was called the Loma Prieta segment. In the course of several meetings, the probability that a major earthquake would occur over the next thirty years was assessed as 0.3 for the Loma Prieta segment and as 0.2 separately for each of the other four segments. On October 17, 1989, a magnitude 7.1 earthquake on the Loma Prieta segment occurred, leading to significant damage and to sixty-two deaths in the San Francisco area.

About a month after the earthquake, some seismologists affiliated with the working group published an article in the prestigious journal *Science* that included the following statements: The earthquake "fulfilled a long-term forecast," "two decades of research . . . allowed an accurate long-term forecast of both the occurrence and consequences" of the earthquake, and the earthquake occurred "where it was anticipated." Obviously there were significant misunderstandings about the meaning of probabilities and their validation. First, the earthquake was less likely to occur (probability 0.3) than not (which therefore had a probability of 0.7) in the next thirty years on the Loma Prieta segment, so how did this earthquake fulfill a long-term forecast? Second, if an earthquake occurred in the San Francisco area, it was more likely to occur on one of the other four segments, so why did this earthquake occur where it was anticipated? The quality of probabilistic forecasts is a complex concept and accuracy cannot be determined from a single event.

Interpreting probabilities even when there is a significant amount of data is often perplexing. A couple of years ago at a military academy, in a questionnaire prior to a seminar, I asked the following: "Suppose a rare medical condition is present in 1 of 1,000 adults, but until recently there was no way to check whether you have the condition. However, a recently developed test to check for the condition is 99 percent accurate. You decide to take the test and the result is positive, indicating that the condition is present. What is your judgment of the chance, in percent, that you have the condition?" Almost half of the more than 300 respondents thought the chance they had the disease was 99 percent, approximately a quarter had an answer between 3 percent and 15 percent, and the remaining quarter were spread thinly over the entire range from 0 to 95 percent. The correct answer is "9 percent," which is almost shocking to many people.

The logic can be explained in simple terms as follows. Suppose there are 1,000 random adults who are to be tested. On average, we would expect only 1 of these adults to have the disease and the test for that individual would almost surely be positive. This gives us 1 positive test. Also, we would expect 999 adults not to have the disease. With an error rate of 1 percent, we would expect essentially 10 of these individuals to have a positive test result. Thus, for the 1,000 individuals, we would expect an average of 11 positive tests, only 1 of which was for an individual with the rare medical condition. Thus, only 1 of 11—or 9 percent—of those with the positive test result really have the rare medical condition. Research in the decision sciences has frequently shown that individuals' intuitions in probabilistic situations are far from accurate.

THE AMPLIFICATION OF RISK

The social amplification of risk is another concept relevant to numerous public policy decisions. Eight years prior to the introduction of the social amplification of risk framework in 1988, I conceptualized an amplification model, without using the word amplification. The model separated the direct personal impacts of fatalities due to a specific cause and the induced indirect societal impact of those fatalities. Then, I constructed a value model and did assessments to preliminarily examine the importance of such amplification. Specifically, this model was developed for government agencies that have responsibility for public safety.

In conceptualizing the model, I stated that "there should be two major governmental concerns regarding impact of fatalities on the public. The first reflects the direct personal impacts of pain, suffering, and economic hardship. These fall most heavily on a very small percent of the total public, those individuals who are the fatalities and their friends and relatives. The second concern involves indirect societal impacts, which include general political, social, and economic turmoil which may occur as a result of the fatalities." Furthermore, I then added: "Formalization of the distinction between personal and societal impacts is appropriate for major problems, such as the public risks from power plant accidents."

The value model separately included personal direct impacts and societal indirect impacts, and the contributors to each of those were differentiated as to whether they pertained to public or worker fatalities. One parameter in the model indicated the relative importance given to the indirect societal impact of the first public fatality compared to the direct personal impact of that fatality. In subsequent assessments of that parameter for decisions that involved the possible misuse of stolen nuclear material with four knowledgeable individuals at Lawrence Livermore Laboratory, the relative importance given to that indirect societal impact versus the direct personal impact was 10, 27, 45, and 118, respectively.

Three aspects of this model and the accompanying assessments are pertinent to policy making. The first is that the model made a clear distinction between the direct personal impacts of fatalities and the indirect societal impacts they induced in important policy areas. Second, it built an explicit value model that allowed one to incorporate these different impacts and keep them distinct from each other. Third, the assessments demonstrated that the societal impact seemed significant at least to a few people who thought hard about the situation.

EDUCATING POLICY MAKERS ABOUT DECISION SCIENCES CONCEPTS

In many government agencies and legislatures, a high proportion of staff and managers influence policy in some way. I believe that a major shortcoming that undermines quality policy making is that many policy makers do not understand many of the concepts relevant to the complex decisions facing them.

The solution, therefore, is to provide focused education and training in decision sciences concepts. The education component might be composed of two courses: a basic course on the fundamental concepts of the decision sciences, with numerous policy examples, and an advanced course on specific concepts in depth. The former course would be for everyone, providing thoughts and information for policy choices, and the latter course would be for decision makers who make or recommend specific policy choices. The courses should be developed with video presentations on the Internet, supported by a central staff for operation of the programs nationwide. The training component should be done in modules developed to be relevant to individual decision makers' responsibilities in order to facilitate the use and application of the learned decision sciences concepts on policy problems. Development of these programs would include identifying the key decision sciences concepts useful for policy analysis. Testing of the educational products would be essential for improvement before opening the program to all who may benefit. Additional adjustments to the programs over time would be partially guided by their contributions to the overall objective—namely, to contribute to better-informed policy decisions and, ultimately, to better policy decisions.

RECOMMENDED READING

Bond, S. D., K. A. Carlson, and R. L. Keeney (2008). "Generating Objectives: Can Decision Makers Articulate What They Want?" *Management Science* 54: 56–70.

Hammond, J.S., R.L. Keeney, and H. Raiffa (1999). *Smart Choices: A Practical Guide to Making Better Decisions.* Cambridge, MA: Harvard University Press.

Kasperson, R. E., O. Renn, P. Slovic, H. S. Brown, J. Emel, R. Goble, J. X. Kasperson, and S. Ratick (1988). "The Social Amplification of Risk: A Conceptual Framework." *Risk Analysis* 8: 177–187.

Keeney, R. L. (1980). "Evaluating Alternatives Involving Potential Fatalities." *Operations Research* 28: 188–205.

U.S. Geological Survey Staff (1990). "The Loma Prieta California Earthquake: An Anticipated Event." *Science* 247: 286–293.

28 Decision Making
A View on Tomorrow

HOWARD RAIFFA

A WIDER SCOPE FOR THE DECISION SCIENCES

When I began studying decision making some sixty years ago, I was mainly oriented toward the ways that analytics can help the decision-making process. As the field has grown, I am now seeing other areas coming more and more into the decision sciences.

For example, the evolution of the study of decision sciences has embraced the area of negotiations, and I am pleased to see that. As the world is becoming more complex, we now grapple with decisions with multiple conflicting objectives. In a sense this area of study is not new, but on the other hand it was not featured in the 1960s and 1970s. And the work of Howard Kunreuther and Paul Slovic and others helped to establish it as a branch of the decision sciences.

Likewise, "organization theory," the design of organizations, overlaps with the decision sciences, broadly interpreted. There is also the practical matter of how people will design the processes of decision making in the future. Setting up constitutions is a good example.

Let's suppose we were setting up a new nation-state and we had to worry about how to decide what to do, and about the process of deciding collectively. We might set up in our constitution schemes that would facilitate and also inhibit certain decisions to be taken in the future. For example, our constitution might make provisions for various commissions; in addition, we might establish a minimum necessary number or percentage of votes, for new laws to be enacted. These are ways of resolving problems in the future, which I think belong in the domain of decision sciences. However, in order to successfully negotiate the constitution, people in charge of these negotiations would have to be trained in decision sciences and be able to use this training purposefully. To ensure successful negotiations, you need to know not only who the key interested parties are but also what their short-term and long-term objectives are. Ideally you also need to know how the other parties process the information you might give them.

Unfortunately, most people who do negotiations do not think of them as constructive joint problem solving—although this is what they are—and we need to look at them in this way. I think that, in the future, negotiations will be thought of as a form of collaborative decision making. The mediator, the arbiter, the conciliator—all play important roles in decision making. I find it troubling that there are books on decision making being published that don't address the idea of arbitration or mediation. That has to change. I would like to see an expository book written covering decision sciences' broadest details, with sections on organization theory and political science, including how to write and negotiate constitutions, with a heavy emphasis on multiple conflicting attributes.

SOME OF MY DISAPPOINTMENTS

I'm very proud of my role in the development of our field of decision analysis, but here are a few of my disappointments:

1 I sometimes wonder whether, over the years, decision analysis and the decision sciences have played an important enough role in public affairs, business affairs, and foreign affairs. I think more use should have been made of the qualitative as opposed to the quantitative aspects of decision science theory. There should also have been more documented debates using decision trees without numbers—that is, without probabilities and utilities. I should have documented the occasional verbal accounts of some of my former students who reported the role of the qualitative decision diagram in structuring the debate of certain ticklish issues within the firms they worked for after leaving Harvard.

2. There is a vigorous, ongoing debate among statisticians about the appropriateness of using judgmental probabilities in statistical analyses of

experimental studies. I am a strong member of the Bayesian camp who argues that those on the opposing side—the classicists in their quest for objectivity—often distort the real decision problem. The classicists report probabilistically about X, because they know how to do this without resorting to judgmental probabilities, instead of reporting about Y, which is more relevant to the decision problem under review but involves judgmentally based probabilities. I get especially perturbed when descriptively motivated decision analysts use the classical paradigm in reporting experimental results about how their subjects behave.

3. I'm disappointed that I didn't co-write *Smart Choices*, with Ralph Keeney and John Hammond, thirty years before we did in 1999, because it features the certainty case of decision, which logically should have preceded the uncertainty case featured so prominently in my other books. Decision analysis started in the 1960s and 1970s, concentrating on problems with uncertainties and probabilities, rather than on problems with multiple conflicting objectives, which could have kept us occupied in the early days of the field's development. Looking at what we wanted for a choice of a career, for example, was not really the central problem of decision analysis as it developed in the last quarter of the twentieth century.

THE INTERDEPENDENCY OF SURPRISE BAD OUTCOMES

This issue of decision frameworks strongly affects public policy and the business world. I do not think that policy makers in Washington, D.C., and elsewhere in the world are sufficiently trained in the decision sciences. Moreover, the field itself is not used enough in terms of discourse, in terms of structuring arguments.

The financial crisis of 2008–2009 is a good illustration. I think what happened is that a lot of people were making financial decisions based on classical utility theory, looking at individual attitudes toward risk, and acting accordingly. But they didn't bring into their analysis an awareness that if there is a surprise on the lower end in one problem, there may be a causal relationship with having a surprise at the lower end in other problems. The problems themselves are treated independently, but they are really dependent. Having a bad outcome in one makes it more likely that you are going to have a bad outcome in another. When the problems are analyzed, they are analyzed as completely independent. I think the interdependency of surprise bad outcomes is something that has to be studied much more, as highlighted by Erwann Michel-Kerjan in his chapter in this book.

A PARADIGM SHIFT FOR ACADEMICS: FROM PROBLEM SOLVERS TO PROBLEM INVENTORS

I myself have not kept up enough with the details of different financial instruments to be able to judge what the responsibility of the decision sciences could have been in averting some of the dilemmas surrounding this recent financial crisis. But whether one considers international negotiations, financial crises, or the management of global risks more generally, I would contend that the way decision analysts have approached these issues could be much improved.

Usually, decision analysts address the problems that are given to them and they have to try to solve them. But much more fundamentally, the analysts, instead of being just problem solvers, should also be problem inventors. They need to make the pie bigger—it is too restrictive in terms of the things that decision analysts are called upon to do. They also have to become much more proactive in the choice of problems that they work on. To solve the as-yet-unforeseen problems of the world they must become problem envisioners. For example, we could have researchers looking at what could happen in the Middle East twenty-five to thirty years from now. What if we had an institution in Crete, Cyprus, or Malta, where researchers from the Middle East could come together to think inventively about how they might collaborate and cooperate to overcome certain problems?

Today's resolutions of international disputes will determine how and when future problems will be negotiated. The lure of potential joint gains from future negotiations should be reflected in the Pareto frontiers of the negotiation problems of today. If some countries are having difficulties resolving their current differences, perhaps they should speculate about the gains coming from future negotiations, if only today's disputes could be collaboratively resolved. So much in the world needs fixing that it is incumbent on today's negotiators to keep in mind that present negotiators are often the gatekeepers for later collaborative negotiations. This strategic "super game" is an awesome responsibility, and analysts must be able to play a productive role in it.

I feel strongly that there is a role for international decision sciences organizations here. There is so much wrong with the world that could be improved if contending groups got together in a collegial way to try to figure out how to get joint gains. This has to done in an experimental situation, where people, as a matter of course, would take a look at the world and say what's wrong and how it might be resolved. This could be accomplished by bringing researchers from different countries to work informally together to map out potential solutions.

An example is the remarkable speech President Lyndon Johnson gave in 1966 in which he called for the scientists of the United States and the Soviet Union to work together on issues other than military and space matters—issues that plagued all advanced societies such as energy, environment, and health. From 1967 to 1972, I was a member of the U.S. team that negotiated with the Soviet Union and six other countries, both East and West, in establishing the International Institute for Applied Systems Analysis (IIASA) in Laxenburg, near Vienna in Austria. The negotiation took place during the height of the Cold War and was a confidence-building gesture. I learned a lot about the theory and practice of many-party negotiations in the presence of extreme cultural differences.

When I served as the first director of IIASA, in 1972–1975, I had that very vision in mind: to bring together distinguished scholars to work on some of the toughest issues confronting the world and to challenge them to think about what new problems the world could be facing twenty years later. We did so by maintaining the importance of neutrality in our work. It is no surprise to me that IIASA is still involved in pressing global negotiations today, climate negotiations and natural disaster management being two of them.

It would be nice if (independent of political processes) there were many more international research centers like IIASA where people would discuss not the decision problems that exist today, or what the world should be like today, but rather what we should be worrying about in the future—say, over the next twenty to twenty-five years. Just imagine what could be accomplished if only people thought about this hard enough.

A FINAL WORD, TO THE NEW GENERATION

If I had one recommendation for the next generation, it is that I would like them to be much more proactive in the choice of their own careers. And when it comes to making decisions in a dangerous world, I would hope that they will conceive of new possibilities that are not being currently pursued. Aspire to be true innovators!

RECOMMENDED READING

Hammond, John S., Ralph L. Keeney, and Howard Raiffa (1999). *Smart Choices: A Practical Guide to Making Better Decisions*. Boston: Harvard Business School Press.

Raiffa, Howard (1992). "How IIASA Began" (http://www.iiasa.ac.at/docs/history .html).

Raiffa, Howard (2002). *The Art of Science and Negotiations: How to Resolve Conflicts and Get the Best Out of Bargaining*. Cambridge, MA: Harvard University Press.

29 Influential Social Science, Risks, and Disasters
A View from the National Science Foundation

ROBERT E. O'CONNOR AND DENNIS E. WENGER

Although there is no shortage of grousing among social scientists who think that policy makers ignore their work, there is much evidence that the findings of social scientists continue to inform policy decisions in significant ways.[1] In this chapter we discuss the influence of social scientists in informing policy makers and ultimately helping to improve public policy.

Following a broad-brush discussion of scientific knowledge and public policy, we describe the particular evolution of research undertaken in the United States involving risk management and disasters. Finally, we comment on the changing role of the National Science Foundation (NSF) in supporting social science research.

ARE ACADEMIC SOCIAL SCIENTISTS MAKING A DIFFERENCE?

In a sense we would like to continue the discussion that Baruch Fischhoff and Ralph Keeney opened in their chapters. Studies of the policy process frequently conclude that social scientists have had significant impact on policy. Broadly over time, in many areas, one can trace drastic policy changes to their scientific origins even in domains of social relations that would not seem amenable to the influence of scientific knowledge.

One example concerns attitudes and policies toward race in America. When the science changed, elite opinion changed, followed by mass opinion. Then, over time, policy changed as well. As late as the early 1920s, the consensus among scientists supported theories of racial superiority. By the late

1920s, however, scientists began to question biological theories of racial superiority so that by the 1950s a consensus among social scientists had emerged that white supremacists suffered from mental disorders or educational deficiencies. The elite media changed to match the scientific consensus, followed by mass opinion. Congress would never have enacted the Civil Rights Act of 1964 and the Voting Rights Act of 1965 if the scientific discourse on race had remained in its 1920s mode of racial superiority.

Another example is the domain of sexual orientation. In 1973 the American Psychiatric Association removed homosexuality from its list of mental disorders. Changes in media discourse, public opinion, and public policy followed. The drastic departure from viewing homosexuality as a disease probably began with the research of Alfred Kinsey in the 1940s. Kinsey's finding that almost half of the adult male population had experienced at least one homosexual encounter implicitly called into question the consensus view that all homosexuals were psychopathic. What changed the scientific consensus, however, was the seminal research of Evelyn Hooker at the University of California at Los Angeles in the 1950s. Using conventional psychological tests, Hooker compared a sample of gay men with a matched sample of straight men. She found no significant differences in personal adjustment and other psychometric measures. When Hooker and others replicated this research, they consistently found few differences. Over time, this new consensus made its way into elite and media discourses. Public opinion changed and new policies emerged.

These two examples of social science leading to policy changes involve mass publics and issues that, for many, engender strong emotions and opinions. Scientific research, however, frequently influences decisions in policy domains that are less emotional. Almost all popular models of policy formation and change find that, most of the time, policy change is slight and incremental, because the distribution and relative power of interest groups are stable. In other words, policy changes only slightly because interest group realities also change only slightly. But new scientific knowledge can produce policy change even during stable political periods. The policy models point to scientific findings as one frequent source of policy change. Often through the work of scientists informing legislative staff and agency administrators, major policy changes can happen with little public arousal.

An example of a major policy change that emerged from scientific findings is passage of the Resource Conservation and Recovery Act (RCRA) of 1976, which established national cradle-to-grave requirements for the management and disposal of hazardous and toxic wastes. At the time, there was no public clamor for action. (The well-publicized Love Canal waste exposure event occurred in 1978 and the Superfund clean-up law was passed in 1980, after RCRA had passed.) Why, then, did Congress pass legislation that, although favored by environmental groups, cost manufacturers large sums of money? One important reason is that since World War II scientists in the biological and geological sciences as well as engineers had produced a compelling literature concerning the dangers of industrial waste and its links with groundwater contamination. Economists and other social scientists had demonstrated that the incentive structures for firms were dysfunctional for society and that reliance on state regulations would not work without national minimal standards. Congress passed the nation's framework legislation for waste management in response not to a mass movement but to concerns expressed by scientists and engineers.

As all three of these cases demonstrate, policy responses to scientific findings are often slow, thus possibly accounting for the disdain that some scientists have toward policy makers. In certain instances, however, a response to findings has not taken decades. An example is the consensus among political scientists that touch-screen voting systems without a paper trail are a bad idea. Studies found that touch-screen-only systems were susceptible to sophisticated computer hackers and that, with no backup paper trail available, officials would be unable either to confirm or reject charges of irregularities.[2] Most states initially ignored this research, which was published after the contested 2000 national election. By the end of the decade, however, most states, including California and Florida, had moved away from touch-screen, no-paper-trail systems.

RISK MANAGEMENT AND DISASTER RESEARCH

Before discussing the policy impacts of risk management and disaster research, we should make a few comments about these two disparate, though inherently related, research fields. Disaster research is a post–World War II phenomenon that was fostered in part in the United States by the Cold War and concerns about nuclear catastrophe. Research first began in geography and sociology at the University of Chicago, although the focus of this research differed dramatically across the two disciplines. Geographers, under the leadership of Gilbert White, focused on issues involving human adaptation to natural phenomena, particularly floods. Sociologists, under the leadership of the Disaster Research Center at Ohio State University and subsequently at the University of Delaware studied individual, organizational, and community responses during the pre-impact, trans-impact, and immediate post-impact periods of disasters. They focused upon things that blew up. These two camps never spoke, let alone collaborated. By the 1960s a modicum of research existed, although the accumulated body of rigorous social science research on hazards and disasters could be held on a few shelves of a modest bookcase.

The risk management field in the social science domain—separate from disaster research—emerged strongly in the 1970s. The field included psychologists who studied judgment and decision making as well as behavioral economists and numerous other social scientists interested in risk communications, perceptions, and management. The "risk management" people have different journals and go to different conferences than the "disaster" people. More than anyone else in the country, Howard Kunreuther has tried to bridge these two communities through his writings on mitigation and insurance, his leadership in the two research communities, and his analysis of multiple risks and disasters, including terrorism.

DISASTER RESEARCH AND PUBLIC POLICY ON MITIGATION AND RECOVERY

The disaster research field has changed in the past forty years. Almost all of the research undertaken can be categorized as involving one of the four phases of the "disaster cycle," namely mitigation of, preparedness for, response to, and recovery from disasters. The field began with a narrow focus—emergency preparedness and response. Throughout the 1960s and 1970s, research still tended to focus on emergency planning, public warnings, population protection, search and rescue, the delivery of emergency medicine, restoration of critical infrastructure, and provision of food, clothing, and shelter. These concerns were inherently related to the dominant policy issues of that era—issues that, in turn, were still influenced by notions of "civil defense." Federal authority for disaster response was spread among more than two dozen agencies. It was not until 1978 that the Federal Emergency Management Agency (FEMA) was created. Prior to this, the primary emphasis at the federal level was on war preparation and nuclear attacks.

Under the influence of economists during the 1980s, urban planners, geographers, psychologists, sociologists, and policy analysts shifted the focus of research to disaster mitigation and recovery. These two areas illustrate both the impact of research on the formulation of mitigation policy and the emerging policy on disaster recovery that is being stimulated by research.

Since then, research has focused on the adoption of both structural and nonstructural mitigation measures by individuals, organizations, communities, and societies. The purpose of mitigation is to implement actions that lessen the likelihood that natural and technological hazards will produce disasters. We will always have hurricanes, for example, but smart actions can reduce their effects on humans and property. Structural mitigation measures include improved building codes, the design of more resilient structures, and physical protection works such as dams and levees. Nonstructural measures include local land-use planning mechanisms, coastal management programs, and augmentation of local capacity and resilience.

Research findings accumulated at an increasing rate over the years, indicating that mitigation was important not only in terms of saving lives and property but also as a strategy for creating more resilient and sustainable communities. Research on the benefits and costs associated with structural and nonstructural measures demonstrated the feasibility of putting in place effective measures that would ensure that the reduction in expected losses would be greater than the cost of such measures. The key to mitigation adoption is strong local capacity that can overcome the barriers of poverty, a lack of resources accessible to governments, competing opposition groups, and the low-probability, high-consequence nature of disaster agents. The 1999 publication of *Disasters by Design: A Reassessment of Natural Hazards in the United States* by Dennis Mileti captured the meaning and importance of such research.

In a process most effectively captured by the Advocacy Coalition Framework, this research attracted "policy entrepreneurs" and champions of mitigation policy. Interest in mitigation stimulated activities ranging from international World Bank actions to FEMA's national Project Impact program (encouraging local disaster mitigation planning) to state and local, public and private initiatives. Consistent with these activities that grew out of research, Congress passed the Disaster Mitigation Act of 2000, which facilitated mitigation planning through a collection of incentives and penalties for compliance and noncompliance. The Act mandated the development of state and local hazard mitigation plans as a precondition for receiving federal pre- and post-disaster mitigation funding, leading to thousands of mitigation plans across the country.

Research on disaster recovery has exploded over the past thirty years as well. The initial research viewed recovery as a straightforward, value-added process that focused on reconstructing and rebuilding communities. Subsequent research discovered that this characterization was suspect. Indeed, community recovery from disasters was found to be a messy, *ad hoc*, serendipitous process of indeterminate length and outcome. As research progressed over the decades, investigators began to focus on the recovery experiences of different social groups and classes; among the most dramatic findings along these lines were those displayed in studies of the recovery from Hurricane Katrina in 2005. The central thrust of recovery research over the past decade, including Katrina research, has been to link disaster recovery to mitigation and sustainability.

The impact of this recovery research, including studies of the National Flood Insurance Program, on public policy has been less dramatic than was the case for mitigation. Legislative proposals have been slower to develop, perhaps due to the smaller number of advocates and the difficulties involved in planning for low-probability, high-consequence events. Nevertheless, the research has stimulated some policy changes, particularly at the state level. A handful of states, such as California and Florida, now require that local communities develop pre-disaster recovery plans for future disasters. Although research into the effectiveness of these planning efforts is now under way, long-term analyses of their impact upon recovery from major disasters have yet to be done.

We still do not have a Disaster Recovery Act that is similar in scope to the Disaster Mitigation Act of 2000. Research on hazard and disaster policy has shown that nonincremental policy change requires both research and "agenda-setting" events. Major extreme events, such as Hurricane Andrew in 1992 and the terrorist attacks of September 11, 2001, can become

precipitating events for policy change. The research base for a Disaster Recovery Act has been undertaken and is present and available. Perhaps the
ongoing recovery efforts following Hurricane Katrina will serve to stimulate
policy innovation. Otherwise, as Erwann Michel-Kerjan and Paul Slovic indicate in the Introduction to this book, disaster recovery may be one of the
cases where political leaders tend to react only to crisis. So it may take another series of major natural disasters for Congress and other top decision
makers to act upon this knowledge.

SUPPORT FOR RISK MANAGEMENT AND DISASTER RESEARCH AT THE NATIONAL SCIENCE FOUNDATION

Research relevant to policy emerges from many sources, including the private
sector and government agencies at all levels. At the national level here in the
United States, mission agencies such as the Department of Homeland Security
and the U.S. Environmental Protection Agency support the work of university
scholars to address issues of particular concern to the agencies. The National
Science Foundation (NSF) is different in that it supports curiosity-driven basic
research that may or may not have relevance to informing policy decisions.

At the NSF, many standing programs, ranging from cultural anthropology through vulcanology, occasionally support projects related to risk management and disaster research. The two programs that focus specifically on
risk management and disaster research, however, are the Decision, Risk and
Management Sciences Program and the Infrastructure Management and
Extreme Events Program, which the present authors respectively direct.
Each of these programs holds biannual competitions that NSF describes as
"nonsolicited" because no specific solicitations of research questions are published. Indeed, the program announcements deliberately avoid identifying
specific topics within the broad frameworks of scholarly activity that are
funded by the programs. The intention is to give scholars leeway in which to
argue that their proposed projects will produce significant new knowledge or
methodological advances, rather than having program officers predetermine
which topics or methods within the fields are most likely to lead to new discoveries. In a sense, this approach is aligned with the view of researchers as
problem inventors rather than problem solvers that Howard Raiffa advocates in his chapter.

We should not infer from the NSF's focus on basic research that NSF-funded research does not inform policy makers. On the contrary, the discoveries of NSF-funded scholars have directly influenced policies as diverse as the adoption of new methods for auctions by the Federal Communication Commission, the design of disaster warning messages, and cap-and-trade programs for pollution control. Aside from intellectual merit, NSF has a funding criterion—"broader impacts"—that includes the usefulness to society of new information. This funding criterion matters, but the quality of the science involved is always the key determinant of funding.

Although the work of NSF-funded scientists has influenced policy decisions, the NSF itself is statutorily prohibited from taking positions on any issues. In short, the NSF funds research but leaves to others interpretation of the relevance of findings to policy. That the NSF takes no policy positions and has no regulatory role may help to explain the popularity of the Foundation among most members of Congress.

The future of disaster and risk management research at the NSF will entail not only a continuation of the current practice of small-team projects, typically lasting three years and costing between $300,000 and $450,000, but also the creation of some longer-term integrated research endeavors. These endeavors, in turn, will support interdisciplinary work involving social scientists and scholars in myriad other fields, including combinatory mathematics, atmospheric physics, ecology, computer science, engineering, and geo-informatics.

If the NSF is going to significantly increase its support for interdisciplinary decision sciences, risk management, and disaster research, integrated social/economic/ecological/geo-science data are needed. Suppose we had these data? What do we do then? How do we aggregate? Traditional probabilistic risk assessment has obvious limitations for understanding extreme events, but what are the alternatives? Are new approaches such as complexity theory part of the answer? What can we learn from these data that will help us better understand individual and collective behaviors in the face of catastrophes?

The NSF itself will not answer these questions, but it is likely to fund leading scholars who will. Their work, informed by both disciplinary and interdisciplinary learning, will ultimately change the way many people think of the world and affect their daily decisions. Beyond influencing policy, academics are indeed making a great difference in the world.

RECOMMENDED READING

Baumgartner, Frank R., and Bryan D. Jones (2009). *Agendas and Instability in American Politics*, 2nd ed. Chicago: University of Chicago Press.

Mileti, Dennis (1999). *Disasters by Design: A Reassessment of Natural Hazards in the United States*. Washington, DC: Joseph Henry Press.

National Research Council of the National Academies (2006). *Facing Hazards and Disasters: Understanding Human Dimensions*. Washington, DC: The National Academies Press.

Sabatier, Paul A., ed. (1999). *Theories of the Policy Process*. Boulder, CO: Westview Press.

Zaller, John R. (1992). *The Nature and Origins of Mass Opinion*. Cambridge: Cambridge University Press.

30 Reflections and Guiding Principles for Dealing with Societal Risks

HOWARD KUNREUTHER

REFLECTIONS OF THINGS PAST

"The Irrational Economist" conference, which brought together friends and colleagues of many years, inevitably led me to focus on past encounters that have influenced my thinking.

I entered the Economics PhD program at MIT in the fall of 1959 with the impression that the field focused on how humans actually behave. It did not take me long to discover that so-called *homo economicus* (economic man) was expected to collect and process large amounts of information and then make optimal decisions as defined by a set of axioms and equations. My dissertation research did not fit into the standard model since I spent almost a year as an observer in a firm focusing on how production and marketing managers made their ordering and scheduling decisions. It became clear to me that everyone in the firm used *simplified* rules and made *suboptimal* decisions. In fact, I showed how one could improve decision making by reducing the variance in managers' behavior.

Following graduate school I found myself interacting with psychologists, geographers, and sociologists who introduced me to views of the world that differed from the standard economists' model of rationality. To this day I am comfortable identifying myself as an economist because the field focuses on developing strategies for utilizing the private and public sectors to improve individual and social welfare through a well-defined set of criteria. Based on a comparison between the normative models of choice utilized by economists (i.e., how decisions should be made) and descriptive models of behavior (i.e., how individuals actually make decisions), prescriptive solutions for improving the choice process can be proposed.

Irrational Behavior Following the Alaska Earthquake

I was introduced to the field of natural disasters, a focal point of much of my research over the years, in September 1964 when I began my first full-time job as a researcher at the Institute for Defense Analysis (IDA). Several economists had been involved over the preceding few months on an IDA study of the recovery of Alaska following an extremely strong earthquake in March 1964. They were surprised to find that food prices on perishable goods were either stable or had gone down despite shortages, and that rents declined despite limited supplies of housing. This *strange* behavior discouraged my colleagues from moving forward on the study and I was asked whether an analysis of the economics of natural disasters using Alaska as a case study would appeal to me. As a budding *irrational economist*, I jumped at this opportunity and with Douglas Dacy began a two-year research project that led to our book on *The Economics of Natural Disasters* in 1968.

The Alaska earthquake also marked a turning point with respect to government disaster relief policy in the United States. Following this disaster, special legislation was passed that provided low-interest loans and forgiveness grants to Alaskan homes and businesses that were affected by the earthquake. In the years following the Alaska earthquake there were a series of floods, hurricanes, and tornadoes that caused extensive damage in the continental United States. Congress passed special legislation following each of these disasters that was justified by representatives from the affected states each contending: "We don't want any special treatment, just the same as was given to Alaska."

Insurance or Disaster Assistance

Congress went to an extreme following Tropical Storm Agnes. Severe flooding from this storm occurred in June 1972 and affected northeast states that were critical battlegrounds for the upcoming presidential election. Very few of the disaster victims had purchased flood insurance, even though the National Flood Insurance Program (NFIP) had been in place since 1968 and premiums on existing structures were highly subsidized by the federal government. Following these storms, Congress provided the uninsured victims with $5,000 forgiveness grants and 1 percent low-interest loans for covering their losses. I undertook a study for the American Enterprise Institute on *Recovery from Natural Disasters: Insurance or Federal Aid* in which I was somewhat critical of this generous disaster assistance, arguing that insurance was a more effective way of dealing with the problem in advance of the disaster.

Dealing with Extreme Events

My interest in natural hazards has extended over the years to the broader question of how society can deal more effectively with low-probability, high-consequence (lp-hc) events. We have learned that those at risk often misperceive the likelihood and consequences of extreme events and act as if these disasters "will not happen to me." Hence, they do not prepare for such contingencies by investing in risk-reducing measures or purchasing insurance. Only after a catastrophe do the key interested parties focus on ways to prevent the next disaster from occurring. And even this behavior is short-lived as the previous crisis fades into the background, as illustrated by the following examples.

Reducing Losses from Chemical Accidents

Edward Bowman and I were involved in a study of managerial behavior with respect to environmental risks at a large chemical company in the Philadelphia area at the time toxic gas was released from a Union Carbide plant in Bhopal, India, on December 3, 1984. It is estimated that 8,000–10,000 people died within seventy-two hours after the disaster occurred and that an additional 25,000 individuals died from gas-related diseases. Bowman and I interviewed the Philadelphia CEO two days after the accident and he encouraged us to interview managers concerned with how his company would respond to such a catastrophe. We found that all of them were now focused on how to avoid a Bhopal-like disaster. They eventually adopted a set of innovations that could have been instituted prior to Bhopal. As we reported in two papers written on this topic, it took a catastrophic accident to focus the attention of this firm and most major chemical companies on ways to reduce risks.

The Bhopal disaster was the impetus for establishing, in 1985, the Wharton School's Risk Management and Decision Processes Center, where Paul

Kleindorfer and I served as co-directors. Its mission from the outset has been to study behavior by individuals, firms, and governments with respect to low-probability, high-consequence events so that more effective strategies can be prescribed for reducing losses from future disasters and aiding the recovery process.

Siting Liquified Natural Gas Terminals

From 1980 to 1982, I spent an extended sabbatical at the International Institute for Applied Systems Analysis (IIASA) outside of Vienna, Austria, focusing much of my attention on the challenges involved in siting liquefied natural gas (LNG) facilities in four countries (Germany, the Netherlands, the United Kingdom, and the United States). During this time I worked closely with John Lathrop, Joanne Linnerooth-Bayer, and Michael Thompson, among other researchers. In particular, we studied the process that each country utilized in finding a home for these technological facilities and analyzed how it dealt with the possibilities of a catastrophic accident, such as a storage tank rupture resulting in an LNG spill. The LNG produces a vapor cloud that could ignite and cause property damage as well as a significant number of injuries and fatalities.

A principal finding from this study was that one cannot zero-in on a specific number to characterize the likelihood of an LNG explosion, even though this aim was the initial impetus for funding the study by the German government. Rather, we concluded that experts are prone to disagree on the likelihood and resulting consequences of an accident, and that it is difficult to reconcile these differences given scientific uncertainty. Each of the key interested parties is thus able to justify its estimates of the risk by finding its favorite guru to defend its positions.

Finding a Home for the High-Level Radioactive Waste Repository

The LNG study at IIASA was a forerunner to a large-scale study on the siting of the high-level nuclear waste (HLNW) facility at Yucca Mountain in Nevada that spanned the fourteen-year period from 1986 to 2000 and involved social scientists from many disciplines such as anthropology, economics, geography, psychology, and sociology. The Nevada study provided an opportunity for a group of us—namely, Doug Easterling, Jim Flynn, Roger Kasperson, Paul Slovic, and me—to focus on issues of equity and social amplification of risk as important components for dealing with siting problems and other lp-hc events.

One incident stands out in my mind as I reflect on the challenges involved in siting an HLNW repository where the nuclear waste would be buried for 10,000 years. During a focus group we conducted in Las Vegas to ascertain citizens' attitudes toward the repository, one woman commented, "I'm not concerned as much about myself as I am about my great-great-great-grandchildren." The focus group discussion then concentrated on the role of future generations in siting the repository, leading us to include several questions on this aspect in our survey of public perceptions toward the facility. We found that "concern with future generations" was one of the most important variables in determining whether people would vote for or against siting an HLNW repository in their backyard.

The Role of Terrorism Insurance

On September 4, 2001, my wife Gail and I arrived in New York City to begin a one-year sabbatical at Columbia University's Earth Institute. I learned about the terrorist attack of 9/11 while riding a bicycle along the Hudson River and listening to my portable radio. There was first an announcement that a small plane had hit the World Trade Center (WTC). I then rode out to the edge of the 69th Street Pier to see the first building on fire but left the scene one minute before the second plane crashed into the second WTC tower. In the aftermath of 9/11, I worked closely with Erwann Michel-Kerjan, who joined the Wharton School in 2002. We wrote a series of papers on the role of terrorism insurance in providing financial protection against future attacks.

The attitude of insurers toward terrorism insurance is instructive. It illustrates their lack of concern with this risk prior to 9/11 and their reluctance to provide coverage after the attacks occurred. Until 9/11, insurers did not exclude damage from a terrorist attack in their policies covering property damage to homeowners and commercial firms. Moreover, they did not attempt to price this risk despite the terroristic attempt on the World Trade Center in 1993 and the Oklahoma City bombing in 1995. In other words, insurers behaved as if a future terrorist attack would not cause any serious losses to their portfolio.

Following 9/11, insurers were reluctant to offer coverage unless they were able to charge an extremely high price because they now felt the potential losses would be too costly to them. One insurance broker reported to us that an industrial firm purchased $9 million worth of terrorism insurance to cover damage to their facilities at an annual premium of $900,000. If the premium reflected the expected loss, this implies an annual probability of 1 in 10 (i.e., $900,000/$9 million) that such an event would occur.

Since 9/11, the Wharton Risk Center has been actively involved in examining the appropriate role of the public and private sectors in providing insurance protection against terrorism coverage and has published widely in this area. Researchers at the Center have a particular interest in ways that insurance can be utilized for encouraging investments by firms in risk-reducing measures so as to reduce the consequences of a future terrorist attack.

Weak Links and Interdependent Security

Another research area stimulated by the 9/11 attacks relates to interdependent security (IDS). From a cost-benefit perspective, the problem facing any consumer or business manager can be stated as follows: What are the economic incentives for incurring the costs of investing in a protective measure if there is some chance that one will still be adversely affected by a weak link in the system? For example, an apartment owner may invest in a sprinkler system to deal with fires that start in her unit but the sprinkler may be ineffective if a fire spreads to her property from a neighbor's dwelling.

A real-life illustration of this type of interdependency was the crash of Pan Am 103 in 1988, caused by a bomb inside an uninspected bag that was placed on a Malta Airlines flight at a small unsecured airport in Malta (*the weak link in the system*), transferred in Frankfurt to a Pan Am feeder line, and then loaded onto Pan Am 103 in London's Heathrow Airport. The IDS paradigm and the necessity of dealing with weak links can be applied to a much broader range of practical problems than Geoffrey Heal and I imagined when we first began working in this area right after 9/11. For example, one of the causes of the financial crisis of 2008–2009 was the potential collapse of the American International Group (AIG), the world's largest insurer. The weak link in AIG was a 377-person London Unit known as AIG Financial Products that was run with almost complete autonomy from the parent company.

More generally, Heal and I have been able to show that there are many situations where if some parties invest in protection then others will follow suit. Hence, there is an opportunity to focus on a few key players to tip or cascade the others in a desirable direction, as demonstrated by the fundamental research carried out by Thomas Schelling in the 1970s.

Take-Aways from These Experiences

These experiences over the years have expanded my understanding of human behavior with respect to uncertainty and risk. They have also led me to think about ways in which individuals' and firms' decision-making processes can be improved. In my view, this can be accomplished by developing a set of *guiding principles* that serve as focal points for designing programs and policies aimed at enhancing both individual and social welfare.

GUIDING PRINCIPLES FOR MANAGING SOCIETAL RISK PROBLEMS

During the past few years, a group of us at the Wharton Risk Center have developed a set of guiding principles for designing strategies to deal with low-probability, high-consequence events.

Three Principles for Encouraging Investment in Protective Measures

In our recently published book, *At War with the Weather* (written with our colleagues Neil Doherty, Martin Grace, Robert Klein and Mark Pauly), Erwann Michel-Kerjan and I suggest strategies for reducing losses from natural disasters.[1] Given our interest in utilizing insurance to encourage investment in risk-reducing measures we formulated the following two insurance principles, which address the issue of setting insurance premiums that reflect risks while trying to deal with issues of equity and affordability.

Insurance Principle 1: Premiums should reflect risk. That is, insurance premiums should be based on risk in order to provide signals to individuals as to the hazards they face and to encourage them to engage in cost-effective mitigation measures to reduce their vulnerability to catastrophes. Risk-based premiums should also reflect the cost of capital that insurers need to integrate into their pricing to ensure adequate return to their investors.

Insurance Principle 2: Equity and affordability issues need to be dealt with. In particular, any special treatment given to homeowners currently residing in hazard-prone areas (e.g., low-income uninsured or inadequately insured homeowners) should come from general public funding and not through insurance premium subsidies.

Note that Insurance Principle 2 applies only to individuals who *currently reside* in a hazard-prone area. Those who require special treatment could be given some type of voucher, such as an insurance stamp for the explicit purpose of purchasing coverage against the risks from natural disasters. This concept is similar to the food stamp program that assists low-income families in the United States. Others who decide to move to the area in the future should be charged premiums that reflect the risk. Note, too, that providing newcomers with financial assistance from public sources to purchase insurance would encourage development in hazard-prone areas and exacerbate the potential for catastrophic losses from future disasters.

Inducing individuals to invest in risk-reducing measures requires an understanding of their decision processes with respect to making tradeoffs between the costs of taking this action and the expected benefits from reducing future losses should an untoward event occur. We thus include the following behavioral principle:

Myopic Behavior: When designing strategies for encouraging investment in protective measures one needs to recognize that individuals focus on short-term horizons in their decision processes. Indeed, there is considerable empirical evidence suggesting that when individuals and businesses plan for the future, they do not fully weigh the long-term benefits of investing in loss reduction measures. They have even less interest in investing in protective measures when there is only a small chance of reaping financial returns from having taken such action. The up-front costs of these protective measures loom disproportionately high relative to the delayed expected benefits over time.

Applied to businesses, short-term horizons can translate into a NIMTOF (Not In My Term of Office) perspective: "If a major crisis occurs, I hope it is not on my watch." The recent financial crisis illustrates this type of behavior. The prospect of a large annual bonus discouraged individuals from hedging their bets or considering the possibility of a financial meltdown such as the one experienced in October 2008.

What to Do? Think Long Term

These three principles suggest that we, as a society, must rethink our strategy for reducing losses from lp-hc events such as natural disasters, terrorism, and financial crises by developing long-term contracts coupled with short-term rewards. An example of such a strategy would be to move from the standard one-year flood insurance contract offered today under the National Flood Insurance Program to long-term insurance contracts tied to the property, so that individuals would not cancel their coverage after two or three years. Today many do just that when they have not suffered a loss and hence cannot make a claim on their policy.

Long-term insurance should also encourage individuals to invest in cost-effective mitigation measures by having either the insurer or the bank holding the mortgage offer a long-term home improvement loan. The reduction in annual premiums due to lower expected losses would exceed the annual costs of the loan for the mitigation measure.

Turning to other extreme events, we find that there are opportunities for developing long-term contracts that take into account the behavioral biases and heuristics utilized by decision makers. For example, the standard *annual* bonus system practiced by many organizations could be modified so that bonuses are contingent on multi-year performance. This might induce managers to more systematically consider the potential consequences of their immediate actions over time and to pay more attention to worst-case scenarios rather than hoping that they will not arise by the end of the current year.

In the same vein, presenting probabilities of extreme events in the context of a multi-year horizon may lead individuals to pay attention to the resulting outcomes. For example, rather than providing information in terms of a 1-in-100 chance of an event occurring next year, one could indicate that the chance of at least one of these events occurring in the next twenty-five years is greater than 1 in 5.

GUIDING PRINCIPLES FOR YOUNG RESEARCHERS

Reflecting back on my own experience, I list below a few principles that have proved helpful to me in my efforts to gain insight into possible solutions for a particular problem and to convince decision makers that they should adopt a proposed course of action.

Researchers' Principle 1: Make sure you are dealing with the right problem.   I had a sobering experience in this regard when I spent a summer during my graduate years working at the Port Authority of New York on an optimal algorithm for assigning toll collectors to booths in the Holland and Lincoln Tunnels. I was given a set of constraints that defined the problem (e.g., toll collectors need to work the first and last hours of an eight-hour shift with two fifty-minute breaks during the day) and told to develop an algorithm for assigning collectors, given a specified number of booths that needed to be kept open at different hours of the day.

After designing a schedule that reduced the number of toll collectors from the current number, I was told by the managers in charge of the process that I really didn't understand their scheduling problem. However, when I pursued this point they never indicated what additional constraints I should have taken into account. An obvious sticking point was that the algorithm reduced the number of toll collectors. I believe there would have been a better chance of developing a strategy that might have been considered by those who had to implement it if we had met at the beginning of the process and had discussed all of the relevant parameters.

Researchers' Principle 2: Consider behavioral biases when designing prescriptive solutions.   Over the years I have learned (sometimes the hard way) that if one does not take into account the way individuals process information and make choices, strategies that appear to be reasonable to economists may not work well in practice. As an illustration of this point, consider the National Flood Insurance Program. When enacted in 1968, it provided highly subsidized premiums for existing homes so as to maintain property values and to encourage individuals to purchase policies. But very few homeowners in flood-prone areas voluntarily bought coverage, even though they were getting a bargain with respect to price. As my colleagues and I later discovered when interviewing these individuals, many believed the probability of a flood in the near future was so low as to justify a lack of concern with protecting themselves. Eventually, Congress passed legislation requiring flood insurance as a condition for a federally insured mortgage.

Researchers' Principle 3: Start with a simple problem before trying to solve a more complex one.   This point was driven home when Geoff Heal and I were tackling the interdependent security (IDS) problem described above. We first looked at the simplest case we could think of: two identical individuals, each of whom had a chance of suffering damage to their apartment unit from a fire. If the fire occurred in Person 1's apartment it was certain to spread to Person 2's unit even if Person 2 had invested in a fire sprinkler system. The same scenario would occur if Person 2 had a fire: It would spread to Person 1's apartment. For this two-player game we discovered that two Nash equilibria were possible: Either both individuals would want to invest in a sprinkler system or neither of them would want to adopt this protective measure.

This was an *Aha* moment for us! We both recognized that we would have had a hard time uncovering this feature of the solution if we'd started with a more complicated problem structure such as having the two individuals differ from each other or considering three or more apartment owners, each deciding whether or not to invest in a fire sprinkler system. Later we added these and other features to make the problem more realistic.

Researchers' Principle 4: As a neutral party, do not advocate a specific program. Rather than lobbying for a specific program, it is often more appropriate to point out the pros and cons of alternative strategies. In this way, one will be viewed more objectively by the interested parties. My colleagues and I learned this lesson firsthand more than thirty years ago while circulating a draft of the final chapter of our book *Disaster Insurance Protection: Public Policy Lessons* to some insurance executives who were working with us on the study. The chapter made a strong pitch for a comprehensive disaster insurance program without noting its advantages and disadvantages relative to other options. One of our insurance colleagues pointed this out to us. We modified the final chapter by providing an assessment of such an insurance program in the context of other strategies, rather than focusing solely on this option.

Researchers' Principle 5: Be aware of loaded words when developing prescriptive solutions.   A few years ago I designed a game as part of a presentation I was giving to practitioners interested in the challenges associated with siting potentially noxious facilities such as landfills. Each person had to determine the amount of *compensation* he or she would require in order to accept a landfill in his or her community. The person stating the lowest amount had the facility sited in his or her backyard; each of the other n participants paid $1/n$ of this dollar figure to the lowest bidder. In other words, if the lowest bid was $200 by Player 1 and there were 11 players (each representing a community) then the 10 higher bidders would each pay $20 (i.e., $200/10) to Player 1 in return for having the landfill in his or her backyard.

After I explained the rules of the game, several participants announced that they were withdrawing because they were being forced to either accept or make unethical payments. They interpreted the word *compensation* to mean a *bribe* and felt compromised. The next time I led the game, I changed the word *compensation* to *benefit-sharing* and there was no objection by anyone to participating in this siting exercise.

One final principle stimulated by these others has guided the activities of the Wharton Risk Center over the past twenty-five years.

Researchers' Principle 6: Early in the process, bring together as many key interested parties as possible and listen carefully to them. If these interested parties take ownership of the ideas that are being discussed, then sit back and let them take over the process. In this regard I am reminded of a dialog that one of my mentors, Gilbert White, had with a colleague at a conference a few years ago. Someone in the audience began advocating a policy that White had proposed in writing without acknowledging that it was White's idea. The colleague suggested to White that he point this out to the conference attendees. Gilbert's reaction was immediate and clear: "We have a much better chance of getting this policy adopted if others believe it is their idea rather than mine!"

RECOMMENDED READING

Auserwald, Philip, Lewis Branscomb, Todd Laporte, and Erwann Michel-Kerjan (2006). *Seeds of Disaster, Roots of Response.* New York: Cambridge University Press.
Moss, David (2002). *When All Else Fails.* Cambridge, MA: Harvard University Press.
Schelling, Thomas (1978). *Micromotives and Macrobehavior.* New York: Norton.
Slovic, Paul (2000). *The Perception of Risk.* London: Earthscan.

ACKNOWLEDGMENTS
An Unusual Journey
Homage to Howard Kunreuther

ON THE WAY BACK FROM BEIJING

September 2007. I was on my way back to the United States from Beijing, China, where I attended the inaugural annual meeting of the "New Champions" jointly organized by the People's Republic of China and the World Economic Forum—a gathering of top leaders in business, politics, nonprofits, the arts, and economics among whom "think new" was the leitmotiv. The fourteen-hour flight offered one of those rare and precious opportunities for deep, uninterrupted contemplation.

My thoughts turned to my senior colleague and friend Howard Kunreuther. Howard was about to turn 70 the following year, and I wanted to give him a party. But the challenge was to organize something different from the usual one-or two-day tribute conference where each invited colleague has about an hour to summarize his or her work with the honoree who is generally about to retire. I had to depart from that format, Kunreuther not being just another academic economist.

HOWARD KUNREUTHER, A GREAT MIND AND A TRUE PIONEER IN THE STUDY OF DECISION MAKING IN A DANGEROUS WORLD

Howard Kunreuther was trained as what many would consider a very rational economist. He received his PhD in economics from MIT in 1965. Among his advisors was Robert Solow, the famous macro-economist who was later awarded the Nobel Prize. Kunreuther easily could have taken the path of hard modeling and theoretical research. But he was deeply interested in how people behave. Soon enough, he started challenging the usual rational model of decision making by looking at how people make decisions in risky environments (at that time, he studied potential victims of major floods and earthquakes). He and his colleagues performed groundbreaking empirical investigations in the 1970s, documenting individual insurance decisions that were difficult to reconcile within the traditional economic paradigm. In that way he became an economist who studies irrationality, an irrational economist.

Today, some forty years later, Kunreuther is recognized as one of the true pioneers in the fields of both decision sciences and catastrophe risk management. He has written or edited nearly thirty books and monographs, as well as hundreds of academic papers, and has always had a passion and enthusiasm for listening to and engaging others' ideas. He is a Fellow of the American Association for the Advancement of Science (AAAS) and a Fellow of the Society for Risk Analysis, from which he received the Society's Distinguished Achievement Award in 2001. He is also a recipient of the Elizur Wright Award for the publication that makes the most significant contribution to the literature of insurance, among many other awards.

But Kunreuther is not only an important scholar. His influence extends to people all over the world—starting, of course, with his family. Profound personal challenges, including the loss of loved ones at an early age and the primary responsibilities that came with it, contributed to the man he is today. There is also his influence on his colleagues and friends of thirty or forty years, who have worked with him and shared his enthusiasm. And there is his influence on a whole new generation of scholars, who have been inspired by his work.

Further, Howard Kunreuther has been, over these four decades, one of those rare economists who always wanted to get down from the "Ivory Tower" to confront knowledgeable and experienced people in the "real world" with research findings. As Paul Slovic and I point out in the Introduction, this approach remains more the exception than the rule. Indeed, one of the key features of Kunreuther's contributions over the years has been his ability to significantly influence yet another important group: policy makers and business leaders.

He does so not by imposing his views but, rather, by learning from them, patiently and in a nonpartisan way. Kunreuther is always the first to share radically new ideas with practitioners, and to ask for sincere feedback. "It works in theory; how can we make it work in practice?" Over the years this approach called not only for respect and trust but also enhanced knowledge, which was ultimately transferred to decision makers, thereby changing behaviors, institutions, and markets, step by step.

In 2008, Klaus Schwab, the founder and chairman of the World Economic Forum (WEF), established several global agenda councils on the most pressing issues facing the world today. These ranged from international security and conflicts, global trade, and education to pandemics and natural disasters. Each group included some of the most brilliant minds on the topic in question. It was no surprise to many of us that when the time came to select the person who would lead the WEF initiative on mitigating natural disasters, Howard Kunreuther was chosen, along with Wharton colleague Michael Useem. This is the perfect illustration of an important bridge between academia and decisions made by world leaders.

LIKE A SUPER VIP CONCERT

Resuming my in-flight musings about what type of party should be organized for Howard's 70th birthday, I realized that a small audience simply would not work. Kunreuther had collaborated with *so many* others in so many different disciplines, and advised so many PhD students, that inviting just a few of them would not make sense. Besides, inviting just academics—while he had interacted for decades with numerous great minds in both the public and the private sectors—would be limiting indeed. Additionally, because Kunreuther had traveled a lot, spending several years in Europe and Asia, the audience would have to be international. Finally, even though Kunreuther was turning 70, he was not planning to retire soon.

Given all of the above, it was clear that this would have to be a somewhat unusual event. The day after coming back to the United States, I called two good friends who would play a critical role: Paul Slovic and Richard Zeckhauser. Slovic is considered by many to be one of the world's leading psychologists concerned with decision making under risk; and Zeckhauser, one of the world's leading experts in public policy and catastrophe management. Life being as surprising as it is, Slovic and Kunreuther have been friends for forty years, and Zeckhauser played bridge with Kunreuther in high school more than fifty years ago. Along with Howard's wife, Gail, our assembled quartet planned The Irrational Economist event.

One year later, more than a hundred of the world's leading economists and other social scientists working on decision sciences and risk management, along with business leaders, gathered for two days in Philadelphia. Any one of these individuals could have been the keynote speaker commanding a large audience at a conference. So in a way, this was like having one hundred rock stars playing continuously for two days at the same place—a super VIP concert.

We asked thirty of them to play the role of catalyst by presenting their most recent ideas. Guideline: Choose any subject that is close to your heart; be new and innovative. One constraint: Speak for no more than seven minutes. (Anyone who is familiar with academia knows that this is a nearly impossible task. Academics like to talk. . .)

Everybody played the game, and in addition to honoring Kunreuther for his significant contributions, this super VIP reunion was quite a success in terms of generating new ideas. Here I would like to thank all the participants at The Irrational Economist conference for sharing their views on the most pressing issues confronting the world today and on research priorities for our disciplines in the next ten years, most of which are discussed in this book. It was clear at the time of the conference that those ideas would reach far beyond the academic world—that they would impact many of us as citizens, businesspeople, and policy makers all over the world. And so, during the next twelve months, Paul Slovic and I continued what had already been a great voyage by taking on the role of editors (or should I say conductors?) to produce this book.

My first debt of gratitude is to Paul Slovic, Gail Loeb Kunreuther, and Richard Zeckhauser, who have been indispensible both in the preparation of conference and as sources of inspiration I often turned to when this book was still in progress. Paul and I worked together very closely to bring the book to fruition. It has been a very humbling experience to work with all the fine people who joined this adventure. I prevailed upon the authors to write innovative contributions and to be responsive to several rounds of comments and editing. For this reason, we all first and foremost share a collective vision in *The Irrational Economist*. I'm happy to say that the book conforms to its own thesis: By ensuring that new knowledge on decision sciences and behavioral economics is established, as well as translated into comprehensive and useful tools for nonspecialists, it can be employed by those in charge of making important decisions for society and, ultimately, help make a difference in the world. I would also like to thank Avinash Dixit and Daniel Kahneman at Princeton University, who, although they are not among the chapter authors, made inspiring contributions to the conference.

I am very grateful for the invaluable help we received on early versions of the book from Carol Heller at the Wharton School of the University of Pennsylvania, a most loyal and creative assistant.

Financial support for this conference provided by the Wharton School's Dean's Office and OPIM Department, as well as the Provost's Office of the University of Pennsylvania, is gratefully acknowledged.

I'm grateful also to my friend Richard Smith, who since our first meeting at Davos a few years ago has provided important guidance to me, including the choice of publisher for this book. The team at PublicAffairs in New York has been fantastic throughout the process of ensuring that *The Irrational Economist* is a "good book about things that matter." Most of all, on behalf of the chapter authors, our gratitude goes to Clive Priddle, editorial director at PublicAffairs, who, along with Peter Osnos, founder and editor-at-large, and Susan Weinberg, publisher, saw early on the potential of this book despite its somewhat atypical format. Thanks to the rest of the team at PublicAffairs as well: Christine Arden, Niki Papadopoulos, Melissa Raymond, Tessa Shanks, Jennifer Thompson, Michelle Welsh-Horst, and Brent Wilcox.

This has been an unusual journey. Honoring someone who is quite special gave rise to a special book. We hope you agree. Remember, (ir)rationality is a matter of perspective.

Erwann Michel-Kerjan
Philadelphia, Pennsylvania
October 2009

NOTES

Introduction Michel-Kerjan and Slovic

1. H. Kunreuther and E. Michel-Kerjan, *At War with the Weather: Managing Large-Scale Risks in a New Era of Catastrophes* (Cambridge, MA: MIT Press, 2009).

2. P. Auerswald, L. Branscomb, T. LaPorte, and E. Michel-Kerjan, *Seeds of Disaster, Roots of Response: How Private Action Can Reduce Public Vulnerability* (New York: Cambridge University Press, 2006).

3. H. A. Simon and A. C. Stedry, "Psychology and Economics," in G. Lindzey and E. Aronson, eds., *The Handbook of Social Psychology*, Vol. 5 (Reading, MA: Addison-Wesley, 1969), p. 272.

4. H. A. Simon, *Models of Man: Social and Rational* (New York: Wiley, 1957), p. 198.

5. S. Lichtenstein and P. Slovic, *The Construction of Preference* (New York: Cambridge University Press, 2006).

6. D. M. Grether and C. R. Plott, "Economic Theory of Choice and the Preference Reversal Phenomenon," *American Economic Review* 69, no. 4 (1979): 623–638.

7. The work of University of Chicago Nobel Laureate Gary Becker constitutes perhaps the most original effort at importing standard economic models to the psychology domain, rather than exporting psychology into economics. In particular, he has applied the standard maximization utility model to a large range of social contexts (e.g., marriages, divorces, love). See G. Becker, *The Economic Approach to Human Behavior* (Chicago: Chicago University Press, 1976); and G. Becker, *A Treatise of the Family* (Cambridge, MA: Harvard University Press, 1981).

8. A. K. Sen, "Rational Fools: A Critique of the Behavioral Foundations of Economic Theory," *Philosophy and Public Affairs* 6 (1977): 317–344.

9. This was apparent in his seminal book *The Wealth of Nations,* published in 1776. Unfortunately, many people forget that in his first and also very influential book, *The Theory of Moral Sentiments* (1759)—in which the image of the "invisible hand" is already employed—he also elaborated a morality centered on sympathy and benevolence to explain the source of mankind's ability to form moral judgments—a critical element of decision making—in spite of man's natural inclinations toward self-interest.

Chapter 2 Akerlof and Shiller: Berserk Weather Forecasters, Beauty Contests, and Delicious Apples on Wall Street

1. This chapter is excerpted from George A. Akerlof and Robert J. Shiller, *Animal Spirits*, Princeton University Press, 2009. Used with permission.

2. These computations use the Standard and Poor's Composite Stock Price Index divided by the Consumer Price Index for All Urban Consumers, as computed by the U.S. Bureau of Labor Statistics; see http://www.robertshiller.com.

3. Paul A. Samuelson has said that the stock market is micro-efficient and macro-inefficient. We have found an element of truth in this statement (Jung and Shiller, 2005).

4. Shiller (2000, 2005).

5. Shiller (1981); Campbell and Shiller (1987).

6. Terry A. Marsh and Robert C. Merton, commenting on papers by LeRoy and Porter (1981) and Shiller (1981), once tried to give "inspiring evidence" that stock prices are indeed a present value of optimally forecasted dividends (Marsh and Merton, 1986). However, they failed in this attempt (Shiller, 1986). The reasons Marsh and Merton gave for thinking that any market inefficiencies will be "arbitraged away" by smart money have a number of limitations (Shleifer and Vishny, 1997; Barberis and Thaler, 2003).

7. These ads are displayed and discussed in Mullainathan and Shleifer (2005).

8. Allen et al. (2002).

9. Higgins (2005).

Chapter 3 Hogarth: Subways, Coconuts, and Foggy Minefields

1. Taleb (2007) refers to coconuts with large consequences as "black swans."

2. For a related approach, see the interesting work by Winter, Cattani, and Dorsch (2007).

3. See, for example, Hogarth and Karelaia (2007).

Chapter 4 Slovic: The More Who Die, the Less We Care

1. Portions of this chapter appeared earlier in P. Slovic, "If I Look at the Mass I Will Never Act: Psychic Numbing and Genocide." *Judgment and Decision Making* 2 (2007): 79–95. This material is based upon work supported by the Hewlett Foundation, and by the National Science Foundation under Grant No. SES-0649509. Any opinions, findings, and conclusions or recommendations expressed in this material are those of the author and do not necessarily reflect the views of the Hewlett Foundation or the National Science Foundation.

2. She struggled to think straight about the great losses that the world ignores: "More than two million children die a year from diarrhea and eight hundred thousand from measles. Do we blink? Stalin starved seven million Ukrainians in one year, Pol Pot killed two million Cambodians" (Dillard, 1999, pp. 130–131).

3. Kogut and Ritov (2005).
4. Västfjäll, Peters, and Slovic (in preparation).
5. Lifton (1967).
6. Haidt (2001).
7. Batson et al. (1983, p. 718).
8. Slovic (2009).

Chapter 5 Michel-Kerjan: Haven't You Switched to Risk Management 2.0 Yet?

1. White House, *The Federal Response to Hurricane Katrina: Lessons Learned* (Washington, DC: Office of the Assistant to the President for Homeland Security and Counterterrorism, 2006).

Chapter 6 Schoemaker: A Two-Edged Sword

1. I thank Eric Horvitz, Ron Howard, Tom Keelin, Paul Kleindorfer, J. Edward Russo, Carl Spetzler, and the editors for their valuable feedback.
2. See, for instance, the chapters by Robert Meyer and Howard Kunreuther in this book.
3. Measuring a person's risk attitude, and applying it consistently to decisions involving risk or uncertainty, is an important part of decision analysis. It entails ranking simple lotteries and then reflecting the person's implied risk preference into the utility numbers assigned to each outcome, as in our simple example.
4. Although its roots are in cognitive psychology, the field is now very much interested in the role of emotion and feeling, as well as in the social context of decisions, thus expanding its disciplinary base.

Chapter 7 Krantz: Constructed Preference and the Quest for Rationality

1. Category (a) includes taking on group identity or group status; enhancing group status; safety (feeling and being secure); efficacy (feeling and being capable or powerful); adherence to group norms; and sharing presence, activities, or experiences with other group members. Category (b) includes aspirations for specialized roles (formal or informal), aspirations for higher status within the group, and being able to make social comparisons within the group. Category (c) comprises a huge variety of obligations that stem from one's achieved role or status, including coordination of others' actions, adding or elaborating group norms, imposing sanctions on group members who violate norms, and working externally with other groups. Finally, category (d) includes both in-group and out-group goals: benefits to others in one's group (reciprocation and nepotism) but also deprivation, discrimination, and negative reciprocation (punishment) directed against others toward whom one feels no affiliation.
2. Using the categories introduced in the previous note, we find that this subtype falls partly under (a), adherence to group norms, and partly under (c), since a standard may depend on one's position (role/status) within a group.

Chapter 8 Kleindorfer: What If You Know You Will Have to Explain Your Choices to Others Afterwards?

1. I am grateful to the editors and Carol Heller, as well as to Stephanie Olen Kleindorfer, Erin L. Krupka, Eric Orts, and Paul Schoemaker, for valuable discussions and comments on this chapter.

2. Kunreuther's early work is reviewed in Chapter 9 of Kleindorfer, Kunreuther, and Schoemaker (1993).

3. See, for example, Easterling and Kunreuther (1995).

4. In one sense, such participation reflects an attempt to counter the mistrust of technocrats, as noted by anthropologist Michael Thompson and sociologist Ulrich Beck. This mistrust is directly connected to the legitimation process in twentieth-century philosophy—for example, in the extensive discussion of hermeneutics by the German philosopher Jürgen Habermas. Indeed, the central question treated by Habermas and his colleagues in the Frankfurt School of critical social theory is the inherent tension between truth-seeking and open access to existing institutions that have the power to interpret knowledge within a particular domain. The same point has been made in the history of science by Thomas Kuhn. For Kuhn the "primacy of paradigms" is a statement not just about the stability of existing intellectual frameworks in particular fields of knowledge but also about the stakes in maintaining allegiance to the status quo of individual scientists who control access to the processes and institutions that validate claims and methods of inquiry in their respective fields.

5. The interested reader can find the full Stern Report at http://www.occ.gov.uk/activities/stern.htm.

Chapter 9 Camerer: Neuroeconomics

1. In this context, *functional* refers to the fact that subjects are performing some task so that brain activity during the task can be analyzed for clues about the function being performed by the activated regions in question.

2. According to the authors of the original "ultimatum game" article (W. Güth, R. Schmittberger, and B. Schwarze, "An Experimental Analysis of Ultimatum Bargaining, *Journal of Economic Behavior and Organization* 3, no. 4 [1982]: 367–388), equilibrium offers were often rejected in one-stage games. Other researchers who studied a two-stage version concluded that equilibrium offers could emerge under suitable learning conditions (K. Binmore, A. Shaked, and J. Sutton, "Testing Noncooperative Bargaining Theory: A Preliminary Study," *American Economic Review* 75, no. 5 [1985]: 1178–1180). A more elaborate experiment performed with two-, three-, and five-stage games found that players appeared to play as if they were self-interested but looked only two stages ahead (Janet Neelin, Hugo Sonnenschein, and Matthew Speigel, "A Further Test of Noncooperative Bargaining Theory: Comment," *American Economic Review* 78, no. 4 [September 1988]: 824–836). That is, using the game structure above, their subjects often offered $2.50, which is the equilibrium offer if the game was truncated to two stages rather than to three.

3. See Crawford (2008) for a summary.

4. In other words, it is possible that they generally knew more about New York temperatures, such that the maximum of p (low in NY) and p (high in NY) was higher than the maximum of p (low in Dushanbe) and p (high in Dushanbe), but in actuality they were not more accurate about the high-information bets.

Chapter 10   Oullier: The Useful Brain

1. Note that by distinguishing between physical and mental boxes I'm providing you with a clear illustration of my own strong tendency to make boxes!

2. J.A.S. Kelso and D.A. Engstrøm, *The Complementary Nature* (Cambridge, MA: MIT Press, 2006); L. Pessoa, "On the Relationship Between Emotion and Cognition," *Nature Reviews Neuroscience* 9 (2008): 148–158.

3. See, for example, Colin Camerer's chapter in this book.

4. M. MacMillan, *An Odd Kind of Fame: Stories of Phineas Gage* (Cambridge, MA: MIT Press, 2000).

5. A. Damasio, *Descartes' Error: Emotion, Reason, and the Human Brain* (New York: Putnam Publishing, 1994).

6. This approach is still used in courts to (attempt to) prove someone's penal (ir)responsibility to the actions he or she committed. See J. Rosen, "The Brain on the Stand," *New York Times*, March 11, 2007.

7. P. W. Glimcher et al., *Neuroeconomics: Decision Making and the Brain* (London: Academic Press, 2008).

8. A.G. Sanfey et al., "The Neural Basis of Economic Decision-Making in the Ultimatum Game," *Science* 300, no. 5626 (2003): 1755–1758.

9. Functional magnetic resonance imaging is the brain imaging technique that is used to make those beautiful 3D pictures of the brain with color blobs that one often sees in the media. These blobs are supposed to indicate where brain activity is significantly higher when tasks are compared. For readers who are not familiar with this methodology a few things need to be added: fMRI does not measure brain activity directly but, rather, estimates it based on the magnetic properties of oxygen consumption in the brain and the assumption that when a part of the brain is more active than another, its metabolic (oxygen) consumption is higher. Also, the fact that only a couple of areas are colored on a brain image does not necessarily mean that the rest of the brain is inactive. Fortunately for all of us, the entire brain is continuously working!

10. As depicted in the previous chapter by Colin Camerer, arguably one of the leading lights in neuroeconomics, the first player in a UG, the *proposer*, offers a share of money he owns to another player, the *responder*. If the responder accepts the proposer's offer, both players keep their respective splits. If the responder doesn't, neither receives any money. If both the proposer and the responder were behaving as rational maximizers, the proposer would offer the minimum amount and the responder would accept it, with even a penny being better than nothing. This is rarely the case in the UG.

11. The technique used in this procedure, which is called repeated transcranial magnetic stimulation (rTMS), momentarily disrupts the workings of a targeted brain area.

12. D. Knoch et al., "Diminishing Reciprocal Fairness by Disrupting the Right Prefrontal Cortex," *Science* 314, no. 5800 (2006): 829–832.

13. Even more puzzling was the fact that their ability to judge the offers as unfair remained unchanged.

14. This study clearly showed that the decision to accept can change while the judgment regarding the (un)fairness of the offer does not, therefore supporting the claim that judgments do not always determine decisions.

15. O. Oullier and F. Basso, "Embodied Economics: How Bodily Information Shapes the Social Coordination Dynamics of Decision Making," *Philosophical Transactions of the Royal Society: Biological Science* (2009), forthcoming.

16. O. Oullier et al., "The Coordination Dynamics of Economic Decision Making: A Multilevel Approach to Social Neuroeconomics," *IEEE Transactions on Neural Systems and Rehabilitation Engineering* 16, no. 6 (2008): 557–571.

17. If you are interested in this question, see the great book by Nobel Laureate Thomas Schelling: *Micromotives and Macrobehavior* (New York: Norton, 1978).

18. Examples include the Neuroscience and the Law program in the United States and, in France, the Neuroscience and Public Policy program, a unique initiative that I am in charge of at the prime minister's Center for Strategic Analysis.

Chapter 11 Kousky, Pratt, and Zeckhauser: Virgin Versus Experienced Risks

1. J. McCune, "Car Crashes into House, Resident in Serious Condition," *The Evening Sun* (Hanover, Pennsylvania), September 22, 2008.

2. Kip Viscusi and Richard Zeckauser, *Journal of Risk and Uncertainty* (2003).

3. Kip Viscusi and Richard Zeckauser, "Recollection Bias and the Combat of Terrorism," *Journal of Legal Studies* 34 (January 2006): 27–55.

4. Carolyn Kousky, "Learning from Extreme Events: Risk Perceptions After the Flood," *Land Economics* forthcoming (2010).

5. Note that if the 1993 floods, say, quadrupled expected losses in the two different floodplains, the effect on housing values in the 100-year floodplain would have been much greater, contrary to our findings but consistent with our conjectures. The factor by which properties in the 500-year floodplain are updated may be greater than that in the 100-year floodplains, but the absolute amount could be less. For example, houses in the 100-year floodplain may already be reduced in price 18 percent and those in the 500-year floodplain by 1 percent. A flood occurs and the homes in the 100-year floodplain have a factor of 3 update, while those in the 500-year floodplain have a factor of 5 update. The factor is thus smaller, but the absolute change in price is larger in the 100-year floodplain.

Chapter 12 Öncüler: How Do We Manage an Uncertain Future?

1. D. Ellsberg, "Risk, Ambiguity and the Savage Axioms," *Quarterly Journal of Economics* 75 (1961): 643–669.

Chapter 14 Sunstein and Zeckhauser: Dreadful Possibilities, Neglected Probabilities

1. Our discussion of probability neglect draws on Sunstein (2002). Thanks to Erwann Michel-Kerjan, Laura Malick, Chris Robert, Paul Slovic, Ngoc Anh Tran, Adrian Vermeule, the participants in the Irrational Economist conference, and others for valuable discussions.

2. The converse is also true. If emotions lead to the neglect of probabilities, there will be insufficient response to a given reduction in probability for high-probability risks ("I'm sure it's going to happen anyway").

3. When the risk is imposed by malicious people, there is often a negative externality associated with the precautions taken by any individual. Those who went to Virginia to fill up made it more dangerous for D.C. fillers. When few citizens walk in an urban area at night, those who still walk find such activity more dangerous.

4. We found similar results in a revised version of the electric shock experiment (Sunstein and Zeckhauser, 2008). There was no significant difference between what people would pay to eliminate a 1 percent chance of a shock and a certain shock.

5. An alternative explanation is that individuals demand substantial compensation for their outrage, and that such compensation is both fairly independent of the probability and large relative to the compensation for risk. Note that efforts to communicate the meaning of differences in risk levels by showing comparisons to normal risk levels reduced the effect of outrage, but only modestly so. Outrage had nearly the same effect as a 2,000-fold increase in risk (Johnson et al.,1993). Did this information provision improve cognitive uptake directly, or indirectly because it dampened the outrage? Further experiments will be required to tell.

6. This should bring to mind a component of the embeddedness phenomenon known from contingent valuation surveys. If seals are appealing and easily visualized, it is not surprising that we might pay more to save them in an oil spill than to save all wildlife.

7. In future work, we expect to examine the complementary concept of payoff neglect: When emotions run high, the size of potential losses will tend to be slighted. The emotion may be stimulated by anger directed at the source of the risk, or merely by a vivid description of the risk itself, apart from its magnitude.

Chapter 16 Pauly: Dumb Decisions or as Smart as the Average Politician?

1. Here is the technical explanation: The optimal deductible is determined by comparing the marginal decrease in the risk premium—what you would be willing to pay to reduce risk over and above the value of the benefits you expect to receive—with the marginal increase in the loading cost, both of which are associated with decreasing the size of the deductible. For example, suppose you have insurance with a $200 deductible, a total premium of $1,300, and a loading percentage of 30 percent. Also suppose that insurance with a $100 deductible sells for $1,365. This means that in the second case, the insurer charges you an additional $50 plus $15 loading cost (30 percent of $50) to decrease your deductible from $200 to $100. Probably many people, if they thought about it this way, would not want the low deductible policy: It increases

their wealth by only $100 when a loss occurs, and they are paying $65 extra to avoid that chance. If you were a very risk-averse person and said that you *would* be willing to pay that penalty, we could then consider whether you would be willing to pay a penalty of the same proportion to cut your loss from $100 to $50. Eventually the loss would be of small enough consequence that you would not pay extra to be protected against it. In technical terms, beginning with a zero deductible, the marginal risk premium starts out at zero (because wealth is the same in all states with full coverage) but increases in absolute value as the deductible and the potential loss exposure grow. Loading, in contrast, is a constant proportion of expected benefits; it always costs something more to protect against any additional risk. At some point a higher deductible would increase risk by too much (relative to the reduction in premium and loading); that is the optimal deductible.

Chapter 17 Viscusi: The Hold-Up Problem

1. A brief summary of their work appears in Kunreuther (1976), with a more detailed exposition of the findings in Kunreuther et al. (1978).

2. Kunreuther (1976, p. 250).

3. These statistics, which are calculated using the data in Kunreuther (1976), are for flood insurance. The statistics for earthquake insurance are similar.

4. Viscusi and Zeckhauser (2006).

5. A fully articulated discussion of this policy proposal is presented in Kunreuther and Pauly (2005).

6. Viscusi and Zeckhauser (2003).

7. National Safety Council (2004, p. 29).

Chapter 18 Moss: The Peculiar Politics of American Disaster Policy

1. Although I am indebted to a great many people for helping me over the years to wrestle with the subject of federal disaster policy, I particularly wish to thank Stephanie Lo and Cole Bolton, who provided outstanding research assistance for this chapter.

2. A partial exception is the Federal Crop Insurance Corporation, though in fact farmers are not charged a premium (only a flat administrative fee) for catastrophic coverage. See the "Catastrophic Coverage (CAT)" listing under the "Crop Policies" section on the FCIC website (http://www.rma.usda.gov/policies/).

3. David Moss, *When All Else Fails: Government as the Ultimate Risk Manager* (Cambridge, MA: Harvard University Press, 2002), p. 254.

4. See President Cleveland's veto statement, February 16, 1887, Ex. Doc. No. 175, as cited in Moss, *When All Else Fails*, pp. 254–255.

5. See Moss, *When All Else Fails*, pp. 258–259; Herbert Hoover, *The Memoirs of Herbert Hoover: The Cabinet and the Presidency, 1920–1933*, Vol. 2 (New York: Macmillan, 1952), p. 126.

6. Howard Kunreuther, *Recovery from Natural Disasters: Insurance and Federal Aid* (Washington, DC: American Enterprise Institute, 1973), p. 9.

7. Moss, *When All Else Fails*, p. 256; David Moss, "Courting Disaster? The Transformation of Federal Disaster Policy Since 1803," in Kenneth A. Froot, ed., *The Financing of Catastrophe Risk* (Chicago: University of Chicago Press, 1999), pp. 314–320.

8. J. David Cummins, Michael Suher, and George Zanjani, "Federal Financial Exposure to Catastrophic Risk," Draft Paper, November 30, 2007, p. 25 (Table 1a). Note that the data presented here are in nominal dollars. The authors also offer estimates in "2006 Exposure and Price Adjusted $," which yield slightly different ratios: an overall federal coverage ratio (federal aid to total losses) of about 40 percent, a federal coverage ratio for uninsured losses of about 65 percent, and an emergency supplemental ratio of about 70 percent (Table 1b).

9. Howard Kunreuther and Louis Miller, "Insurance Versus Disaster Relief: An Analysis of Interactive Modelling for Disaster Policy Planning," *Public Administration Review* 45, Special Issue: Emergency Management (January 1985): 148; also cited in Cummins, Suher, and Zanjani, "Federal Financial Exposure," p. 2.

10. See, for example, Moss, "Courting Disaster," pp. 338–339.

11. Moss, *When All Else Fails*, pp. 260–264. See also Howard Kunreuther, "The Case for Comprehensive Disaster Insurance," *Journal of Law & Economics* 11, no. 1 (April 1968): 133–163; Douglas Dacy and Howard Kunreuther, *The Economics of Natural Disasters: Implications for Federal Policy* (New York: Free Press, 1969), esp. p. 235; and Kunreuther, *Recovery from Natural Disasters*.

12. Mancur Olson, Jr., *The Logic of Collective Action: Public Goods and the Theory of Groups* (Cambridge, MA: Harvard University Press, 1965).

13. See CBS News/New York Times Poll, "The Economy, Gas Prices, and Hurricane Katrina," September 9–13, 2005 (http://www.cbsnews.com/htdocs/CBSNews_polls/poll_091405_Katrina.pdf, accessed on February 28, 2009); Associated Press/Ipsos poll conducted by Ipsos-Public Affairs, September 16–18, 2005 (http://www.pollingreport.com/disasters.htm, accessed on February 28, 2009).

14. See also 1995 Insurance Research Council poll (cited in Moss, "Courting Disaster"), which found "87 percent of Americans either strongly approved (51 percent) or moderately approved (36 percent) of the federal government providing disaster relief" (p. 334).

15. Thomas Eisensee and David Strömberg, "News Droughts, News Floods, and U.S. Disaster Relief," *Quarterly Journal of Economics* 122, no. 2 (May 2007): 693. See also David Strömberg and James M. Snyder, Jr., "The Media's Influence on Public Policy Decisions," in Roumeen Islam, ed., *Information and Public Choice: From Media Markets to Policymaking* (Washington, DC: The World Bank, 2008), pp. 17–31.

16. Although television news broadcasts were introduced as early as the 1940s, technological limits placed significant constraints on the medium. Writes Phillip Kierstead: "Early television news broadcasts were crude. . . . Much of the newsfilm came from newsreel companies. . . . [T]here was no adequate recording medium for preserving television pictures other than the fuzzy and inadequate kinescopes. Still pictures were mounted on easels so that studio cameras could photograph them. Developing film for moving pictures and transporting it to New York usually meant that the film available for newscasts was outdated by the time of broadcast." See Phillip Kierstead, "News, Network," *The Encyclopedia of Television* (http://www.museum.tv/archives/etv/N/htmlN/newsnetwork/newsnetwork.htm, accessed on February 28, 2009).

17. Kierstead, "News, Network"; Newton N. Minow (Chairman of the Federal Communications Commission), "Television and the Public Interest," Address to National Association of Broadcasters, Washington, DC, May 9, 1961 (http://www.american rhetoric.com/speeches/newtonminow.htm, accessed on February 28, 2009).

18. Kierstead, "News, Network."

19. Ralph B. Levering, "Kennedy, John F., and the Media," in Stephen L. Vaughn, ed., *Encyclopedia of American Journalism* (New York: Routledge, 2008), p. 243; "The History of Film, Television and Video," online chronology (http://www.high-techproductions .com/historyoftelevision.htm, accessed on February 28, 2009).

20. See CBS News Video, "1964 Alaska Earthquake—This Week in History: A Look Back at the March 27, 1964, earthquake in Alaska" (http://www.cbsnews.com/ video/watch/?id=1439412n, accessed on February 28, 2009). The quoted passage is from Kunreuther, *Recovery from Natural Disasters*, p. 9.

21. David Moss and Mary Oey, "The Paranoid Style in the Study of American Politics," in Edward Balleisen and David Moss, eds., *Government and Markets: Toward a New Theory of Regulation* (Cambridge: Cambridge University Press, forthcoming). See also Alexander Dyck, David A. Moss, and Luigi Zingales, "Media Versus Special Interests," NBER Working Paper Series, No. 14360, September 2008.

22. Regarding the "slow response to Hurricane Andrew," for example, James F. Miskel maintains that "there is no doubt that dissatisfaction with the relief effort contributed to the victory of Bill Clinton, a Democrat, over the Republican incumbent George H. W. Bush" (Miskel, *Disaster Response and Homeland Security: What Works, What Doesn't* [Westport, CT: Praeger Security International, 2006], p. 86). Regarding President George W. Bush in 2005, Daniel Béland writes, "Unfortunately for the president and the Republican Party, ten months after the 2004 presidential election, public and media outcry over their slow response to the Hurricane Katrina disaster in New Orleans seriously tarnished their carefully built image as relentless national defenders. Although local and state officials shared the blame for that slow response, President Bush's apparent indecision in the aftermath of this catastrophe eroded the credibility of an administration that already faced mounting criticism about American losses in Iraq" (Béland, *States of Global Insecurity: Policy, Politics, and Society* [New York: Worth Publishers, 2007], p. 102). President George W. Bush's pollster and chief campaign strategist in 2004 was quoted in *Vanity Fair* as saying, "Katrina to me was the tipping point. The president broke his bond with the public. Once that bond was broken, he no longer had the capacity to talk to the American public. State of the Union addresses? It didn't matter. Legislative initiatives? It didn't matter. P.R.? It didn't matter. Travel? It didn't matter. I knew when Katrina—I was like, man, you know, this is it, man. We're done." See Cullen Murphy and Todd S. Purdum, "Farewell to All That: An Oral History of the Bush White House," *Vanity Fair*, February 2009 (http://www.vanityfair.com/politics/ features/2009/02/bush-oral-history200902, accessed on February 28, 2009).

23. See Kunreuther, "The Case for Comprehensive Disaster Insurance," esp. pp. 154–157; and Moss, "Courting Disaster," pp. 345–351. See also David Moss, Testimony Before the U.S. Senate Committee on Commerce, Science, and Transportation, Hearing on Insuring Terrorism Risks, Panel II, October 30, 2001.

Chapter 19 Jaffee: Catastrophe Insurance and Regulatory Reform After the Subprime Mortgage Crisis

1. See Kunreuther and Pauly (2006) and Jaffee, Kunreuther, and Erwann Michel-Kerjan (2008). The former considers possible government actions to rectify such short-comings, including a comprehensive all-risk catastrophe insurance plan, whereas the latter examines the possible role of long-term insurance.

2. Direct losses on subprime mortgages have been estimated at about $500 billion, representing a one-time loss of only about 1 percent averaged across all U.S. investment portfolios. The systemic aspects of the crisis arose because the losses were highly concentrated in the portfolios of a small number of financial firms that were then threatened with bankruptcy, thereby creating a contagion to other interconnected financial firms and markets.

3. In most cases, insurers simply discontinued the coverage. One factor is that unexpected losses bring into question whether the proper model is being used, so ambiguity aversion may be involved. Capital market imperfections provide another set of factors. In particular, investors may be unwilling to provide new capital for fear it will be used primarily to pay off existing losses, a form of the debt overhang problem from corporate finance.

4. See Kunreuther and Michel-Kerjan (2009) for an extended discussion.

5. TRIA has created provisions for the U.S. Treasury that allow it to recapture some of its expenditures by imposing surcharges on all property and casualty insurance policies in subsequent years. It is unclear, of course, whether these fees will be imposed in the event of an actual terrorist act. In any case, they would apply to all policies and thus would not be risk-based.

6. TRIA does include biological, chemical, nuclear, and radiological risks, but insurers are not required to cover these risks under the "make available" clause, and very little such coverage is available.

7. The subprime mortgage crisis, however, has bankrupted large financial firms, whereas few insurers have been bankrupted in recent years as a result of natural disasters or terrorist attacks. Nine insurers reportedly became bankrupt as a result of the 1992 Hurricane Andrew, and one insurer of significant size, Poe, was bankrupted by Hurricane Katrina; on the other hand, no insurer or reinsurer bankruptcies occurred as a result of the 1994 Northridge attack or the 9/11 terrorist attack. The latter findings indicate that the catastrophe insurers were adequately capitalized for these events.

8. This is in line with earlier plans for governmental excess of loss insurance suggested for natural disasters. Alternatively, the problem could be solved if the lenders issued catastrophe bonds, but to date the markets for these bonds remain too inefficient for this application.

9. The American International Group (AIG)—in effect, a hybrid consisting of an insurer and an investment bank—also deserves comment, since it, too, has suffered enormous losses by insuring CDO and CDS subprime mortgage risks, and without appropriate regulatory controls. As a result, the firm has received an extremely costly

government bailout. Literally, more taxpayer money was spent to save this company than was provided to victims of the 2005 hurricane season—the most devastating season in the history of the country.

10. A unique feature of monoline capital requirements is that the firms are not allowed to distribute "earned premiums" as dividends for an extended period, often ten years. The idea is to match the holding period for the capital with the long-term recurrence rates of the catastrophe risks.

11. Government bailouts of entire firms are particularly costly because they indemnify all the firm's creditors—a version of the debt overhang issue from corporate finance. This inefficiency is reflected in all of the government's subprime mortgage bailouts. I thank Ken Froot for emphasizing for me this application of the debt overhang issue.

12. See Jaffee (2009).

Chapter 20 Froot: Toward Financial Stability

1. I modify markets with dealer-centric to indicate the many dealer-intermediated markets that exist, and to contrast them from exchange-centric markets.

2. The London Interbank Offered Rate (LIBOR) is a daily reference rate based on the interest rates at which banks borrow funds from other banks in the London wholesale money market (or interbank market). Overnight index swaps (OIS) are instruments that allow financial institutions to swap the interest rates they are paying without having to refinance or change the terms of the loans they have taken from other financial institutions.

3. A credit default swap (CDS) is a credit derivative contract between two counterparties. The buyer makes periodic payments to the seller, and in return receives a payoff if an underlying financial instrument defaults. CDS contracts have been compared with insurance, because the buyer pays a premium and, in return, receives a sum of money if one of the specified events occur. Sources: Wikipedia.

4. The average duration of the corporate bonds and CDS is about seven and five years, respectively.

Chapter 21 Arrow: Economic Theory and the Financial Crisis

1. I wish to thank the William and Flora Hewlett Foundation for research support.

2. Expected prices were taken to be functions of current prices, so that the functional relation between current demands and supplies and current prices becomes somewhat complicated.

3. This inconsistency between perfect foresight and informational limitations had already been argued by Morgenstern (1935). In a way, his involvement with the creation of game theory meant that a perfect foresight equilibrium could be shown, by the use of fixed-point theorems, to be a consistent concept, and so represents a step away from his earlier work. I now think his original position had important merits.

4. For a general survey, see Laffont and Martimort (2002).

5. Arguments of this type had already been raised in connection with the savings and loan crisis of the 1980s (see Kane [1989], though he was also concerned with government guarantees and regulation).

Chapter 22 Heal: Environmental Politics

1. This chapter is an extract from *Whole Earth Economics*, forthcoming.

2. He also won the Nobel Peace Prize in 1906, but for his role in mediating in the Russo-Japanese War rather than for his environmental work.

3. Quoted from the section titled "Lyndon B. Johnson and the Environment" at the EPA's website (www.epa.org).

4. Quoted in J. Brooks Flippen, *Nixon and the Environment* (Alberquerque: University of New Mexico Press, 2000), p. 102.

Chapter 23 Collier: Act Now, Later, or Never?

1. The so-called Ramsey Rule states that the socially efficient discount rate equals the real growth rate of consumption multiplied by the elasticity of the marginal utility of consumption. This Rule, including its underlying wealth effect, is the cornerstone of the current debate about the discount rate.

Chapter 24 Doherty: Climate Change

1. Howard Kunreuther, Jacqueline Meszaros, Robin Hogarth, and Mark Spranca, "Ambiguity and Underwriter Decision Processes," *Journal of Economic Behavior and Organization* 26 (1995): 337–352. See also Neil Doherty and Paul Kleindorfer, "Ambiguity and the Insurance of Catastrophe Losses," Working Paper, Risk and Decision Processes Center, Wharton School.

2. I should note, in all fairness, that such rate increases reflect both the change in estimated expected loss and the higher cost of capital that results from post-loss capital rationing.

3. For simplicity, Figure 24.1 depicts the variances as seemingly the same. Of course, we would also be unsure about all moments.

4. "The Economics of Climate Change," *Stern Review*, ch. 1. The science behind this hinges on the interaction of three main effects—ocean surface temperatures, vertical wind shear, and atmospheric humidity—but these may not all act in the same direction. For example, while higher water temperatures and higher humidity can increase the intensity of cyclones, increased vertical shear may tend to destroy the vortex and thereby break up the storms. See "Hurricanes in a Warmer World," *Union of Concerned Scientists* (2006).

5. This is a tricky issue. Paul Samuelson's well-known paper ("Risk and Uncertainty: A Fallacy of the Law of Large Numbers," *Scientia*, April/May 1963) urges caution regarding the pitfalls in repeated gambles and the issue of how far risk can be diversified through inter-temporal mechanisms.

6. Dwight Jaffee, Howard Kunreuther, and Erwann Michel-Kerjan, "Long-Term Insurance for Addressing Catastrophe Risk," Working Paper # 14210, National Bureau of Economic Research (2008). Insurers can "insure" the premium risk for their policyholders by offering premiums that do not vary over time, or at least do not vary annually according to changes in the estimated level of risk.

7. Karl Borch, "Equilibrium in a Reinsurance Market," *Econometrica* 30, no. 3. (1962): 424–444. See also Georges Dionne and Neil Doherty, "Insurance with Undiversifiable Risk: Contract Structure and Organizational Form of Insurance Firms," *Journal of Risk and Uncertainty* 6 (1993): 187–203.

Chapter 25 Linnerooth-Bayer: International Social Protection in the Face of Climate Change

1. Shu Zukang, p. xxiv.

2. Decision 1/CP.13, Bali Action Plan (www.unfccc.int/files/meetings/cop_13/application/pdf/cp_bali_action.pdf).

3. S. Solomon et al., "Technical Summary," in S. Solomon, D. Qin, M. Manning, Z. Chen, M. Marquis, K. B. Averyt, M. Tignor, and H. L. Miller, eds., *Climate Change 2007: The Physical Science Basis* (Contribution of Working Group I to the Fourth Assessment Report of the Intergovernmental Panel on Climate Change, Cambridge University Press, Cambridge).

4. Food and Agriculture Organization (FAO), "Public Assistance and Agricultural Development in Africa," twenty-first FAO regional conference for Africa, Yaounde, Cameroon.

5. J. R. Skees, B. J. Barnett, and A. G. Murphy, "Creating Insurance Markets for Natural Disaster Risk in Lower-Income Countries: The Potential Role for Securitization," *Agricultural Finance Review* 68 (2008): 151–157.

6. J. Linnerooth-Bayer, M. J. Bals, and R. Mechler (in press). "Insurance as Part of a Climate Adaptation Strategy," in M. Hulme and H. Neufeldt, eds., *Making Climate Change Work for Us: European Perspectives on Adaptation and Mitigation Strategies* (Cambridge: Cambridge University Press, 2009).

7. Howard Kunreuther and Erwann Michel-Kerjan, *At War with the Weather* (Cambridge, MA: MIT Press, 2009).

8. Skees et al., "Creating Insurance Markets for Natural Disaster Risk in Lower-Income Countries," p. 9.

Chapter 27 Keeney: Thinking Clearly About Policy Decisions

1. Bond, Carlson, and Keeney (2008).

Chapter 29 O'Connor and Wenger: Influential Social Science, Risks, and Disasters

1. The opinions expressed in this chapter are the sole view of the authors and do not necessarily reflect the views of the National Science Foundation or anyone else.

2. See, for example, A. Rubin, *Brave New Ballot: The Battle to Safeguard Democracy in the Age of Electronic Voting* (New York: Morgan Road Books, 2006), and R. M. Alvarez and T. E. Hall, *Electronic Elections: The Perils and Promises of Digital Democracy* (Princeton: Princeton University Press, 2008).

Chapter 30 Kunreuther: Reflections and Guiding Principles for Dealing with Societal Risks

1. Howard Kunreuther and Erwann Michel-Kerjan, *At War with the Weather: Managing Large-Scale Risks in a New Era of Catastrophes* (Cambridge, MA: MIT Press, 2009).

2. Howard Kunreuther, with R. Ginsberg, L. Miller, P. Sagi, P. Slovic, B. Borkan, and N. Katz, *Disaster Insurance Protection: Public Policy Lessons* (Wiley Interscience, 1978).

ABOUT THE CONTRIBUTORS

George A. Akerlof, University of California, Berkeley
George Akerlof is the Daniel E. Koshland, Sr., Distinguished Professor of Economics at the University of California, Berkeley. He was educated at Yale and the Massachusetts Institute of Technology. In 2001, Professor Akerlof received the Nobel Prize in Economic Science; he was honored for his theory of asymmetric information and its effect on economic behavior. In 2006, he became president of the American Economic Association, having served earlier as vice president and member of the executive committee. He is also on the North American Council of the Econometric Association. Professor Akerlof's research interests include sociology and economics, theory of unemployment, assymetric information, staggered contract theory, money demand, labor market flows, theory of business cycles, economics of social customs, measurement of unemployment, and economics of discrimination.

Kenneth J. Arrow, Stanford University
Kenneth Arrow is the Joan Kenney Professor of Operations Research (Emeritus) at Stanford University. His work has been primarily in economic theory and operations, focusing on such areas as social choice theory, risk bearing, medical economics, general equilibrium analysis, inventory theory, and the economics of information and innovation. He was one of the first economists to note the existence of a learning curve, and he also showed that under certain conditions an economy reaches a general equilibrium. In 1972, together with Sir John Hicks, he received the Nobel Prize in Economic Science for his pioneering contributions to general equilibrium theory and welfare theory. In addition to the Nobel Prize, he has received the American Economic Association's John Bates Clark Medal. Professor Arrow is a member of the National Academy of Sciences and the Institute of Medicine. He received a BS from City College and an MA and PhD from Columbia University, and he holds approximately twenty honorary degrees.

Colin F. Camerer, California Institute of Technology
Colin Camerer is the Rea and Lela Axline Professor of Business Economics at the California Institute of Technology (located in Pasadena, California), where he teaches cognitive psychology and economics. He earned an MBA in finance and a PhD in decision theory from the University of Chicago Graduate School of Business. Before coming to Caltech in 1994, Professor Camerer worked at the Kellogg, Wharton, and University of

Chicago business schools. He studies both behavioral and experimental economics. His most recent books include *Behavioral Game Theory* (Princeton University Press, 2003), *Foundations of Human Sociality*, with fourteen co-authors (Oxford University Press, 2004), and *Advances in Behavioral Economics*, co-edited with George Loewenstein and Matthew Rabin (Princeton University Press, 2004).

Neil Doherty, The Wharton School

Neil Doherty is the Frederick H. Ecker Professor of Insurance and Risk Management and past chair of the Department of Insurance and Risk Management at The Wharton School of the University of Pennsylvania. His principal area of interest is corporate risk management, with a focus on financial strategies for managing risks that traditionally have been insurable. Such strategies include the use of existing derivatives, the design of new financial products, and the use of capital structure. Professor Doherty has written three books in this area—*Corporate Risk Management: A Financial Exposition* (McGraw Hill, 1985), *The Financial Theory of Insurance Pricing*, with S. D'Arcy (1987), and *Integrated Risk Management* (McGraw Hill, 2000)—as well as several recent papers. His other areas of interest include the economics of risk and information, adverse selection, the value of information, and the design of insurance contracts with imperfect information and related issues.

Baruch Fischhoff, Carnegie Mellon University

Baruch Fischhoff is Howard Heinz University Professor in the Department of Social and Decision Sciences and the Department of Engineering and Public Policy at Carnegie Mellon University, where he heads the Decision Sciences Major. He holds a BS in mathematics and psychology from Wayne State University and an MA and PhD in psychology from the Hebrew University of Jerusalem. Professor Fischhoff's research areas include risk communication, analysis and management, adolescent decision making, informed consent, security, and environmental protection. He has co-authored or edited four books: *Acceptable Risk* (Cambridge University Press, 1981), *A Two-State Solution in the Middle East: Prospects and Possibilities* (Carnegie Mellon University Press, 1993), *Preference Elicitation* (Klewer, 1999), and *Risk Communication: The Mental Models Approach* (Cambridge University Press, 2001). He is a member of the Institute of Medicine of the U.S. National Academy of Sciences and past president of the Society for Judgment and Decision Making and of the Society for Risk Analysis. He chairs the Food and Drug Administration Risk Communication Advisory Committee and the Environmental Protection Agency's Homeland Security Advisory Committee. He is also a member of the Environmental Protection Agency Scientific Advisory Board, the Department of Homeland Security Science and Technology Advisory Committee, and the Department of State Global Expertise Program, and was a founding member of the Commission on the Rights of Women in Eugene, Oregon.

Kenneth A. Froot, Harvard University

Kenneth Froot is André R. Jakurski Professor of Business Administration at Harvard University's Graduate School of Business Administration. He received his BA from Stanford University and his PhD from the University of California at Berkeley. His research on a wide range of topics in finance, risk management, and international markets has been published in many journals and books. He is co-chair of the National Bureau of Economic Research's Insurance Group as well as a member of the American Finance Association, the American Economics Association, and the Behavioral Finance Working Group, and has served as a term member of the Council on Foreign Relations. Professor Froot has been a consultant to many companies, countries, and official institutions, including the International Monetary Fund, the World Bank, and the Board of Governors of the Federal Reserve on international financial, risk management, and investment management issues. He has also acted as a financial advisor to the prime minister of the Republic of Slovenia and to the finance minister of Poland, and has served on the staff of the Economic Advisory Board of the Export-Import Bank of the United States and the U.S. President's Council of Economic Advisers.

Christian Gollier, Toulouse School of Economics

Christian Gollier is currently deputy director at the Toulouse School of Economics (TSE), research director at the Institut d'Economie Industrielle (IDEI), and director of the Laboratory of Environment and Resources Economics, Toulouse, France. He holds a PhD in economics and an MA in applied mathematics from the Catholic University of Louvain. His current research ranges from decision theory under uncertainty to environmental economics, with a special focus on long-term effects. He has been a consultant for various industries and public institutions, on issues such as social security reforms, the economics of climate change, and corporate social responsibility. He has written and edited seven books on risk, including *The Economics of Risk and Time* (MIT Press, 2001), and was a lead author of the 2007 Report of the Intergovernmental Panel of Climate Change. Among many prizes and honors, Professor Gollier has received several awards, including that of Junior Member of the "Institut Universitaire de France," the Paul A. Samuelson award, and, in 2005, the "GSU-ARIA" award for the best paper presented at the first World Risk and Insurance Congress. He is the former president of the Risk Theory Society and of the European Group of Risk and Insurance Economists.

Geoffrey Heal, Columbia University

Geoffrey Heal is Garrett Professor of Public Policy and Corporate Responsibility, professor of Economics and Finance at Columbia University's Graduate School of Business, and professor of Public and International Affairs at the School of International and Public Affairs. He received his PhD in physics and economics at Cambridge University, where he obtained a First Class Honors degree and a doctorate, and then taught at Cambridge, Stanford, Yale, and Princeton. Professor Heal's research fields include the securitization of catastrophic risks and analysis of the systemic risks associated with the growth of derivative markets as well as the interaction between society and its natural resource base. The latter agenda focuses, in part, on the extent to which market mechanisms can be instrumental in environmental conservation. His recent books include *Valuing the Future* (Columbia University Press, 2000), *Nature and the Marketplace* (Island Press, 2000), *Topological Social Choice* (Springer Verlag), *Sustainability: Dynamics and Uncertainty* (Klewer, 1998), and *Environmental Markets* (Columbia University Press, 2000).

He has published 8 other books and over 150 articles. Professor Heal is a member of the Pew Oceans Commission, a director of the Union of Concerned Scientists (www .ucsusa.org), a director of the Beijer Institute of the Royal Swedish Academy of Sciences, and chair of the National Academy/National Research Council's Committee on the Valuation of Ecosystem Services.

Robin M. Hogarth, Universitat Pompeu Fabra
Robin Hogarth is ICREA Research Professor at Universitat Pompeu Fabra, Barcelona. He was formerly the Wallace W. Booth Professor of Behavioral Science at the University of Chicago's Booth School of Business, where he served as deputy dean from 1993 to 1998. He earned his MBA from INSEAD and his PhD from the University of Chicago. His research has focused mainly on the psychology of judgment and decision making, and he has published several books, including *Judgment and Choice*, 2nd ed. (Wiley, 1987) and *Educating Intuition* (University of Chicago, 2001), as well as numerous articles in leading professional journals (e.g., *Psychological Bulletin*, *Psychological Review*, *Management Science*, the *Journal of the American Statistical Association*, and the *Journal of Risk and Uncertainty*). He is a past president of both the Society for Judgment and Decision Making and the European Association for Decision Making. His most recent book, *Dance with Chance: Making Luck Work for You*, written with Spyros Makridakis and Anil Gaba, was published by Oneworld in 2009. In June 2007, Hogarth was awarded the degree of "doctor honoris causa" by the University of Lausanne.

Dwight M. Jaffee, University of California at Berkeley
Dwight Jaffee is the Willis Booth Professor of Banking, Finance, and Real Estate at the Haas School of Business, University of California at Berkeley. He is a member of the Haas School's Finance and Real Estate groups, and co-chair of the Fisher Center for Real Estate and Urban Economics. He received his doctorate from the MIT. His primary areas of research include real estate finance (especially mortgage-backed securitization and government-sponsored enterprises) and insurance (especially earthquake, terrorism, and auto). He recently co-authored a book titled *Globalization and a High-Tech Economy: California, the U.S., and Beyond* (Klewer Academic Publishers, 2004). Professor Jaffee has been a Distinguished Visiting Professor at the National University of Singapore and has been a visiting scholar at the Federal Reserve Bank of San Francisco. He has also served in numerous advisory roles for the World Bank, the Board of Governors of the Federal Reserve System, the Office of Federal Housing Enterprise Oversight, and the U.S. Department of Housing and Urban Development.

Ralph L. Keeney, Duke University
Ralph Keeney is Research Professor of Decision Sciences at the Fuqua School of Business of Duke University. He earned his PhD in Operations Research from MIT. Previously, Professor Keeney was a research scholar at the International Institute for Applied Systems Analysis (IIASA) in Austria as well as the founder of the decision and risk analysis group of a large geotechnical and environmental consulting firm. Professor Keeney is the author of many books and articles, including *Decisions with Multiple*

Objectives, co-authored with Howard Raiffa (reprinted by Cambridge University Press, 1993), which won the ORSA Lanchester Prize, and *Value-Focused Thinking: A Path to Creative Decision Making* (Harvard University Press, 1992), which received the Decision Analysis Society Best Publication Award. His book *Smart Choices: A Practical Guide to Making Better Decisions*, co-authored with John S. Hammond and Howard Raiffa (Harvard Business School Press, 1999), also received the Decision Analysis Society Best Publication Award. It has been translated into thirteen languages. Professor Keeney was awarded the Ramsey Medal for Distinguished Contributions in Decision Analysis by the Decision Analysis Society and is a member of the U.S. National Academy of Engineering.

Paul R. Kleindorfer, INSEAD
Paul Kleindorfer is the Paul Dubrule Professor of Sustainable Development and Distinguished Research Professor at INSEAD, Fontainebleau, France. He is also Anheuser-Busch Professor of Management Science (Emeritus) at The Wharton School of the University of Pennsylvania. He graduated with distinction from the U.S. Naval Academy and studied on a Fulbright Fellowship in Mathematics at the University of Tübingen, Germany, followed by doctoral studies in the Graduate School of Industrial Administration at Carnegie Mellon University. Professor Kleindorfer has held university appointments at Carnegie Mellon University, Massachusetts Institute of Technology, The Wharton School, and several other universities and international research institutes. Until 2005, he was the co-director of the Wharton Risk Management and Decision Processes Center. He is currently the Director of the Sustainability Programme in the INSEAD Social Innovation Centre, where his research is concerned with climate change and the transition to the low-carbon economy. His most recent book is *The Network Challenge* (Wharton Publishing, 2009), co-authored with Jerry Wind.

Carolyn Kousky, Resources for the Future
Carolyn Kousky is a Fellow at Resources for the Future in Washington, D.C. Her research focuses on natural resource management, land use, decision making under uncertainty, and individual and societal responses to natural disaster risk. Her work assesses the ways in which decisions are made regarding low-probability events, at both the individual and societal levels, and how such decision making can be improved. In particular, she has researched the management of flood risk in the United States, analyzing insurance decisions, floodplain management, and what individuals learn from the occurrence of extreme events. In 2006–2007, she was a visiting scholar at the Wharton Risk Center, working on flood insurance in the United States. She received a BS in earth systems from Stanford University and a PhD in public policy from Harvard University.

David H. Krantz, Columbia University
David Krantz graduated from Yale University (mathematics) and received his PhD (psychology) from the University of Pennsylvania. He joined the Columbia faculty in 1985 and is currently professor of psychology and statistics. He is founding director of Columbia's Center for the Decision Sciences and the Center for Research on Environmental Decisions (CRED) and has been a Fellow of the Guggenheim Foundation and

the Center for Advanced Studies in the Behavioral Sciences. He has also been active in a number of roles in the Earth Institute at Columbia over the past ten years. Professor Krantz's research focuses on problem solving, especially decision making, multiple goals, risky and inter-temporal choice, and the use of statistical concepts in everyday reasoning. His recent publications include "Goals and Plans in Decision-Making" (with Howard Kunreuther) in *Judgment and Decision Making* and "Individual Values and Social Goals in Environmental Decision Making" (with several CRED co-authors) in *Decision Modeling and Behavior in Uncertain and Complex Environments.*

Howard Kunreuther, The Wharton School

Howard Kunreuther is the Cecilia Yen Koo Professor of Decision Sciences and Public Policy at The Wharton School as well as co-director of the Risk Management and Decision Processes Center. He received his PhD in economics from MIT. He has a long-standing interest in ways that society can better manage low-probability/high-consequence events related to technological and natural hazards and has published extensively on this topic. He is a member of the OECD's High Level Advisory Board on Financial Management of Large-Scale Catastrophes, a member of the World Economic Forum (WEF) Global Agenda Council on Natural Disasters, a Fellow of the American Association for the Advancement of Science (AAAS), and a Distinguished Fellow of the Society for Risk Analysis, receiving the Society's Distinguished Achievement Award in 2001. Professor Kunreuther has written and co-edited 200 papers and over 30 books, including *At War with the Weather*, with Erwann Michel-Kerjan (MIT Press, 2009), *Catastrophe Modeling: A New Approach to Managing Risks*, with Patricia Grossi (Klewer Academic Publishers, 2005), and *Wharton on Making Decisions* (with Stephen Hoch) (John Wiley and Sons, 2001), and is a recipient of the Elizur Wright Award for the publication that makes the most significant contribution to the literature of insurance.

Joanne Linnerooth-Bayer, IIASA

Joanne Linnerooth-Bayer is leader of the Risk and Vulnerability Program at the International Institute for Applied Systems Analysis (IIASA) in Laxenburg, Austria. She is an economist by training, and has received a BS and a PhD at Carnegie-Mellon University and the University of Maryland, respectively. Her current interests are global change and the risk of catastrophic events, and she is investigating options for improving the financial management of catastrophic risks in transition and developing countries. She and her colleagues have carried out extensive research on this topic and are developing options for the donor communities, as well as the climate adaptation community, to support insurance and other forms of proactive disaster assistance. She is an associate editor of the *Journal for Risk Research* and on the editorial board of *Risk Analysis* and *Risk Abstracts*. Her other affiliations include the faculty of Beijing Normal University and the Science Committee of the Chinese Academy of Disaster Reduction and Emergency Management.

Robert Meyer, The Wharton School

Robert Meyer is the Gayfryd Steinberg Professor of Marketing and co-director of Wharton's Risk Management and Decision Processes Center. He received his PhD in transportation geography from the University of Iowa in 1980. His research focuses on consumer decision analysis, sales response modeling, and decision making under uncertainty. Using laboratory simulations Professor Meyer and his colleagues have been able to show that the much-publicized failures of preparation that contributed to the losses from such recent events as the Asian Tsunami and Hurricane Katrina are consistent with a number of hard-wired biases in the ways that people respond to risk. Professor Meyer's work has appeared in a wide variety of professional journals and books, including the *Journal of Consumer Research*, the *Journal of Marketing Research*, *Marketing Science*, and *Management Science*. He has served as the editor of *Marketing Letters* and as an associate editor of *Marketing Science* and the *Journal of Consumer Research*.

Erwann Michel-Kerjan, The Wharton School
Erwann Michel-Kerjan teaches value creation in The Wharton School's MBA program. He is the managing director of the Wharton Risk Management and Decision Process Center, a center with over twenty five years of experience in developing strategies and policies for dealing with catastrophic risks. He is also research associate at the École Polytechnique in France, where he completed his doctoral studies in economics and mathematics in 2002; he has also studied at McGill and Harvard Universities. He has published extensively on how to better manage extreme events, ranging from terrorism and nuclear proliferation to floods, hurricanes, earthquakes, and pandemics. Specifically, he works at developing new solutions to provide the necessary financial protection against such large-scale risks and advises governments, companies, and organizations in several countries to develop concrete responses. His books include *Seeds of Disaster, Roots of Response* (Cambridge University Press, 2006) and *At War with the Weather*, with Howard Kunreuther (MIT Press, 2009). He currently serves as chairman of the OECD's Secretary General High Level Advisory Board on Financial Management of Large-Scale Catastrophes. In 2007, Professor Michel-Kerjan was named a Young Global Leader by the World Economic Forum (in Davos, Switzerland), a five-year nomination bestowed to recognize and acknowledge the most extraordinary leaders of the world under the age of 40.

David A. Moss, Harvard University
David Moss is the John G. McLean Professor at Harvard Business School, where he teaches classes in business, government, and the international economy. He earned a BA in history and government from Cornell University and an MA in economics and a PhD in history from Yale University. Professor Moss is the author of numerous articles, book chapters, and case studies, mainly in the fields of institutional and policy history, political economy, and comparative social policy. He has also written three books, including *Socializing Security: Progressive-Era Economists and the Origins of American Social Policy* (Harvard University Press, 1996), which traces the intellectual and institutional origins of the American welfare state, and *When All Else Fails: Government as the Ultimate Risk Manager* (Harvard University Press, 2002), which explores the government's pivotal role as a risk manager in policies ranging from limited liability and bankruptcy law to social insurance and federal disaster relief. Professor Moss is a member of the U.S. National Academy of Social Insurance. Among the recent honors

he has received are the Robert F. Greenhill Award, the Editors' Prize from the American Bankruptcy Law Journal, the Student Association Faculty Award for outstanding teaching at the Harvard Business School, and the American Risk and Insurance Association's Kulp-Wright Book Award.

Robert E. O'Connor, National Science Foundation

Robert O'Connor has been directing the Decision, Risk and Management Sciences Program at the National Science Foundation since 2001. He earned his undergraduate degree at Johns Hopkins University and his doctorate in political science at the University of North Carolina at Chapel Hill. At NSF he also manages the Decision, Risk and Uncertainty area of emphasis of the Human and Social Dynamics initiative. In addition, he serves on the management teams for the Decision Making Under Uncertainty for Climate Change (DMUU) centers and the Dynamics of Coupled Natural and Human Systems Program. Prior to coming to NSF, he was a professor of political science at the Pennsylvania State University. The U.S. Department of Energy, U.S. Environmental Protection Agency, the National Oceanographic and Atmospheric Administration, and the National Science Foundation funded his research into public perceptions of cumulative, uncertain long-term risks, of technologies perceived as risky, and of agency risk communications. Professor O'Connor represents the National Science Foundation on two interagency groups: the U.S. Climate Change Science Program's Interagency Working Group on Human Contributions and Responses and the Subcommittee on Disaster Reduction of the National Science and Technology Council of the Executive Office of the President.

Ayse Öncüler, ESSEC

Ayse Öncüler is associate professor of marketing at ESSEC Business School in France. She holds a master's degree in applied economics and a PhD in decision sciences (under the supervision of Howard Kunreuther), both from The Wharton School, University of Pennsylvania. Her academic research focuses on risky decision making over time, covering a variety of applications from risk mitigation investments to consumer behavior. Her work has been published in academic journals such as the *Journal of Risk and Uncertainty*, the *Journal of Behavioral Decision Making*, *Management Science*, and *Social Psychology Quarterly* and has been reviewed in media outlets such as the *Financial Times* and *CFO Europe*. Recently she has been working on ambiguity and probability transformation in intertemporal choice.

Olivier Oullier, Aix-Marseille University

Olivier Oullier is an associate professor of neuroscience at Aix-Marseille University (France) and a research associate at the Center for Complex Systems and Brain Sciences (Florida Atlantic University). His work focuses on multi-level social coordination dynamics, embodied cognition, and neuroeconomics. A member of the World Economic Forum's Global Agenda Council on Decision-Making and Incentive, he is scientific advisor to the French prime minister's Center for Strategic Analysis in charge of the "Neuroscience and Public Policy" program—the world's first institutional initiative to specifically evaluate and implement the applications of newfound knowledge on brain sciences to health prevention, risk management, education, and justice. Founder of the first graduate course on neuroeconomics and neuroethics in France, Professor Oullier serves as an expert on these topics for various public and private institutions including the French Parliament and the European Commission. His book *The State of Mind in Economics: Neuroeconomics and Beyond* (with Alan Kirman and Scott Kelso) is forthcoming from Cambridge University Press.

Mark V. Pauly, The Wharton School

Mark Pauly is the Bendheim Professor in the Department of Health Care Systems at The Wharton School of the University of Pennsylvania. He received his PhD in economics from the University of Virginia and is a former commissioner on the Physician Payment Review Commission, an active member of the Institute of Medicine, and one of the nation's leading health economists. His classic study on the economics of moral hazard was the first to point out how health insurance coverage may affect patients' use of medical services. Professor Pauly's interest in health policy has led him to investigate ways to reduce the number of uninsured people through tax credits for public and private insurance and to create an appropriate design for Medicare in a budget-constrained environment. He has served on Institute of Medicine panels on public accountability for health insurers under Medicare and on improving the financing of vaccines and was recently also a member of the Medicare Technical Advisory Panel. Currently he is a co-editor-in-chief of the *International Journal of Health Care Finance and Economics* and an associate editor of the *Journal of Risk and Uncertainty*.

John W. Pratt, Harvard University

John Pratt is the William Ziegler Professor of Business Administration (Emeritus) at Harvard Business School. He received his education at Princeton and Stanford, specializing in mathematics and statistics, and was the editor of the *Journal of the American Statistical Association* from 1965 to 1970. He has also chaired National Academy of Sciences committees on environmental monitoring, census methodology, and the future of statistics. Professor Pratt is a fellow of five professional societies and has co-authored or edited books on statistical decision theory, statistical and mathematical aspects of pollution problems, social experimentation, nonparametric statistics, and principals and agents. His other research interests have included statistical inference, approximation of probability distributions, utility theory, risk aversion, risk sharing, incentives, statistical causality, and, currently, fair division.

Howard Raiffa, Harvard University

Howard Raiffa is the Frank P. Ramsey Professor (Emeritus) of Managerial Economics, a joint chair held by the Business School and the Kennedy School of Government at Harvard University. He received his doctorate in mathematics from the University of Michigan. A mathematician by training, Professor Raiffa is an originator of the now-famous "decision tree" and has done extensive work on developing techniques to help decision makers think more systematically about complex choices involving uncertainties and tradeoffs. He has received numerous honorary degrees and, in 2000, was awarded the prestigious Dickson Prize for Science, conferred annually by professors at Carnegie Mellon University. As a scientific advisor to McGeorge Bundy, White House assistant for national security under Presidents Kennedy and Johnson, and Philip Handler, president of the National Academy of Sciences, he helped to negotiate the creation of an East-West think tank with the aim of reducing Cold War tensions. Professor Raiffa has published extensively; his books include *Games and Decisions: Introduction and Critical Survey*, with R. Luce (Wiley & Sons, 1957), *Decision Analysis: Introductory Lectures on Choices Under Uncertainty* (McGraw-Hill, 1997), and *Applied Statistical Decision Theory*, with R. Schaifer (Wiley Classics Library, 2000).

Thomas Schelling, University of Maryland

Thomas Schelling is Emeritus Distinguished University Professor at the School of Public Policy of the University of Maryland. Professor Schelling came to the Maryland School of Public Affairs after twenty years at the John F. Kennedy School of Government, Harvard University. Recipient of the 2005 Nobel Prize in Economic Science, he has been elected to the National Academy of Sciences, the Institute of Medicine, and the American Academy of Arts and Sciences. In 1991 he was president of the American Economic Association, of which he is a Distinguished Fellow. He was the recipient of the National Academy of Sciences award for Behavioral Research Relevant to the Prevention of Nuclear War. He served in the Economic Cooperation Administration in Europe, and has held positions in the White House and Executive Office of the President, Yale University; the RAND Corporation; and the Department of Economics and Center for International Affairs, Harvard University. He has published on military strategy and arms control, energy and environmental policy, climate change, nuclear proliferation, terrorism, organized crime, foreign aid and international trade, conflict and bargaining theory, racial segregation and integration, health policy, tobacco and drugs policy, and ethical issues in public policy and in business.

Paul J. H. Schoemaker, Decision Strategies International

Paul Schoemaker is the founder, chairman, and CEO of Decision Strategies International, a consulting and training company specializing in strategic planning, executive development, and multi-media software. He currently serves as the research director of the Mack Center for Technological Innovation at The Wharton School of the University of Pennsylvania, where he teaches strategy and decision making. His main research interests are in the areas of business strategy, decision sciences, scenario planning, organizational dynamics, and emerging technologies. He has written eight books and over a hundred papers, which have appeared in such journals as the *Harvard Business Review*, the *Journal of Mathematical Psychology*, *Management Science*, and the *Journal of Economic Literature*. His 1995 paper on scenario planning ranks in the all-time top-five reprints of the *Sloan Management Review*. Professor Schoemaker received an MBA in finance, an MA in management, and a PhD in decision sciences from The Wharton School at the University of Pennsylvania. He was Howard Kunreuther's first PhD student at Wharton, with whom he co-authored several papers and the book *Decision Sciences, An Integrated Perspective*, with Paul Kleindorfer and Howard Kunreuther (Cambridge University Press, 1993).

Robert J. Shiller, Yale University

Robert Shiller is the Arthur M. Okun Professor of Economics at Yale University and Professor of Finance and Fellow at the International Center for Finance, Yale School of Management. He received his PhD in economics from MIT in 1972. Professor Shiller has written on financial markets, financial innovation, behavioral economics, macroeconomics, real estate, and statistical methods as well as on public attitudes, opinions, and moral judgments regarding markets. He is the author of many books including *Subprime Solution: How the Global Financial Crisis Happened and What to Do About It* (Princeton University Press, 2008), which offers an analysis of the housing and economic crisis and a plan of action against it. He co-authored, with George Akerlof, *Animal Spirits* (Princeton University Press, 2009). He has been research associate of the National Bureau of Economic Research since 1980, and has been co-organizer of National Bureau of Economic Research workshops on behavioral finance, and on macroeconomics and individual decision making (behavioral macroeconomics). He served as vice president of the American Economic Association in 2005 and as president of the Eastern Economic Association in 2006–2007. He writes two regular columns: "Finance in the 21st Century" for Project Syndicate and "Economic View" for the *New York Times*.

Paul Slovic, University of Oregon

Paul Slovic is a professor of psychology at the University of Oregon and a founder and president of Decision Research. He holds both an MA (1962) and a PhD (1964) from the University of Michigan. He has received honorary doctorates from the Stockholm School of Economics (1996) and the University of East Anglia (2005). He studies human judgment, decision making, and risk analysis. He and his colleagues worldwide have developed methods to describe risk perceptions and measure their impacts on individuals, industry, and society. He publishes extensively and serves as a consultant to industry and government. His most recent books include *The Perception of Risk* (Earthscan, 2000), *The Social Amplification of Risk*, with N. Pidgeon and R. Kasperson (Cambridge University Press, 2003), and *The Construction of Preference*, with S. Lichtenstein (Cambridge University Press, 2006). Professor Slovic is a past president of the Society for Risk Analysis and, in 1991, received its Distinguished Contribution Award. In 1993, he received the Distinguished Scientific Contribution Award from the American Psychological Association. In 1995, he received the Outstanding Contribution to Science Award from the Oregon Academy of Science.

Cass R. Sunstein, Harvard Law School

Cass Sunstein is the Felix Frankfurter Professor of Law at Harvard Law School and the most cited law professor on any faculty in the United States. He currently serves as administrator of the Office of Information and Regulatory Affairs (OMB) at the White House. Professor Sunstein graduated in 1975 from Harvard College and in 1978 from Harvard Law School, both magna cum laude. After graduation, he clerked for Justice Benjamin Kaplan of the Massachusetts Supreme Judicial Court and Justice Thurgood Marshall of the U.S. Supreme Court, and then he worked as an attorney-advisor in the Office of the Legal Counsel of the U.S. Department of Justice. Before joining Harvard, he was a faculty member at the University of Chicago Law School from 1981 to 2008. Sunstein's many books include *After the Rights Revolution* (Harvard University Press, 1990), *Risk and Reason* (Cambridge University Press, 2002), *Laws of Fear: Beyond the Precautionary Principle* (Cambridge University Press, 2005), *Worst-Case Scenarios* (Harvard University Press, 2007), and *Nudge: Improving Decisions About Health, Wealth, and Happiness*, with Richard H. Thaler (Yale University Press, 2008). He is also co-author of leading casebooks in both constitutional law and administrative law, with academic specialties in these two fields as well as in regulatory policy.

W. Kip Viscusi, Vanderbilt University Law School

Kip Viscusi is Vanderbilt's first University Distinguished Professor, with appointments in the Owen Graduate School of Management and the Department of Economics as well as in the Law School. He is the award-winning author of more than 20 books and 250 articles, most of which deal with various aspects of health and safety risk. Professor Viscusi is widely regarded as one of the world's leading authorities on cost-benefit analysis, and his estimates of the value of risks to life and health are currently used throughout the federal government. He has served as a consultant to the U.S. Office of Management and Budget, the Environmental Protection Agency, the Occupational Safety and Health Administration, the Federal Aviation Administration, and the U.S. Department of Justice. He was deputy director of the Council on Wage and Price Stability in the Carter administration. He also served on the Science Advisory Board of the U.S. Environmental Protection Agency for seven years and is currently on the EPA Homeland Security Committee. Professor Viscusi is the founding editor of the *Journal of Risk and Uncertainty*, now housed at Vanderbilt. He is also the founding editor of the journal *Foundations and Trends: Microeconomics*.

Dennis E. Wenger, National Science Foundation

Dennis Wenger is the program director for Infrastructure Systems Management and Extreme Events at the National Science Foundation. He is also the acting program director for the Civil Infrastructure Systems. Previously at Texas A&M University, he was a professor of urban and regional science as well as the founding director and Senior Scholar of the Hazard Reduction & Recovery Center. Professor Wenger has been engaged in research on hazards and disasters for over forty years, focusing on the social and multidisciplinary aspects of natural, technological, and human-induced disasters (emergency management capabilities and response, police and fire planning and response, search and rescue, mass media coverage of disasters, warning systems and public response, factors related to local community recovery success, and disaster beliefs and emergency planning). He is the author of numerous books, research monographs, articles, and papers. Professor Wenger currently serves as one of the nine members of the United Nations Scientific and Technical Committee to the International Strategy for Disaster Reduction. For NSF, Professor Wenger serves as the Foundation's representative to the Roundtable on Disasters of the National Academy of Science, and he is co-chair for science of the Subcommittee on Disaster Reduction of the National Science and Technology Council of the Executive Office of the President.

Richard Zeckhauser, Harvard University

Richard Zeckhauser is Frank P. Ramsey Professor of Political Economy, Kennedy School, Harvard University. In his research—comprising 12 books and 250 articles—and his life, he seeks ways to effectively confront the unknown and the unknowable, hence to be a rational economist. He played bridge with Howard Kunreuther in high school. With that training, he won his first major national bridge championship in 1967, and another in 2007, after returning to the game after a significant hiatus. His most recent books are *Targeting in Social Programs: Avoiding Bad Bets, Removing Bad Apples*, with Peter Schuck (Brookings Institution Press, 2006), *The Patron's Payoff: Conspicuous Commissions in Italian Renaissance Art*, with Jonathan Nelson (Princeton University Press, 2008), and *2+2=5: Private Roles for Public Goals*, with John Donahue (forthcoming).

INDEX